TEACH YOURSELF
WINDOWS® 95
VISUALLY™

D1318766

IDG's **3-D Visual**™ Series

IDG BOOKS *From* **maranGraphics**™

IDG Books Worldwide, Inc.
An International Data Group Company
Foster City, CA • Indianapolis • Chicago • Southlake, TX

Teach Yourself Windows® 95 VISUALLY™

Published by
IDG Books Worldwide, Inc.
An International Data Group Company
919 E. Hillsdale Blvd., Suite 400
Foster City, CA 94404
(415) 655-3000

Copyright © 1995, 1996 by maranGraphics Inc.
5755 Coopers Avenue
Mississauga, Ontario, Canada
L4Z 1R9

Screen shots reprinted with permission from Microsoft Corporation.

All rights reserved. No part of this book, including interior design, cover design, and icons, may be reproduced or transmitted in any form, by any means (electronic, photocopying, recording, or otherwise) without prior written permission from maranGraphics.

Library of Congress Catalog Card No.: 96-076723
ISBN: 0-7645-6001-8
Printed in the United States of America
10 9 8 7 6 5 4 3 2

Distributed in the United States by IDG Books Worldwide, Inc.

Distributed by Transworld Publishers Limited in the United Kingdom; by IDG Norge Books for Norway; by IDG Sweden Books for Sweden; by Woodslane Pty. Ltd. for Australia; by Woodslane Enterprises Ltd. for New Zealand; by Longman Singapore Publishers Ltd. for Singapore, Malaysia, Thailand, and Indonesia; by Simron Pty. Ltd. for South Africa; by Toppan Company Ltd. for Japan; by Distribuidora Cuspide for Argentina; by Livraria Cultura for Brazil; by Ediciencia S.A. for Ecuador; by Addison-Wesley Publishing Company for Korea; by Ediciones ZETA S.C.R. Ltda. for Peru; by WS Computer Publishing Corporation, Inc., for the Philippines; by Unalis Corporation for Taiwan; by Contemporanea de Ediciones for Venezuela; by Computer Book & Magazine Store for Puerto Rico; by Express Computer Distributors for the Caribbean and West Indies. Authorized Sales Agent: Anthony Rudkin Associates for the Middle East and North Africa.

For corporate orders, please call maranGraphics at 800-469-6616.
For general information on IDG Books Worldwide's books in the U.S., please call our Consumer Customer Service department at 800-762-2974.
For reseller information, including discounts and premium sales, please call our Reseller Customer Service department at 800-434-3422.
For information on where to purchase IDG Books Worldwide's books outside the U.S., please contact our International Sales department at 415-655-3200 or fax 415-655-3295.
For information on foreign language translations, please contact our Foreign & Subsidiary Rights department at 415-655-3021 or fax 415-655-3281.
For sales inquiries and special prices for bulk quantities, please contact our Sales department at 415-655-3200.
For information on using IDG Books Worldwide's books in the classroom or for ordering examination copies, please contact our Educational Sales department at 800-434-2086 or fax 817-251-8174.
For press review copies, author interviews, or other publicity information, please contact our Public Relations department at 415-655-3000 or fax 415-655-3299.
For authorization to photocopy items for corporate, personal, or educational use, please contact maranGraphics at 800-469-6616.

LIMIT OF LIABILITY/DISCLAIMER OF WARRANTY: AUTHOR AND PUBLISHER HAVE USED THEIR BEST EFFORTS IN PREPARING THIS BOOK. IDG BOOKS WORLDWIDE, INC., AND AUTHOR MAKE NO REPRESENTATIONS OR WARRANTIES WITH RESPECT TO THE ACCURACY OR COMPLETENESS OF THE CONTENTS OF THIS BOOK AND SPECIFICALLY DISCLAIM ANY IMPLIED WARRANTIES OF MERCHANTABILITY OR FITNESS FOR A PARTICULAR PURPOSE. THERE ARE NO WARRANTIES WHICH EXTEND BEYOND THE DESCRIPTIONS CONTAINED IN THIS PARAGRAPH. NO WARRANTY MAY BE CREATED OR EXTENDED BY SALES REPRESENTATIVES OR WRITTEN SALES MATERIALS. THE ACCURACY AND COMPLETENESS OF THE INFORMATION PROVIDED HEREIN AND THE OPINIONS STATED HEREIN ARE NOT GUARANTEED OR WARRANTED TO PRODUCE ANY PARTICULAR RESULTS, AND THE ADVICE AND STRATEGIES CONTAINED HEREIN MAY NOT BE SUITABLE FOR EVERY INDIVIDUAL. NEITHER IDG BOOKS WORLDWIDE, INC., NOR AUTHOR SHALL BE LIABLE FOR ANY LOSS OF PROFIT OR ANY OTHER COMMERCIAL DAMAGES, INCLUDING BUT NOT LIMITED TO SPECIAL, INCIDENTAL, CONSEQUENTIAL, OR OTHER DAMAGES.

Trademark Acknowledgments

maranGraphics Inc. has attempted to include trademark information for products, services and companies referred to in this guide. Although maranGraphics Inc. has made reasonable efforts in gathering this information, it cannot guarantee its accuracy.

All other brand names and product names used in this book are trademarks, registered trademarks, or trade names of their respective holders. maranGraphics Inc. and IDG Books Worldwide are not associated with any product or vendor mentioned in this book.

FOR PURPOSES OF ILLUSTRATING THE CONCEPTS AND TECHNIQUES DESCRIBED IN THIS BOOK, THE AUTHOR HAS CREATED VARIOUS NAMES, COMPANY NAMES, MAILING ADDRESSES, E-MAIL ADDRESSES AND PHONE NUMBERS, ALL OF WHICH ARE FICTITIOUS. ANY RESEMBLANCE OF THESE FICTITIOUS NAMES, COMPANY NAMES, MAILING ADDRESSES, E-MAIL ADDRESSES AND PHONE NUMBERS TO ANY ACTUAL PERSON, COMPANY AND/OR ORGANIZATION IS UNINTENTIONAL AND PURELY COINCIDENTAL.

maranGraphics has used their best efforts in preparing this book. As Web sites are constantly changing, some of the Web site addresses in this book may have moved or no longer exist. maranGraphics does not accept responsibility nor liability for losses or damages resulting from the information contained in this book. maranGraphics also does not support the views expressed in the Web sites contained in this book.

©**1995, 1996**
maranGraphics, Inc.

The 3-D illustrations are the copyright of maranGraphics, Inc.

U.S. Corporate Sales	**U.S. Trade Sales**
Contact maranGraphics at (800) 469-6616 or Fax (905) 890-9434.	Contact IDG Books at (800) 434-3422 or (415) 655-3000.

Welcome to the world of IDG Books Worldwide.

IDG Books Worldwide, Inc., is a subsidiary of International Data Group, the world's largest publisher of computer-related information and the leading global provider of information services on information technology. IDG was founded more than 25 years ago and now employs more than 8,500 people worldwide. IDG publishes more than 270 computer publications in over 75 countries (see listing below). More than 90 million people read one or more IDG publications each month.

Launched in 1990, IDG Books Worldwide is today the #1 publisher of best-selling computer books in the United States. We are proud to have received eight awards from the Computer Press Association in recognition of editorial excellence and three from Computer Currents' First Annual Readers' Choice Awards. Our best-selling ...For Dummies® series has more than 25 million copies in print with translations in 30 languages. IDG Books Worldwide, through a joint venture with IDG's Hi-Tech Beijing, became the first U.S. publisher to publish a computer book in the People's Republic of China. In record time, IDG Books Worldwide has become the first choice for millions of readers around the world who want to learn how to better manage their businesses.

Our mission is simple: Every one of our books is designed to bring extra value and skill-building instructions to the reader. Our books are written by experts who understand and care about our readers. The knowledge base of our editorial staff comes from years of experience in publishing, education, and journalism - experience which we use to produce books for the '90s. In short, we care about books, so we attract the best people. We devote special attention to details such as audience, interior design, use of icons, and illustrations. And because we use an efficient process of authoring, editing, and desktop publishing our books electronically, we can spend more time ensuring superior content and spend less time on the technicalities of making books.

You can count on our commitment to deliver high-quality books at competitive prices on topics you want to read about. At IDG Books Worldwide, we continue in the IDG tradition of delivering quality for more than 25 years. You'll find no better book on a subject than one from IDG Books Worldwide.

John Kilcullen
President and CEO
IDG Books Worldwide, Inc.

IDG Books Worldwide, Inc., is a subsidiary of International Data Group, the world's largest publisher of computer-related information and the leading global provider of information services on information technology. International Data Group publishes over 276 computer publications in over 75 countries. Ninety million people read one or more International Data Group publications each month. International Data Group's publications include: Argentina: Annuario de Informatica, Computerworld Argentina, PC World Argentina; Australia: Australian Macworld, Client/Server Journal, Computer Living, Computerworld, Computerworld 100, Digital News, IT Casebook, Network World, On-line World Australia, PC World, Publishing Essentials, Reseller, WebMaster; Austria: Computerwelt Österreich, Networks Austria, PC Tip; Belarus: PC World Belarus; Belgium: Data News; Brazil: Annuário de Informática, Computerworld Brazil, Connections, Super Game Power, Macworld, PC Player, PC World Brazil, Publish Brazil, Reseller News; Bulgaria: Computerworld Bulgaria, Networkworld/Bulgaria, PC & MacWorld Bulgaria; Canada: CIO Canada, Client/Server World, ComputerWorld Canada, InfoCanada, Network World Canada; Chile: Computerworld Chile, PC World Chile; Colombia: Computerworld Colombia, PC World Colombia; Costa Rica: PC World Centro America; The Czech and Slovak Republics: Computerworld Czechoslovakia, Elektronika Czechoslovakia, Macworld Czech Republic, PC World Czechoslovakia; Denmark: Communications World, Computerworld Danmark, Macworld Danmark, PC Privat Danmark, PC World Danmark, PC World Danmark Supplements, TECH World; Dominican Republic: PC World Republica Dominicana; Ecuador: PC World Ecuador; Egypt: Computerworld Middle East, PC World Middle East; El Salvador: PC World Centro America; Finland: MikroPC, Tietoverkko, Tietoviikko; France: Distributique, Golden, Hebdo-Distributique, Info PC, Le Guide du Monde Informatique, Le Monde Informatique, Reseaux & Telecoms; Germany: Computer Partner, Computerwoche, Computerwoche Extra, Computerwoche Focus, I/M Information Management, Macwelt, PC Welt; Greece: GamePro, Multimedia World; Guatemala: PC World Centro America; Honduras: PC World Centro America; Hong Kong: Computerworld Hong Kong, PCWorld Hong Kong, Publish in Asia; Hungary: ABCD CD-ROM, Computerworld Szamitastechnika, PC & Mac World Hungary, PC-X Magazine; Iceland: Tolvuheimur/PC World Island; India: Information Systems Computerworld, PC World India, Publish in Asia; Indonesia: InfoKomputer PC World, Komputek Computerworld, Publish in Asia; Ireland: ComputerScope, PC Live!; Israel: People & Computers; Italy: Computerworld Italia, Computerworld Italia Special Editions, Macworld Italia, Networking Italia, PC Shopping, PC World/Walt Disney; Japan: DTP World, HP Open World Japan, Macworld Japan, Nikkei Personal Computing, Open World Japan, OS/2 World Japan, SunWorld Japan, Windows World Japan; Kenya: East African Computer News; Korea: Hi-Tech Information/Computerworld, Macworld Korea, PC World Korea; Macedonia: PC World Macedonia; Malaysia: Computerworld Malaysia, PC World Malaysia, Publish in Asia; Mexico: Computerworld Mexico, Macworld, PC World Mexico; Myanmar: PC World Myanmar; Netherlands: Computer! Totaal, LAN Magazine, LanWorld Buyers Guide, Macworld, Net Magazine, Totaal! Beurskrant; New Zealand: Absolute Beginner's Guide, Computer Buyer, Computer Industry Directory, Computerworld New Zealand, MTB, Network World, PC World New Zealand; Nicaragua: PC World Centro America; Nigeria: PC World Nigeria; Norway: Computerworld Norge, Computerworld Privat (Datamagasinet), CW Rapport Norge, IDG's KURSGUIDE, Macworld Norge, Multimediaworld, PC World Ekspress, PC World Nettverk, PC World Norge, PC World's Produktguide, Windows World Spesial; Pakistan: Computerworld Pakistan, PC World Pakistan; Panama: PC World Panama; P. R. of China: China Computer Users, China Computerworld, China Infoworld, China Telecom World Weekly, Computer & Communication, Electronic Design China, Electronics Today, Electronics Weekly, Game Camp, Game Soft, Network World China, PC World China, Popular Computer Weekly, Software Weekly, Software World, Telecom World; Peru: Computerworld Peru, PC World Profesional Peru, PC World Peru; Poland: Computerworld Poland, Computerworld Special Report, Macworld, Networld, PC World Komputer; Philippines: Computerworld Philippines, PC World Philippines, Publish in Asia; Portugal: Cerebro/PC World, Computerworld/Correio Informático, Dealer World Portugal, Mac*In/PC*In, Multimedia World Portugal; Puerto Rico: PC World Puerto Rico; Romania: Computerworld Romania, PC World Romania, Telecom Romania; Russia: Computerworld Russia, Mir PK, Sety; Singapore: Computerworld Singapore, PC World Singapore, Publish in Asia; Slovenia: MONITOR; South Africa: Computing S.A., InfoWorld S.A., Network World S.A., Software World; Spain: Computerworld Espa-a, COMUNICACIONES WORLD, Dealer World, Macworld Espa-a, PC World Espa-a; Sweden: CAP&Design, Computer Sweden, Corporate Computing, MacWorld, Maxi Data, MikroDatorn, Nätverk & Kommunikation, PC/Aktiv, PC World, Windows World; Switzerland: Computerworld Schweiz, Macworld Schweiz, PCtip; Taiwan: Computerworld Taiwan, Macworld Taiwan, PC World Taiwan, Publish Taiwan, Windows World; Thailand: Thai Computerworld, Publish in Asia; Turkey: Computerworld Turkiye, MACWORLD Turkiye, PC WORLD Turkiye; Ukraine: Computerworld Kiev, Computers & Software, Multimedia World Ukraine, PC World Ukraine; United Kingdom: Acorn User, Amiga Action, Amiga Computing, Appletalk, Computing, GamePro, Macworld, Network News, Parents and Computers, PC Advisor, PC Home, PSX Pro UK, The WEB; United States: Cable in the Classroom, CD Review, CIO Magazine, Computerworld, Computerworld Client/Server Journal, Digital Video Magazine, DOS World, Federal Computer Week, GamePro, InfoWorld, I-Way, JavaWorld, Macworld, Multimedia World, Netscape World Online, Network World, PC Entertainment, PC World, Publish, SunWorld Online, SWATPro Magazine, Video Event, WebMaster; Uruguay: PC World Uruguay; Venezuela: Computerworld Venezuela, PC World Venezuela; and Vietnam: PC World Vietnam.

**Every maranGraphics book represents
the extraordinary vision and commitment of a unique family:
the Maran family of Toronto, Canada.**

Back Row (from left to right):   *Sherry Maran, Rob Maran, Richard Maran,
Maxine Maran, Jill Maran.*

Front Row (from left to right):   *Judy Maran, Ruth Maran.*

Richard Maran is the company founder and its inspirational leader. He developed maranGraphics' proprietary communication technology called "visual grammar." This book is built on that technology—empowering readers with the easiest and quickest way to learn about computers.

Ruth Maran is the Author and Architect—a role Richard established that now bears Ruth's distinctive touch. She creates the words and visual structure that are the basis for the books.

Judy Maran is Senior Editor. She works with Ruth, Richard, and the highly talented maranGraphics illustrators, designers, and editors to transform Ruth's material into its final form.

Rob Maran is the Technical and Production Specialist. He makes sure the state-of-the-art technology used to create these books always performs as it should.

Sherry Maran manages the Reception, Order Desk, and any number of areas that require immediate attention and a helping hand.

Jill Maran is a jack-of-all-trades and dynamo who fills in anywhere she's needed anytime she's back from university.

Maxine Maran is the Business Manager and family sage. She maintains order in the business and family—and keeps everything running smoothly.

CREDITS

Author & Architect:
Ruth Maran

Copy Editor:
Alison MacAlpine

Project Manager:
Judy Maran

Editor:
Brad Hilderley

Proofreaders:
Kelleigh Wing
Susan Beytas

Layout & Cover Design:
Christie Van Duin

Illustrators:
Tamara Poliquin
Chris K.C. Leung
Russell Marini
Andrew Trowbridge

Screen Artist:
Greg Midensky

Indexer:
Kelleigh Wing

Post Production:
Robert Maran

ACKNOWLEDGMENTS

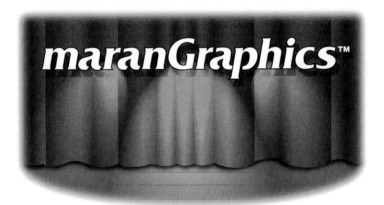

Thanks to the dedicated staff of maranGraphics, including Susan Beytas, Francisco Ferreira, Brad Hilderley, Julie Lane, Chris K.C. Leung, Alison MacAlpine, Jill Maran, Judy Maran, Maxine Maran, Robert Maran, Sherry Maran, Russ Marini, Greg Midensky, Tamara Poliquin, Andrew Trowbridge, Christie Van Duin and Kelleigh Wing.

Finally, to Richard Maran who originated the easy-to-use graphic format of this guide. Thank you for your inspiration and guidance.

TABLE OF CONTENTS

Chapter 6 : Time-Saving Features

Chapter 7 : Personalize Windows

Chapter 8 : Entertaining Features

Chapter 9 : Object Linking and Embedding

TABLE OF CONTENTS

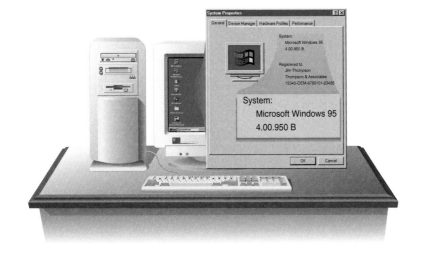

INTRODUCTION TO WINDOWS

Microsoft® Windows® 95 is a program that controls the overall activity of your computer.

Windows ensures that all parts of your computer work together smoothly and efficiently.

CONTROLS YOUR HARDWARE

Windows controls the different parts of your computer system, such as the printer and monitor, and enables them to work together.

ORGANIZES YOUR INFORMATION

Windows provides ways to organize and manage files stored on your computer. You can use Windows to sort, copy, move, delete and view your files.

RUNS YOUR PROGRAMS

Windows starts and operates programs, such as Microsoft Word and Lotus 1-2-3. Programs let you write letters, analyze numbers, manage finances, draw pictures and even play games.

USING THE MOUSE

The mouse is a hand-held device that lets you select and move items on your screen.

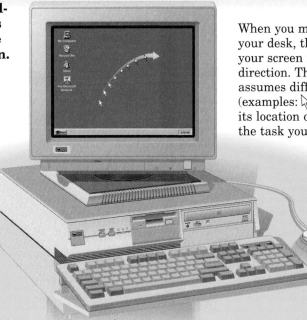

When you move the mouse on your desk, the mouse pointer on your screen moves in the same direction. The mouse pointer assumes different shapes (examples: ⃔, I) depending on its location on your screen and the task you are performing.

Resting your hand on the mouse, use your thumb and two rightmost fingers to move the mouse on your desk. Use your two remaining fingers to press the mouse buttons.

REMEMBER THESE MOUSE TERMS

CLICK
Press and release the left mouse button.

DOUBLE-CLICK
Quickly press and release the left mouse button twice.

DRAG
When the mouse pointer is over an object on your screen, press and hold down the left mouse button. Still holding down the button, move the mouse to where you want to place the object and then release the button.

START WINDOWS

Windows provides an easy, graphical way for you to use your computer.

START WINDOWS

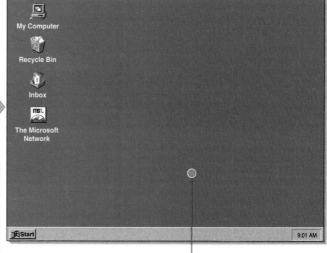

■ When you start Windows, the **Welcome** dialog box appears. It displays a tip about using Windows.

1 If you do not want this dialog box to appear every time you start Windows, click this option (✔ changes to ☐).

2 To close the dialog box, click **Close**.

■ The dialog box disappears and you can clearly view your desktop. The **desktop** is the background area of your screen.

4

THE WINDOWS 95 SCREEN

**The Windows screen displays
various items. The items that appear
depend on how your computer is set up.**

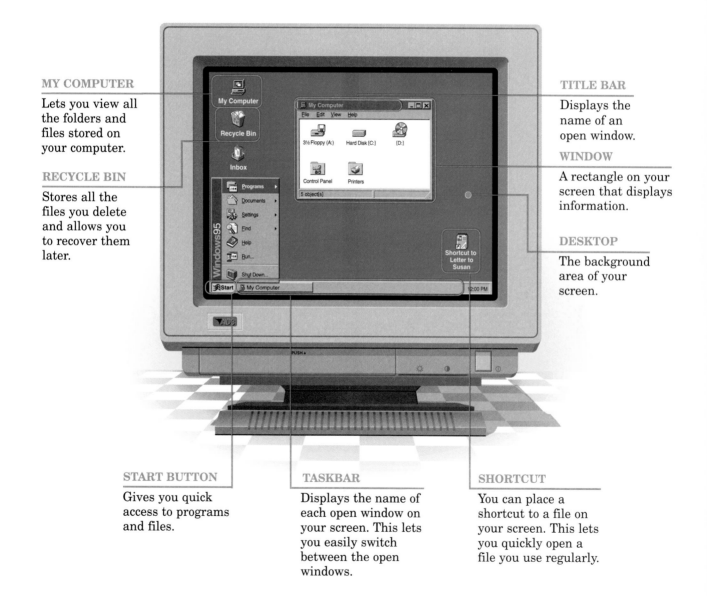

MY COMPUTER

Lets you view all
the folders and
files stored on
your computer.

RECYCLE BIN

Stores all the
files you delete
and allows you
to recover them
later.

TITLE BAR

Displays the
name of an
open window.

WINDOW

A rectangle on your
screen that displays
information.

DESKTOP

The background
area of your
screen.

START BUTTON

Gives you quick
access to programs
and files.

TASKBAR

Displays the name of
each open window on
your screen. This lets
you easily switch
between the open
windows.

SHORTCUT

You can place a
shortcut to a file on
your screen. This lets
you quickly open a
file you use regularly.

DISPLAY THE DATE

You can easily
display the date
on your screen.

DISPLAY THE DATE

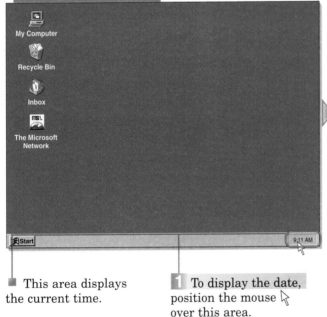

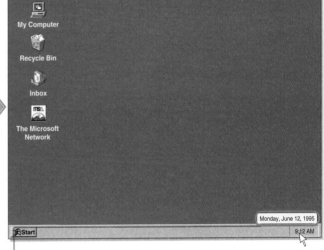

■ This area displays
the current time.

1 To display the date,
position the mouse
over this area.

■ After a few seconds,
the date appears.

Note: If Windows displays
the wrong date or time, you
can change the date or time
set in your computer. For
more information, refer to
page 102.

SHUT DOWN WINDOWS

When you finish using
your computer, you should
shut down Windows before
turning off the computer.

*It's now safe to turn off
your computer.*

Do not turn off
your computer until
this message appears
on your screen.

SHUT DOWN WINDOWS

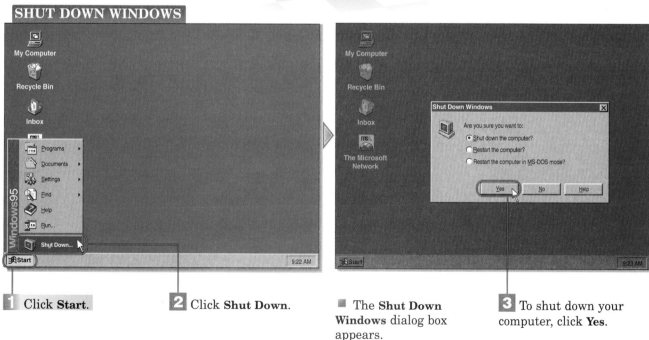

1 Click **Start**.

2 Click **Shut Down**.

■ The **Shut Down
Windows** dialog box
appears.

3 To shut down your
computer, click **Yes**.

**In this chapter you will learn
the basic skills you need to
work in Windows 95.**

CHAPTER 2: WINDOWS BASICS

START A PROGRAM

You can use the Start button to start your programs.

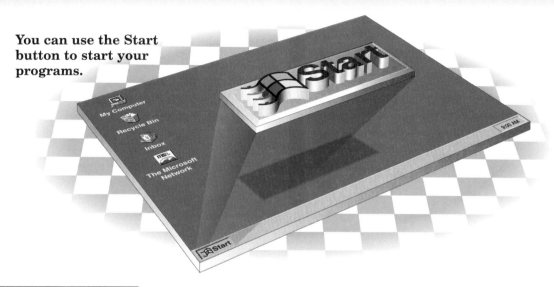

START A PROGRAM

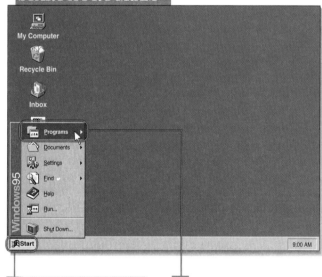

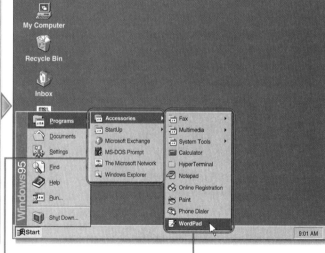

1 Click **Start**. A menu appears.

Note: To display the Start menu using the keyboard, press and hold down **Ctrl** *and then press* **Esc**.

2 Click **Programs**.

*Note: To select a menu item using the keyboard, press the underlined letter (example: **P** for **P**rograms).*

■ A list of items appears.

3 To view the programs for an item displaying an arrow (▶), click the item (example: **Accessories**).

4 To start a program, click the program (example: **WordPad**).

Note: To close the Start menu without selecting a program, click outside the menu area or press **Alt** *on your keyboard.*

10

Windows comes with many useful programs. Here are some examples:

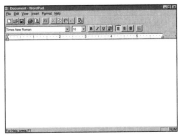

WordPad
is a word processing program that lets you create letters, reports and memos.

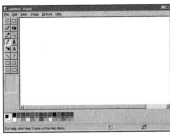

Paint
is a drawing program that lets you draw pictures and maps.

Microsoft Exchange
is a program that lets you exchange electronic mail and faxes.

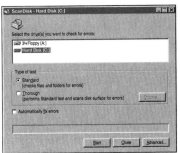

ScanDisk
is a program that searches for and repairs disk errors.

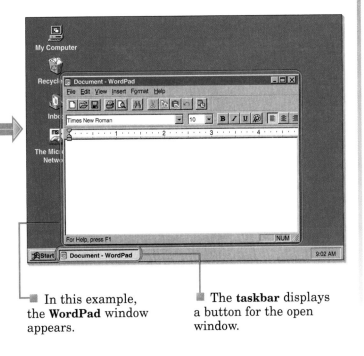

In this example, the **WordPad** window appears.

The **taskbar** displays a button for the open window.

MINIMIZE A WINDOW

If you are not using a window, you can minimize the window to remove it from your screen. You can redisplay the window at any time.

MINIMIZE A WINDOW

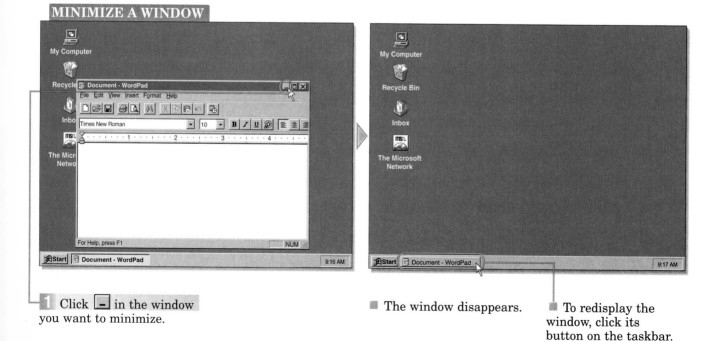

1 Click ☐ in the window you want to minimize.

■ The window disappears.

■ To redisplay the window, click its button on the taskbar.

12

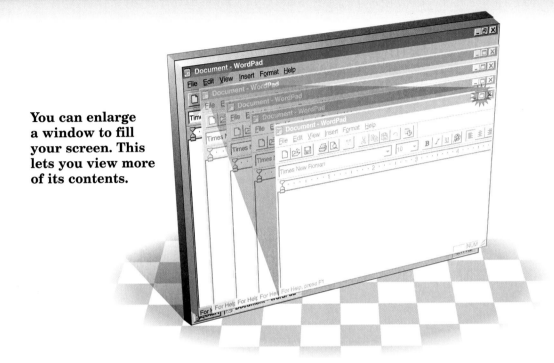

You can enlarge
a window to fill
your screen. This
lets you view more
of its contents.

MAXIMIZE A WINDOW

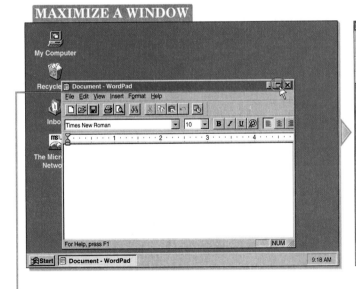

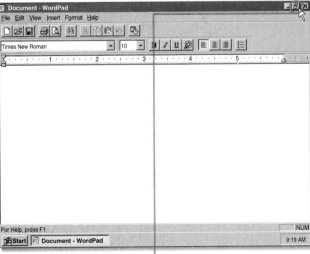

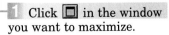

1 Click ▢ in the window
you want to maximize.

■ The window fills
your screen.

■ To return the window to
its previous size, click ▣.

13

MOVE A WINDOW

If a window covers items on your screen, you can move the window to a different location.

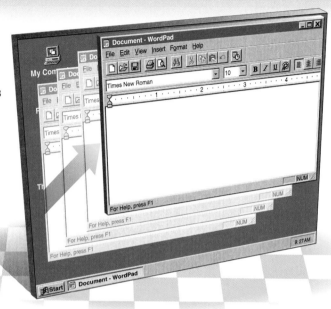

MOVE A WINDOW

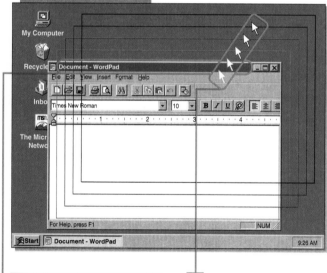

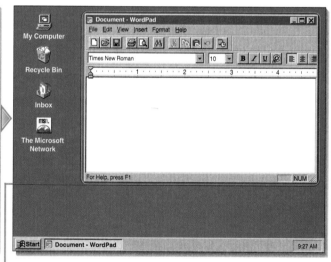

1 Position the mouse ⬉ over the title bar of the window you want to move.

2 Drag the mouse ⬉ to where you want to place the window.

◼ An outline of the window indicates the new location.

3 The window moves to the new location.

14

You can easily change the size of a window displayed on your screen.

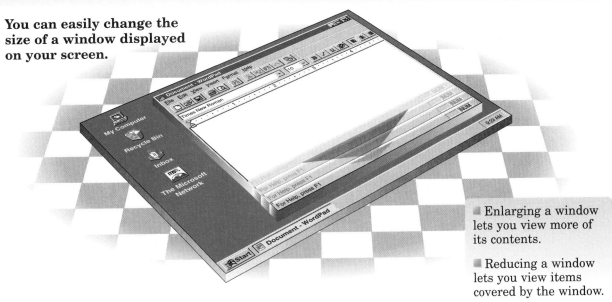

◀ Enlarging a window lets you view more of its contents.

◀ Reducing a window lets you view items covered by the window.

SIZE A WINDOW

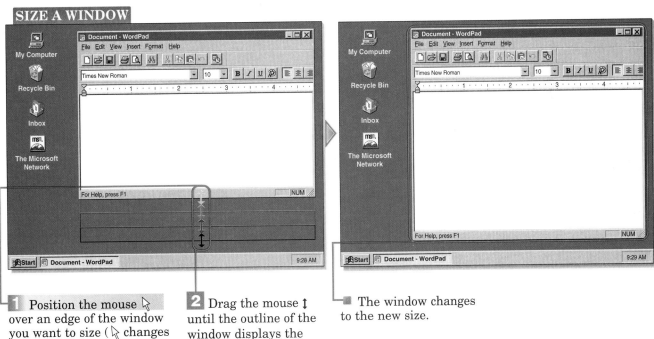

1 Position the mouse ◱ over an edge of the window you want to size (◱ changes to ↕ or ↔).

2 Drag the mouse ↕ until the outline of the window displays the size you want.

◀ The window changes to the new size.

SWITCH BETWEEN WINDOWS

You can have more than one window open at a time. You can easily switch between all open windows.

SWITCH BETWEEN WINDOWS

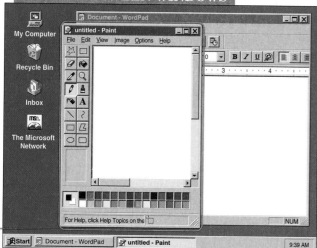

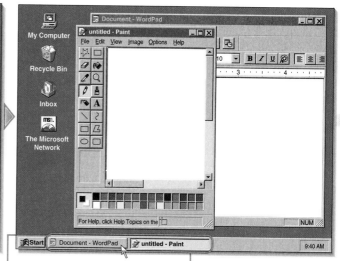

■ You can only work in one window at a time. The active window (example: **Paint**) appears in front of all other windows.

Note: To start a program, such as Paint, refer to page 10.

■ The taskbar displays a button for each open window on your screen.

1 To move the window you want to work with to the front, click its button on the taskbar.

Think of each window as a separate piece of paper. Switching between windows lets you place a different piece of paper at the top of the pile.

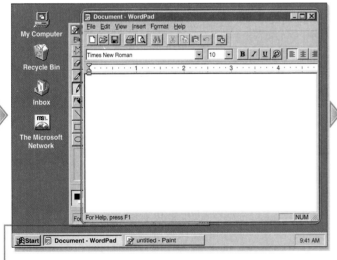

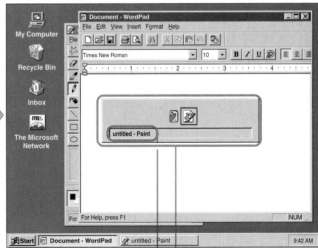

■ The window appears in front of all other windows. This lets you clearly view its contents.

You can also use your keyboard to quickly switch between the open windows on your screen.

1 Press and hold down **Alt** on your keyboard.

2 Still holding down **Alt**, press **Tab** and a box appears.

3 Press **Tab** until this area displays the name of the window you want to work with. Then release **Alt**.

CASCADE WINDOWS

If you have several windows open, some of them may be hidden from view. The Cascade command lets you display your open windows one on top of the other.

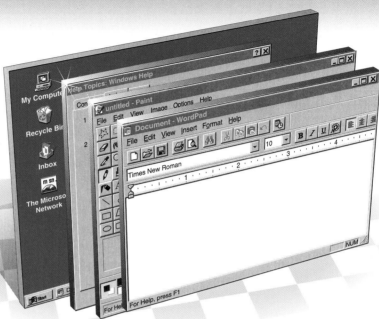

CASCADE WINDOWS

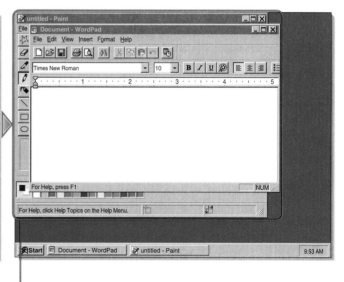

1 Click an empty area on the taskbar using the **right** button. A menu appears.

2 Click **Cascade**.

■ The windows neatly overlap each other.

You can use the
Tile command to
view the contents
of all your open
windows at once.

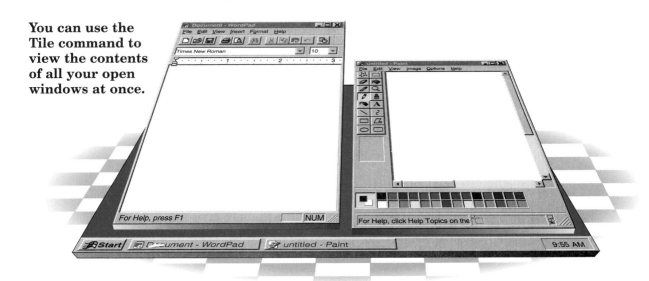

TILE WINDOWS

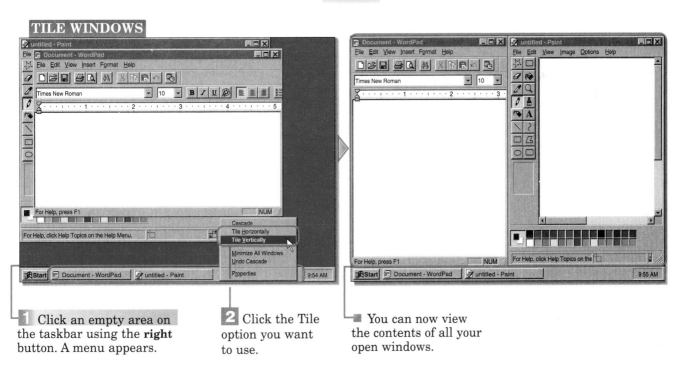

1 Click an empty area on
the taskbar using the **right**
button. A menu appears.

2 Click the Tile
option you want
to use.

You can now view
the contents of all your
open windows.

MINIMIZE ALL WINDOWS

You can minimize all
your open windows
to remove them from
your screen. You can
redisplay a window
at any time.

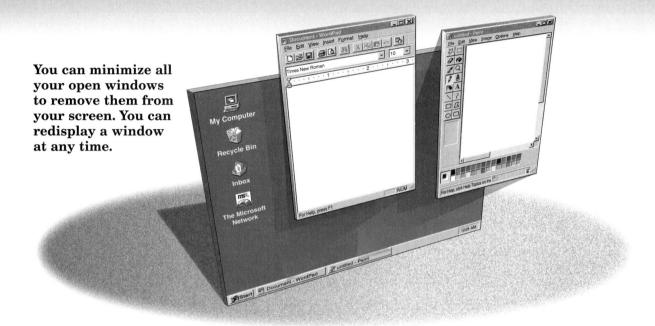

MINIMIZE ALL WINDOWS

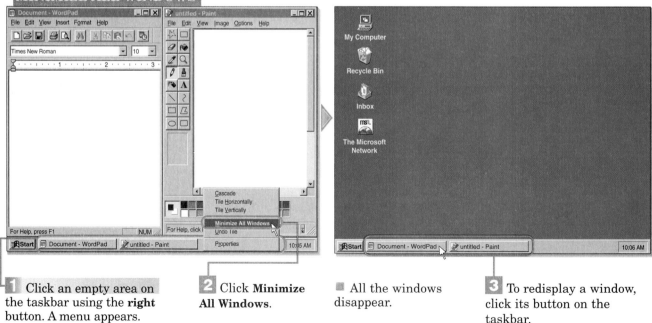

1 Click an empty area on
the taskbar using the **right**
button. A menu appears.

2 Click **Minimize
All Windows**.

▧ All the windows
disappear.

3 To redisplay a window,
click its button on the
taskbar.

When you finish working
with a window, you can
close the window to
remove it from your
screen.

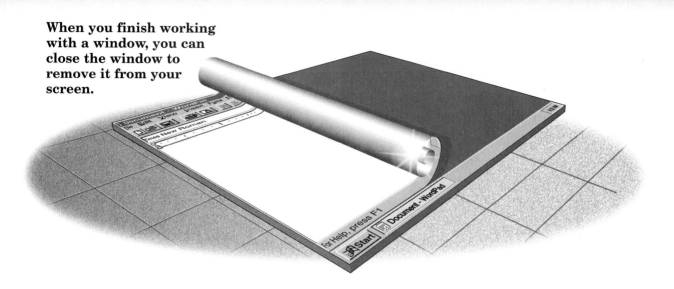

CLOSE A WINDOW

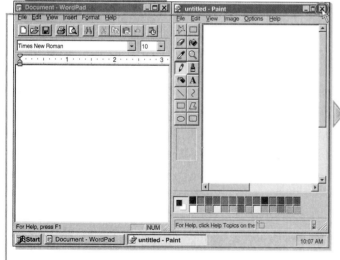

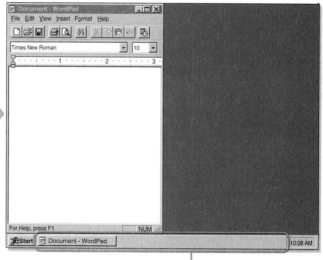

1 Click **X** in the window
you want to close.

■ The window disappears
from your screen.

■ The button for the
window disappears
from the taskbar.

GETTING HELP

If you do not know
how to perform a
task, you can use
the Help feature to
get information.

GETTING HELP

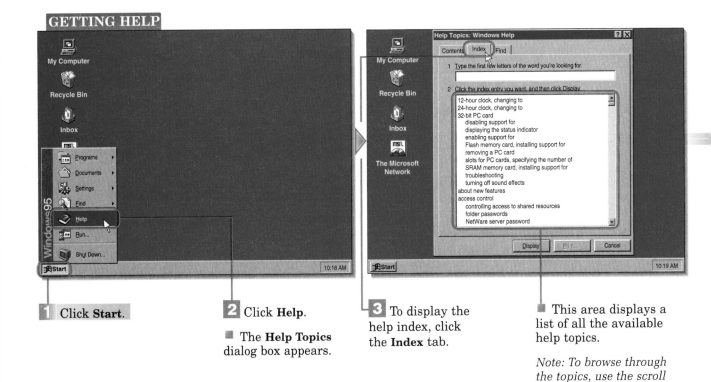

1 Click **Start**.

2 Click **Help**.

■ The **Help Topics**
dialog box appears.

3 To display the
help index, click
the **Index** tab.

■ This area displays a
list of all the available
help topics.

*Note: To browse through
the topics, use the scroll
bar. For more information,
refer to page 24.*

TIP

**There are three ways to find information
in the Help Topics dialog box.**

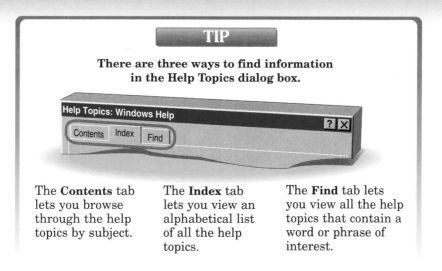

The **Contents** tab lets you browse through the help topics by subject.

The **Index** tab lets you view an alphabetical list of all the help topics.

The **Find** tab lets you view all the help topics that contain a word or phrase of interest.

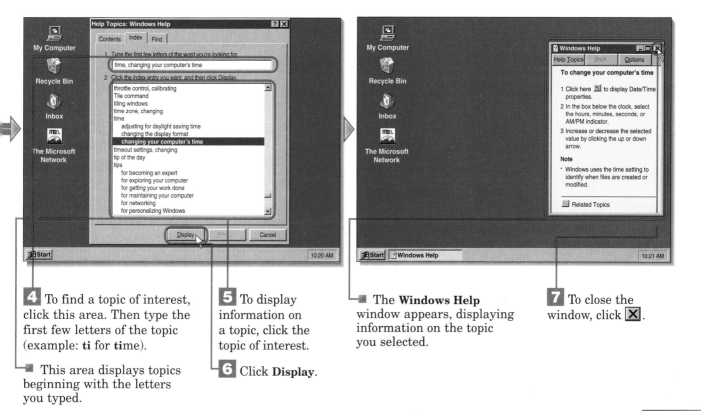

4 To find a topic of interest, click this area. Then type the first few letters of the topic (example: **ti** for **ti**me).

This area displays topics beginning with the letters you typed.

5 To display information on a topic, click the topic of interest.

6 Click **Display**.

The **Windows Help** window appears, displaying information on the topic you selected.

7 To close the window, click ⊠.

23

SCROLL THROUGH A WINDOW

A scroll bar lets you browse through information in a window. This is useful when a window is not large enough to display all the information it contains.

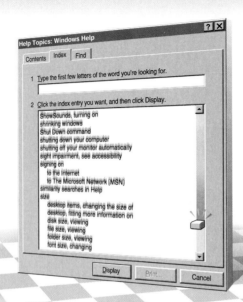

SCROLL DOWN

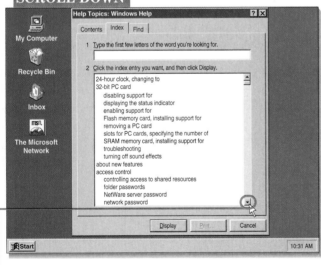

1 To scroll down, click ▼.

*Note: In this example, we scroll through the **Help Topics** dialog box. To display the dialog box, perform steps 1 and 2 on page 22.*

SCROLL UP

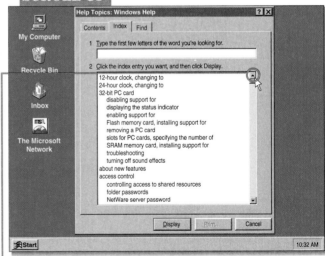

1 To scroll up, click ▲.

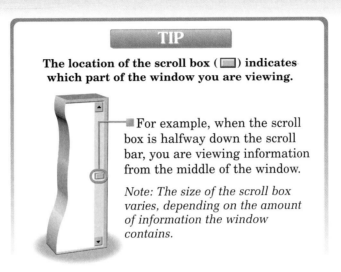

TIP

The location of the scroll box (▭) indicates which part of the window you are viewing.

For example, when the scroll box is halfway down the scroll bar, you are viewing information from the middle of the window.

Note: The size of the scroll box varies, depending on the amount of information the window contains.

SCROLL TO ANY POSITION

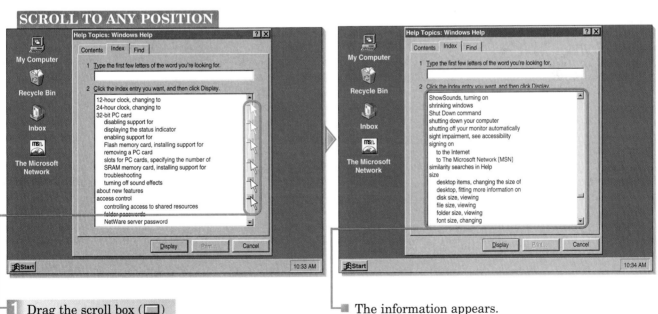

1 Drag the scroll box (▭) along the scroll bar until you see the information you want.

■ The information appears.

USING THE MS-DOS PROMPT

You can work with DOS programs and commands in Windows.

USING THE MS-DOS PROMPT

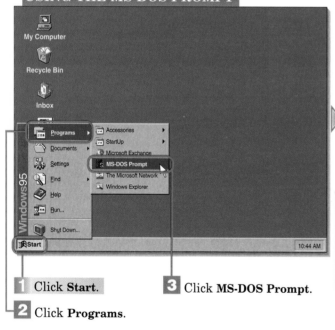

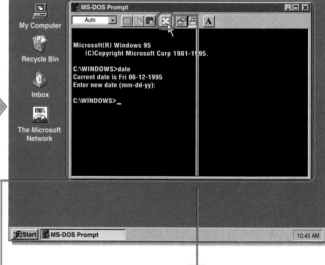

1 Click **Start**.

2 Click **Programs**.

3 Click **MS-DOS Prompt**.

■ The **MS-DOS Prompt** window appears. You can enter DOS commands and start DOS programs in the window.

*Note: In this example, we use the **date** command to display the date set in the computer.*

4 To fill your screen with the MS-DOS prompt, click ▦ .

**If a DOS program will not run in a window,
try restarting the computer in MS-DOS mode.**

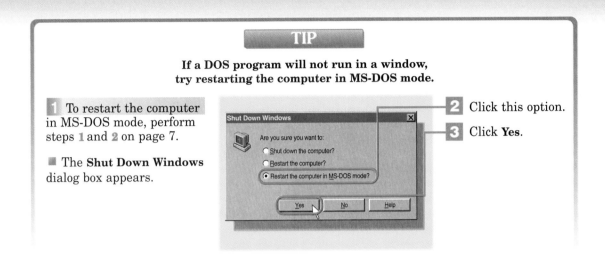

1 To restart the computer in MS-DOS mode, perform steps **1** and **2** on page 7.

■ The **Shut Down Windows** dialog box appears.

2 Click this option.

3 Click **Yes**.

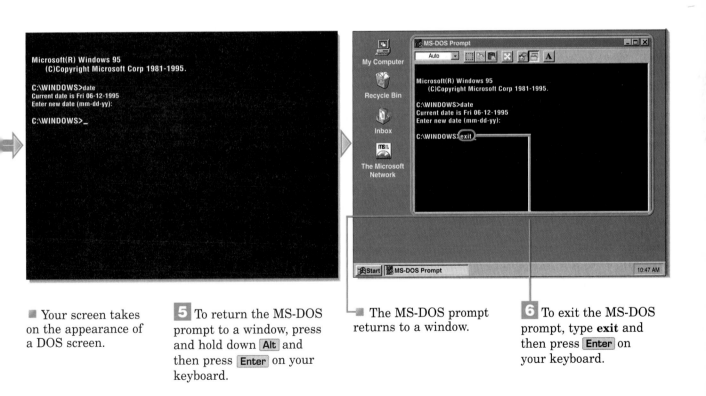

■ Your screen takes on the appearance of a DOS screen.

5 To return the MS-DOS prompt to a window, press and hold down **Alt** and then press **Enter** on your keyboard.

■ The MS-DOS prompt returns to a window.

6 To exit the MS-DOS prompt, type **exit** and then press **Enter** on your keyboard.

**In this chapter you will learn
how to create drawings using
the Paint program.**

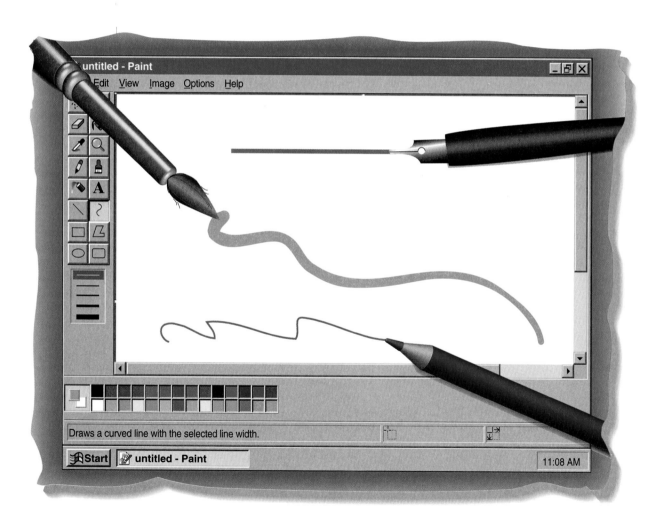

CHAPTER 3: PAINT

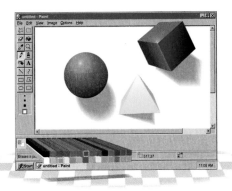

START PAINT

Paint lets you use your artistic abilities to draw pictures and maps on your computer.

START PAINT

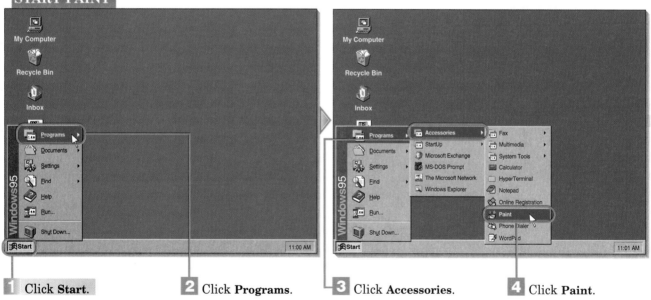

1 Click **Start**.

2 Click **Programs**.

3 Click **Accessories**.

4 Click **Paint**.

TIP

You can place Paint drawings in other programs. For example, you can add your company logo to a business letter you created.

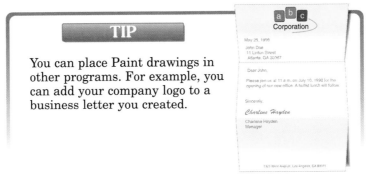

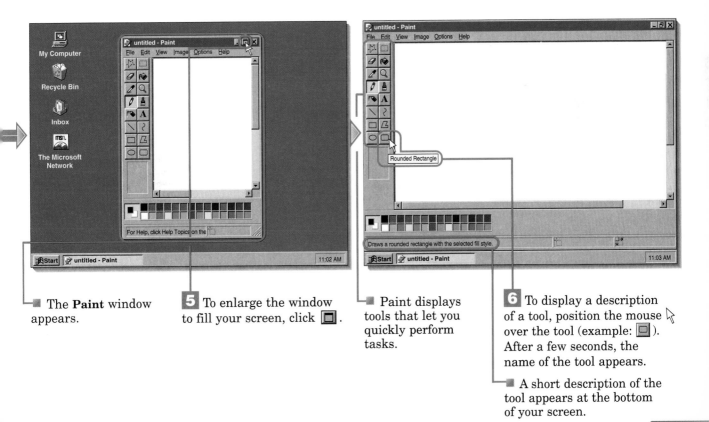

■ The **Paint** window appears.

5 To enlarge the window to fill your screen, click ▣.

■ Paint displays tools that let you quickly perform tasks.

6 To display a description of a tool, position the mouse over the tool (example: ▣). After a few seconds, the name of the tool appears.

■ A short description of the tool appears at the bottom of your screen.

31

DRAW SHAPES

You can draw shapes such as circles and squares in any color displayed at the bottom of your screen.

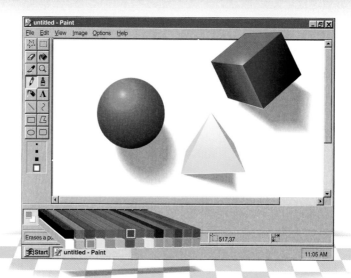

DRAW SHAPES

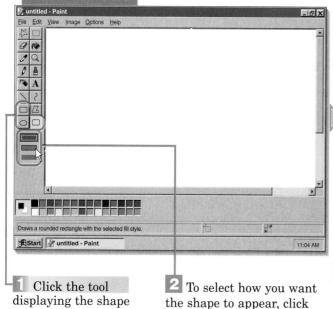

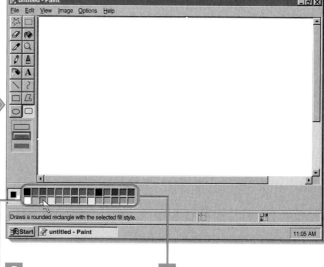

1 Click the tool displaying the shape you want to draw (example: ).

2 To select how you want the shape to appear, click one of the options in this area.

Note: For more information, refer to the top of page 33.

3 To select a color for the outline of the shape, click the color (example: ■).

4 To select a color for the inside of the shape, click the color using the **right** button (example: ■).

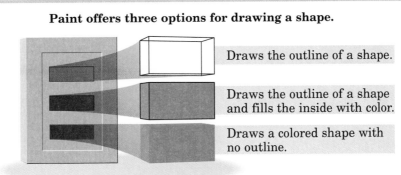

Paint offers three options for drawing a shape.

Draws the outline of a shape.

Draws the outline of a shape and fills the inside with color.

Draws a colored shape with no outline.

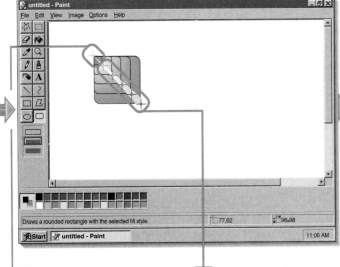

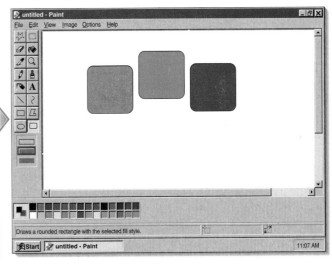

5 Position the mouse ⊳ where you want to begin drawing the shape (⊳ changes to ┼).

6 Drag the mouse ┼ until the shape is the size you want.

Note: To draw a perfect circle or square, press and hold down **Shift** *on your keyboard before and during step 6.*

■ Repeat steps **1** to **6** for each shape you want to draw.

DRAW LINES

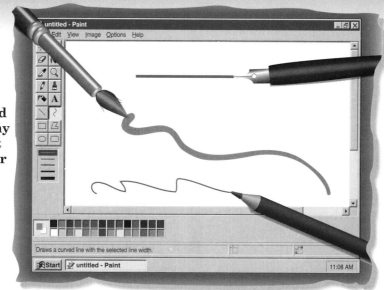

You can draw straight, wavy and curved lines in any color displayed at the bottom of your screen.

DRAW LINES

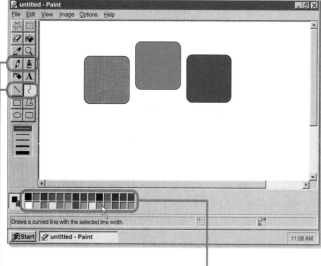

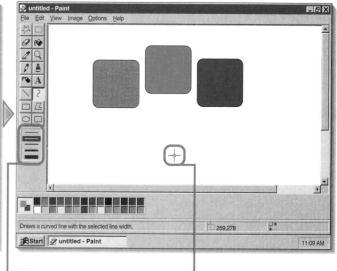

1 Click the tool for the type of line you want to draw (example: ?).

Note: For more information, refer to the top of page 35.

2 To select a color for the line, click the color (example: ■).

3 To select a line thickness, click one of the options in this area.

Note: The ⊘ tool does not provide any line thickness options. The ▲ tool provides a different set of options.

4 Position the mouse ⌖ where you want to begin drawing the line (⌖ changes to + or ⊘).

34

Paint lets you draw these types of lines.

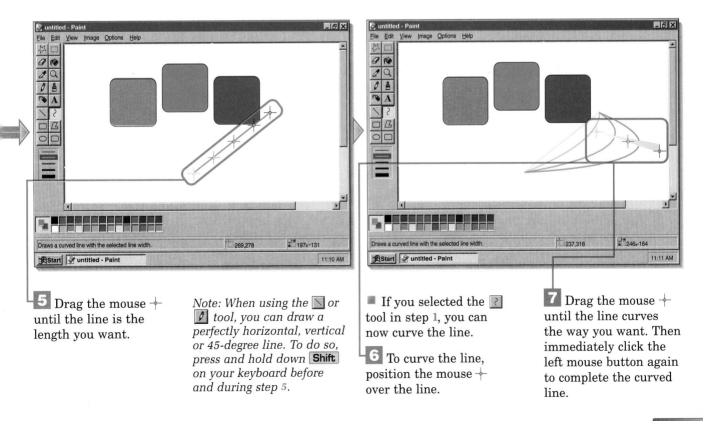

Draws thin, wavy lines.

Draws wavy lines of different thicknesses.

Draws straight lines of different thicknesses.

Draws curved lines of different thicknesses.

5 Drag the mouse ✛ until the line is the length you want.

Note: When using the ▨ or ✎ tool, you can draw a perfectly horizontal, vertical or 45-degree line. To do so, press and hold down **Shift** *on your keyboard before and during step 5.*

■ If you selected the ▨ tool in step 1, you can now curve the line.

6 To curve the line, position the mouse ✛ over the line.

7 Drag the mouse ✛ until the line curves the way you want. Then immediately click the left mouse button again to complete the curved line.

ERASE AN AREA

You can use the Eraser
tool to remove part of
your drawing.

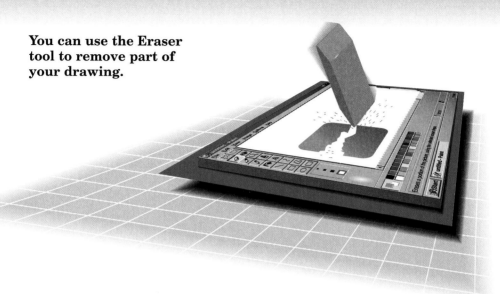

ERASE AN AREA

You can use any color to erase an
area on your screen.

Use a white eraser
when the area you
want to erase has
a white background.

Use a colored eraser
when the area you
want to erase has a
colored background.

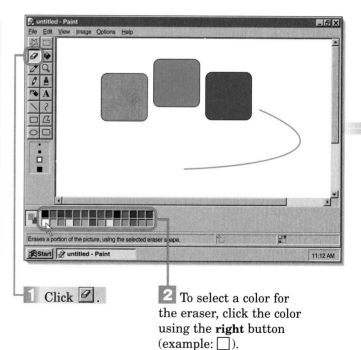

1 Click 🖉 .

2 To select a color for
the eraser, click the color
using the **right** button
(example: ☐).

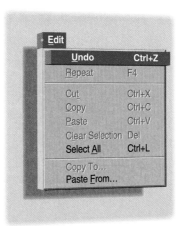

Paint remembers the last change you made to your drawing. If you regret this change, you can cancel it by using the Undo feature.

UNDO LAST CHANGE

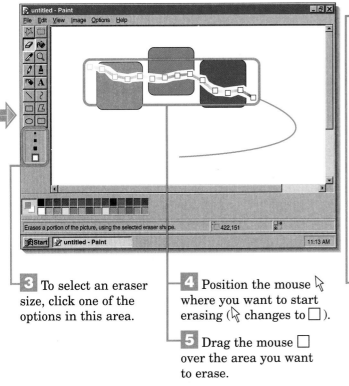

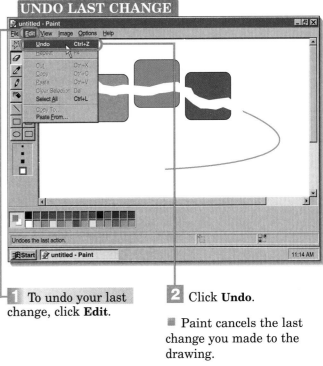

3 To select an eraser size, click one of the options in this area.

4 Position the mouse ▷ where you want to start erasing (▷ changes to □).

5 Drag the mouse □ over the area you want to erase.

1 To undo your last change, click **Edit**.

2 Click **Undo**.

■ Paint cancels the last change you made to the drawing.

ADD TEXT

You can add a title
or explanation
to your drawing.

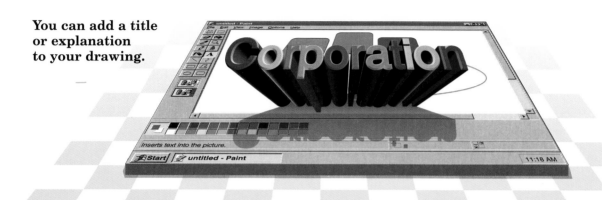

ADD TEXT

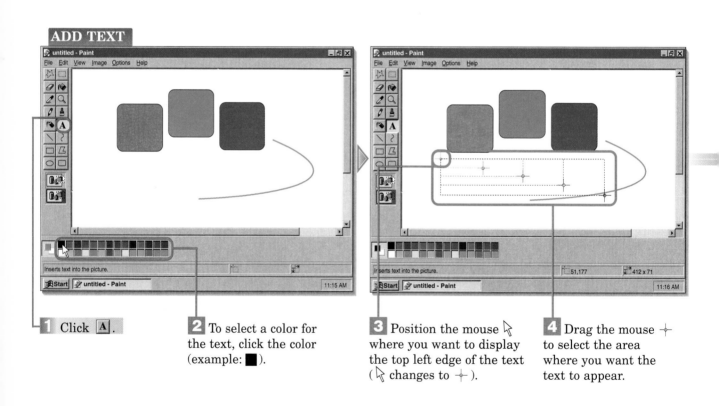

1 Click **A**.

2 To select a color for
the text, click the color
(example: ■).

3 Position the mouse ⌖
where you want to display
the top left edge of the text
(⌖ changes to ✛).

4 Drag the mouse ✛
to select the area
where you want the
text to appear.

TIP

If the Text Toolbar does not appear
after you perform step **5** below, you can easily
display the toolbar on your screen.

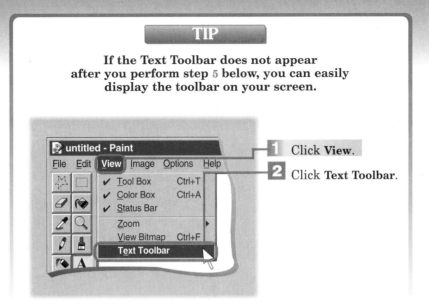

1 Click **View**.

2 Click **Text Toolbar**.

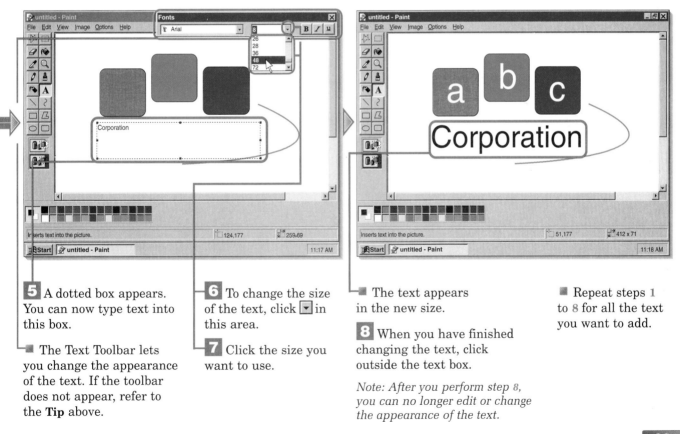

5 A dotted box appears. You can now type text into this box.

■ The Text Toolbar lets you change the appearance of the text. If the toolbar does not appear, refer to the **Tip** above.

6 To change the size of the text, click ▼ in this area.

7 Click the size you want to use.

■ The text appears in the new size.

8 When you have finished changing the text, click outside the text box.

Note: After you perform step 8, you can no longer edit or change the appearance of the text.

■ Repeat steps **1** to **8** for all the text you want to add.

SAVE A DRAWING

You should save your
drawing to store it for
future use. This lets you
later review and make
changes to the drawing.

SAVE A DRAWING

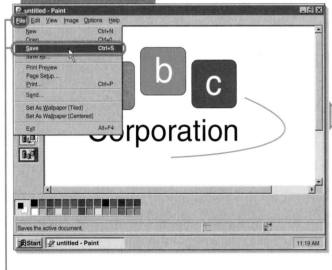

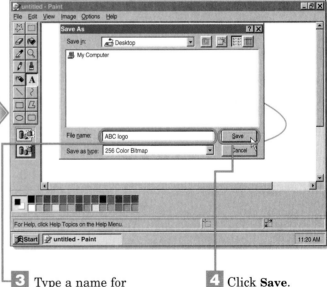

1 Click **File**.

2 Click **Save**.

■ The **Save As** dialog
box appears.

*Note: If you previously saved
your drawing, the **Save As**
dialog box will not appear,
since you have already
named the drawing.*

3 Type a name for
your drawing.

*Note: You can use up to
255 characters to name
your drawing. The name
cannot contain the
characters \ ? : * " < > or |.*

4 Click **Save**.

When you finish using Paint, you can exit the program.

EXIT PAINT

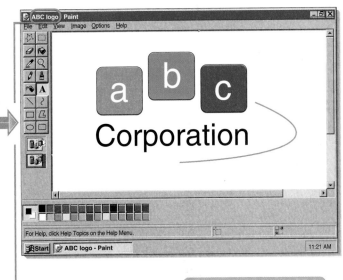

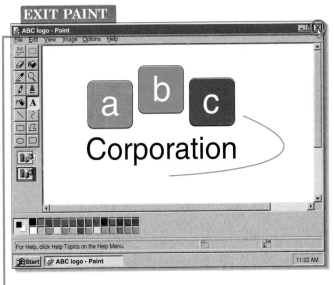

■ Paint saves your drawing and displays the name at the top of your screen.

SAVE CHANGES

To avoid losing your work, you should save your drawing every 5 to 10 minutes.

■ To save changes, repeat steps 1 and 2 on page 40.

1 To exit Paint, click ⊠.

Note: To restart Paint, refer to page 30.

41

OPEN A DRAWING

You can open a saved
drawing and display
it on your screen.
This lets you view
and make changes
to the drawing.

OPEN A DRAWING

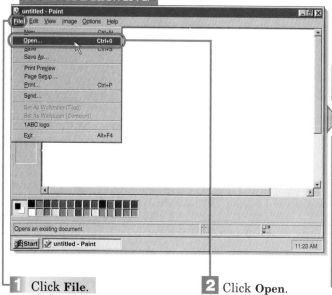

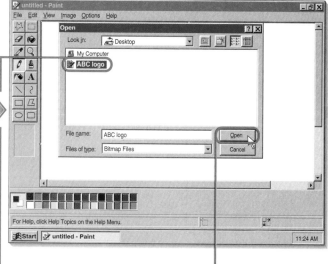

1 Click **File**.

2 Click **Open**.

■ The **Open** dialog
box appears.

3 Click the name of the
drawing you want to open.

*Note: If you cannot find the
drawing you want to open,
refer to page 90 to find the
drawing.*

4 Click **Open**.

IMPORTANT

Paint only lets you work with one drawing at a time. If you are currently working with a drawing, save the drawing before opening another.

Note: For information on saving a drawing, refer to page 40.

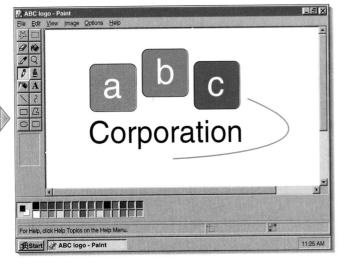

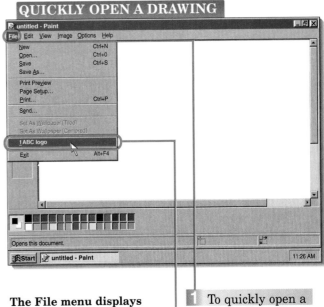

■ Paint opens the drawing and displays it on your screen. You can now review and make changes to the drawing.

The File menu displays the names of the last four drawings you opened.

Note: In this example, only one drawing has been opened.

1 To quickly open a drawing, click **File**.

2 Click the name of the drawing you want to open.

43

**In this chapter you will learn
how to view the information stored
on your computer.**

CHAPTER 4: VIEW CONTENTS OF COMPUTER

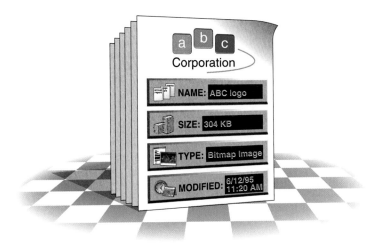

STORAGE DEVICES

HARD DRIVE (C:)

The hard drive is the primary device your computer uses to store information.

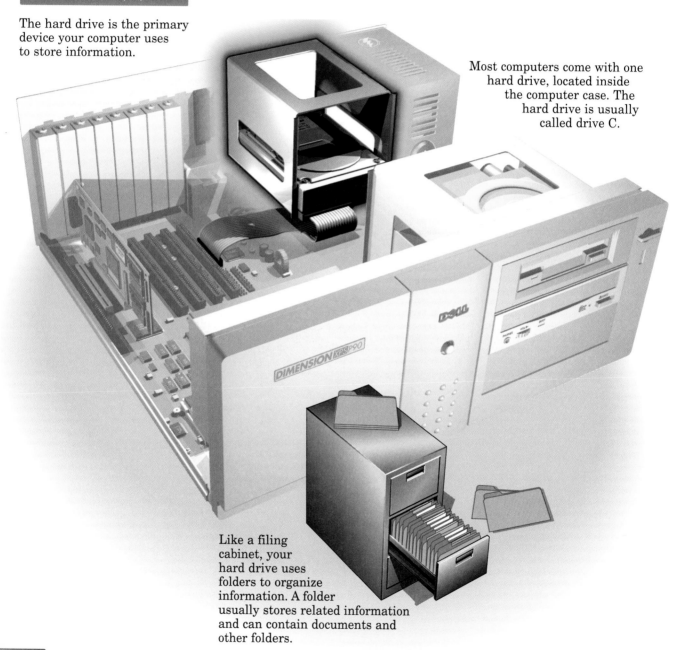

Most computers come with one hard drive, located inside the computer case. The hard drive is usually called drive C.

Like a filing cabinet, your hard drive uses folders to organize information. A folder usually stores related information and can contain documents and other folders.

FLOPPY DRIVE (A:)

A floppy drive stores and retrieves information on floppy disks (diskettes). If your computer has only one floppy drive, the drive is called drive A. If your computer has two floppy drives, the second drive is called drive B.

CD-ROM DRIVE (D:)

A CD-ROM drive is a device that reads information stored on compact discs. You cannot change information stored on a compact disc.

Note: Your computer may not have a CD-ROM drive.

VIEW CONTENTS OF COMPUTER

You can easily view
the folders and files
stored on your
computer.

VIEW CONTENTS OF COMPUTER

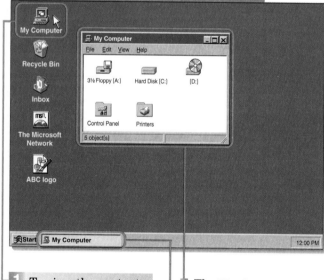

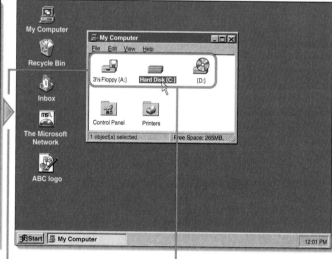

■ 1 To view the contents
of your computer, double-
click **My Computer**.

■ The **My Computer**
window appears.

■ The taskbar displays
the name of the open
window.

■ These objects
represent the drives
on your computer.

■ 2 To display the contents
of a drive, double-click the
drive.

*Note: If you want to view
the contents of a floppy or
CD-ROM drive, make sure
you insert a floppy disk
or CD-ROM disc before
performing step 2.*

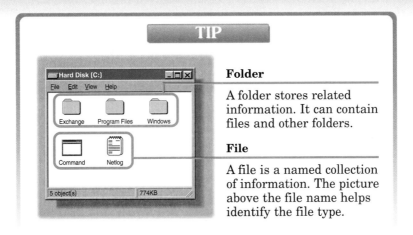

Folder

A folder stores related information. It can contain files and other folders.

File

A file is a named collection of information. The picture above the file name helps identify the file type.

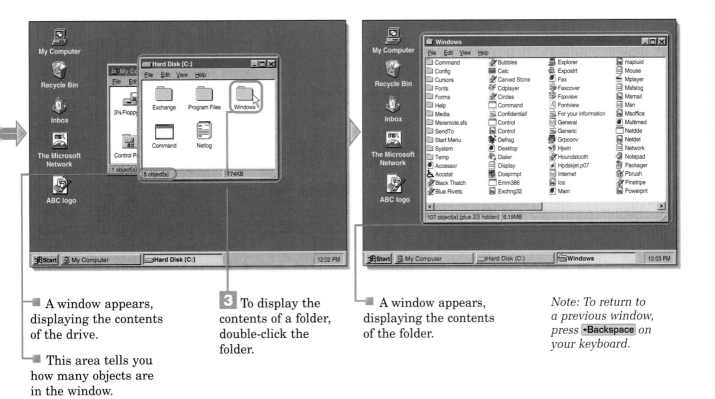

◼ A window appears, displaying the contents of the drive.

◼ This area tells you how many objects are in the window.

3 To display the contents of a folder, double-click the folder.

◼ A window appears, displaying the contents of the folder.

Note: To return to a previous window, press ◆Backspace on your keyboard.

CHANGE SIZE OF ITEMS

You can change the size of items displayed in a window. Enlarging items lets you view the items more clearly.

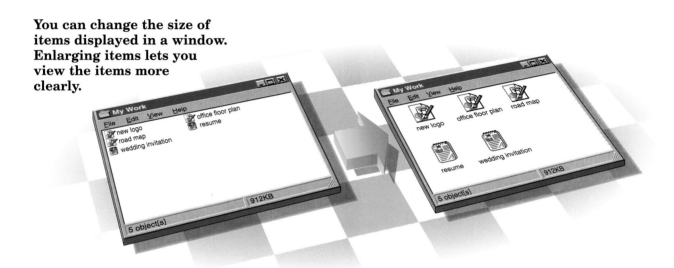

CHANGE SIZE OF ITEMS

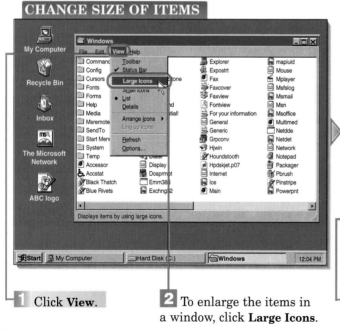

1 Click **View**.

2 To enlarge the items in a window, click **Large Icons**.

■ The items change to a larger size.

*Note: To return to the smaller item size, repeat steps 1 and 2, selecting **Small Icons** in step 2.*

You can move an item to a new
location in a window. This
lets you rearrange items
as you would rearrange
objects on your desk.

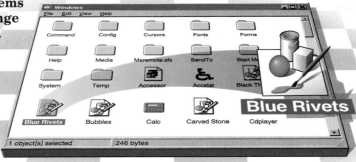

MOVE AN ITEM

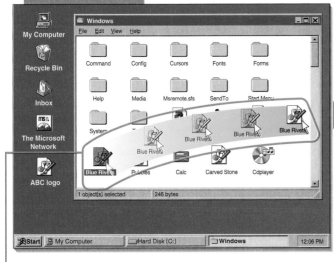

1 Drag the item you
want to move to a new
location.

2 The item moves
to the new location.

*Note: If the **Auto Arrange**
feature is on, other items
will automatically adjust
to make room for the item.
For more information,
refer to page 52.*

ARRANGE ITEMS

You can have Windows
automatically arrange
items to fit neatly
in a window.

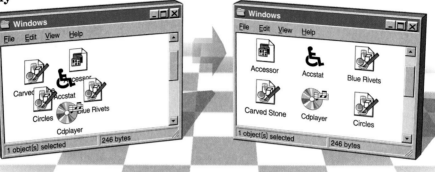

ARRANGE ITEMS

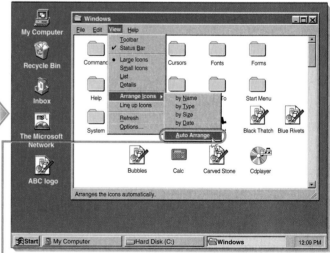

1 Click **View**.

2 Click **Arrange Icons**.

■ If this area does not display a check mark (✔), the Auto Arrange feature is off.

3 To turn on the feature, click **Auto Arrange**.

Note: If the area displays a check mark (✔) and you want to leave the feature on, press **Alt** *on your keyboard to close the menu.*

Note: For information on changing the size of a window, refer to page 15.

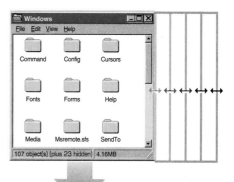

TIP

If you change the size of a window when the Auto Arrange feature is on, Windows will automatically rearrange the items to fit the new size.

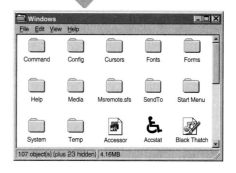

■ The items fit neatly in the window.

■ To turn off the Auto Arrange feature, repeat steps 1 to 3.

Note: You cannot move an item to a blank area in a window when the Auto Arrange feature is on.

DISPLAY FILE INFORMATION

Windows lets you display information about the files listed in a window.

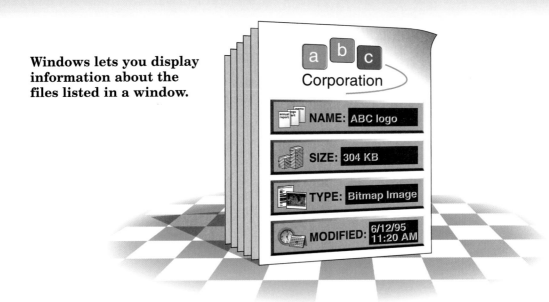

DISPLAY FILE INFORMATION

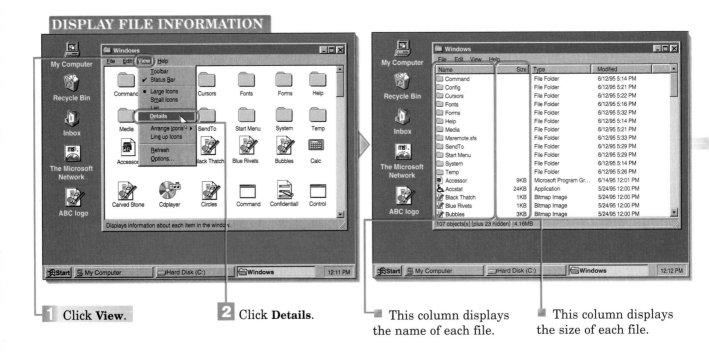

1 Click **View**.

2 Click **Details**.

■ This column displays the name of each file.

■ This column displays the size of each file.

TIP

The size of a file is measured in kilobytes (KB). A kilobyte is approximately 1,000 characters, or one page of double-spaced text.

DISPLAY NAMES ONLY

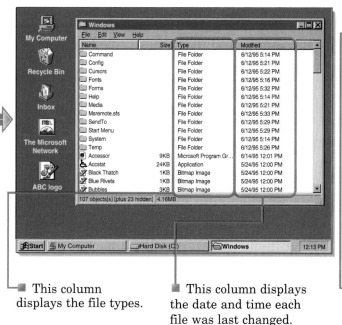

■ This column displays the file types.

■ This column displays the date and time each file was last changed.

1 To hide the file information and display only the file names, click **View**.

2 Click **List**.

SORT ITEMS

You can sort the items displayed in a window. This can help you find files and folders more easily.

SORT BY NAME

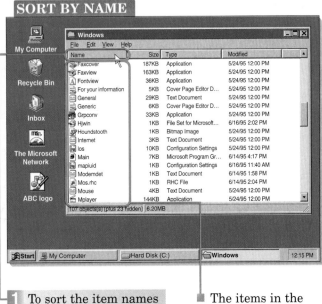

1 To sort the item names from A to Z, click **Name**.

*Note: If the **Name** button is not displayed, perform steps 1 and 2 on page 54.*

■ The items in the window are sorted.

■ To sort the item names from Z to A, repeat step 1.

SORT BY SIZE

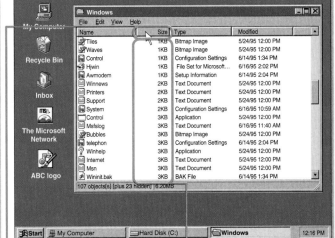

1 To sort the items from smallest to largest, click **Size**.

*Note: If the **Size** button is not displayed, perform steps 1 and 2 on page 54.*

■ The items in the window are sorted.

■ To sort the items from largest to smallest, repeat step 1.

TIP

No matter how you sort items,
Windows always lists the
folders separately from
the files.

SORT BY TYPE

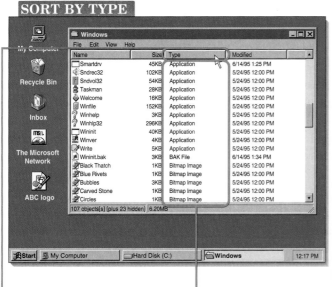

SORT BY DATE

◀ **1** To sort the item types
from A to Z, click **Type**.

*Note: If the Type button
is not displayed, perform
steps 1 and 2 on page 54.*

◾ The items in the
window are sorted.

◾ To sort the item
types from Z to A,
repeat step 1.

◀ **1** To sort the items
from newest to oldest,
click **Modified**.

*Note: If the Modified button
is not displayed, perform
steps 1 and 2 on page 54.*

◾ The items in the
window are sorted.

◾ To sort the items
from oldest to newest,
repeat step 1.

57

**In this chapter you will learn
how to work with files and folders
stored on your computer.**

CHAPTER 5: WORK WITH FILES AND FOLDERS

SELECT FILES

Before working with files, you must first select the files you want to work with. Selected files appear highlighted on your screen.

SELECT A FILE

1 Click the file you want to select.

■ The file is highlighted.

Note: To deselect files, click a blank area in the window.

■ This area displays the number of files you selected.

■ This area displays the total size of the files you selected.

Note: One byte equals one character. One kilobyte (KB) equals approximately one page of double-spaced text.

TIP

SELECT FOLDERS

You can select folders the same way you select files.

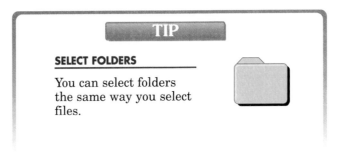

SELECT A GROUP OF FILES

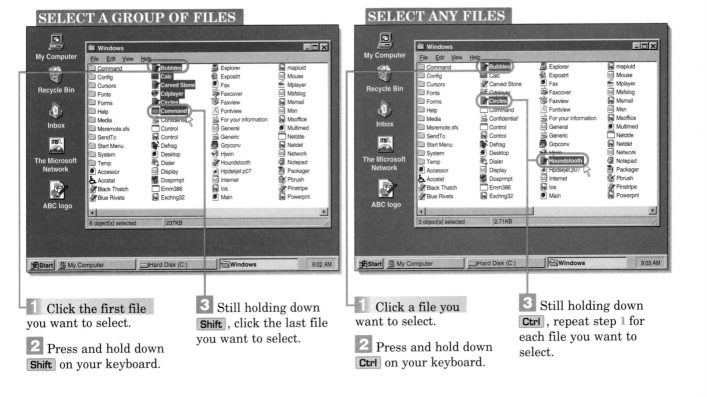

1 Click the first file you want to select.

2 Press and hold down **Shift** on your keyboard.

3 Still holding down **Shift**, click the last file you want to select.

SELECT ANY FILES

1 Click a file you want to select.

2 Press and hold down **Ctrl** on your keyboard.

3 Still holding down **Ctrl**, repeat step 1 for each file you want to select.

CREATE A NEW FOLDER

You can create a new folder to better organize the information stored on your computer. Creating a folder is like placing a new folder in a filing cabinet.

A folder is also called a directory.

CREATE A NEW FOLDER

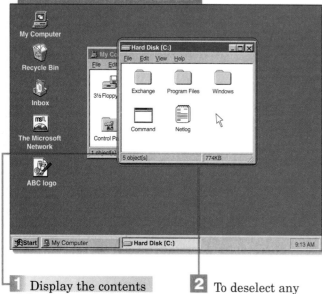

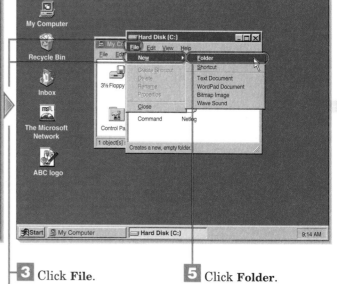

1 Display the contents of the drive or folder where you want to place the new folder.

Note: For more information, refer to page 48.

2 To deselect any selected files, click a blank area in the window.

3 Click **File**.

4 Click **New**.

5 Click **Folder**.

62

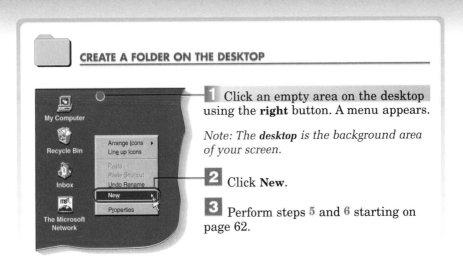

CREATE A FOLDER ON THE DESKTOP

1 Click an empty area on the desktop using the **right** button. A menu appears.

*Note: The **desktop** is the background area of your screen.*

2 Click **New**.

3 Perform steps **5** and **6** starting on page 62.

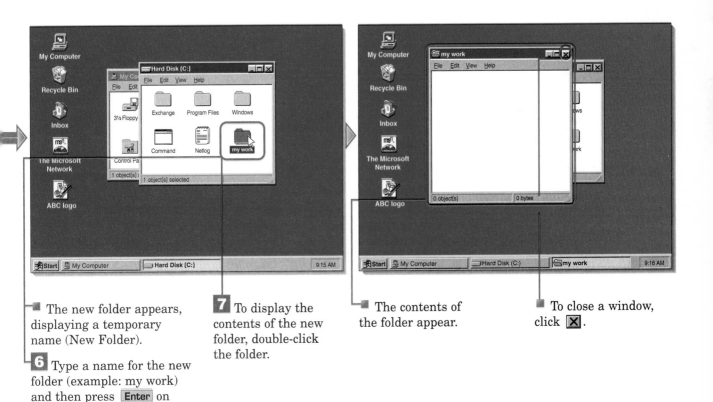

◆ The new folder appears, displaying a temporary name (New Folder).

6 Type a name for the new folder (example: my work) and then press **Enter** on your keyboard.

7 To display the contents of the new folder, double-click the folder.

◆ The contents of the folder appear.

◆ To close a window, click **X**.

MOVE A FILE TO A FOLDER

You can organize the files stored on your computer by placing them in folders.

Moving files to folders is similar to rearranging documents in a filing cabinet to make them easier to find.

MOVE A FILE TO A FOLDER

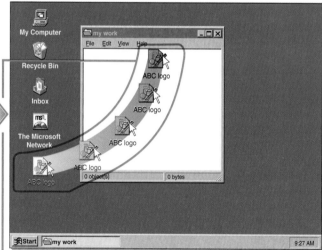

1 Position the mouse ⟨ over the file you want to move.

■ To move more than one file, select all the files you want to move. Then position the mouse ⟨ over one of the files.

Note: To select multiple files, refer to page 61.

2 Drag the file to a folder.

64

TIP

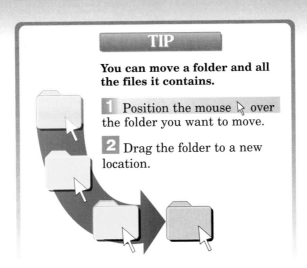

You can move a folder and all the files it contains.

1 Position the mouse 🖰 over the folder you want to move.

2 Drag the folder to a new location.

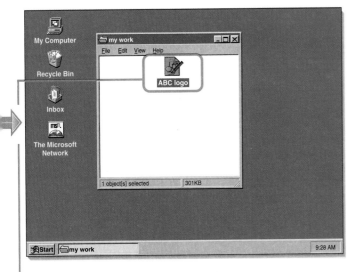

◾ The file moves to the folder.

COPY A FILE TO A FOLDER

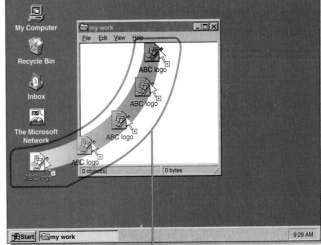

You can make an exact copy of a file and then place the copy in a folder. This lets you store the file in two locations.

1 Press and hold down **Ctrl** on your keyboard.

2 Still holding down **Ctrl**, drag the file to the folder.

COPY A FILE TO A FLOPPY DISK

You can make an exact copy of a file and then place the copy on a floppy disk. This is useful if you want to give a copy of a file to a colleague.

COPY A FILE TO A FLOPPY DISK

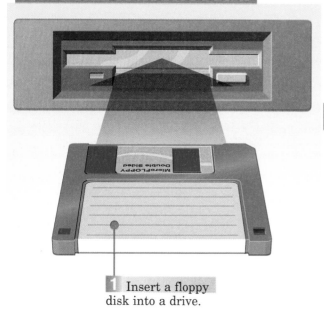

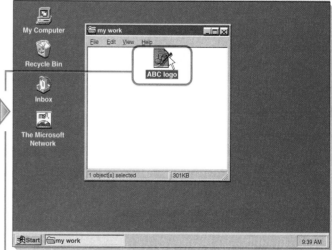

1 Insert a floppy disk into a drive.

2 Click the file you want to copy.

■ To copy more than one file, select all the files you want to copy.

Note: To select multiple files, refer to page 61.

Windows provides a backup program that helps you copy all your important files to floppy disks. This provides you with extra copies in case the original files are lost or damaged.

Note: To back up files, refer to the Back Up Your Files chapter starting on page 228.

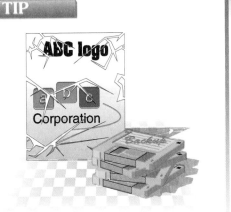

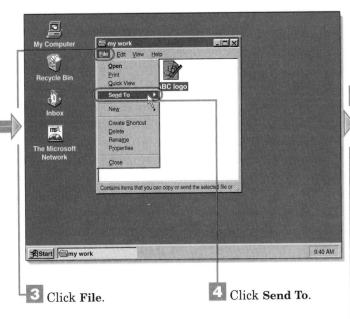

3 Click **File**.

4 Click **Send To**.

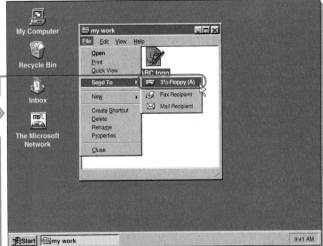

This area lists the floppy drive(s) on your computer.

5 Click the drive where you want to place a copy of the file.

COPY A FOLDER

You can copy a folder and all the files it contains to a floppy disk.

1 Perform steps 1 to 5 starting on page 66, except click the folder you want to copy in step 2.

RENAME A FILE

You can give a file a new name to better describe its contents. This makes it easier to find the file.

RENAME A FILE

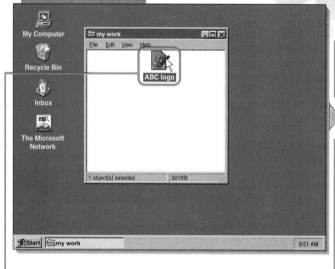

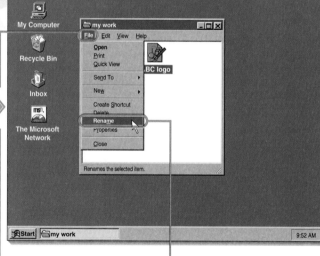

1 Click the file you want to rename.

2 Click **File**.

3 Click **Rename**.

You can easily rename a file on the desktop.

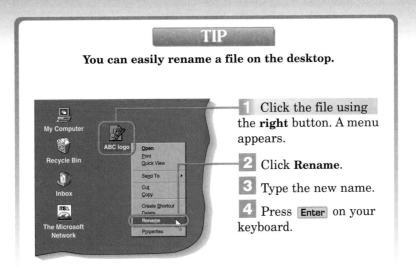

1 Click the file using the **right** button. A menu appears.

2 Click **Rename**.

3 Type the new name.

4 Press **Enter** on your keyboard.

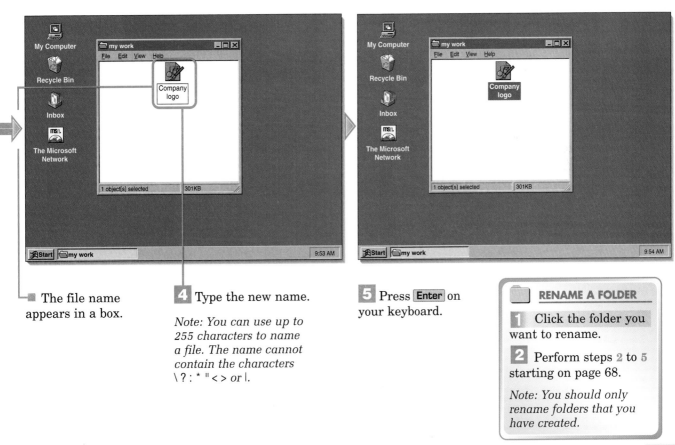

■ The file name appears in a box.

4 Type the new name.

*Note: You can use up to 255 characters to name a file. The name cannot contain the characters \ ? : * " < > or |.*

5 Press **Enter** on your keyboard.

RENAME A FOLDER

1 Click the folder you want to rename.

2 Perform steps **2** to **5** starting on page 68.

Note: You should only rename folders that you have created.

OPEN A FILE

You can open a file to
display its contents on
your screen. This lets
you review and make
changes to the file.

OPEN A FILE

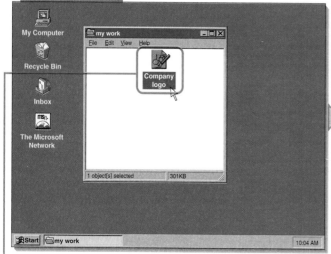

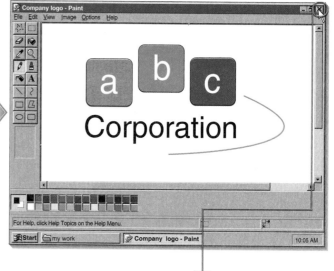

1 Double-click the
file you want to open.

■ The file opens. You
can review and make
changes to the file.

2 To close the file,
click  .

Windows remembers the files you most recently used. You can quickly open any of these files.

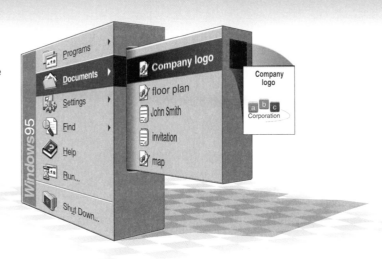

OPEN A RECENTLY USED FILE

1 Click **Start**.

2 Click **Documents**.

■ A list of the files you most recently used appears.

Note: Some files may not appear in this list.

3 Click the file you want to open.

■ The file opens. You can review and make changes to the file.

4 To close the file, click ☒.

PREVIEW A FILE

You can quickly view the contents of a file without starting the program that created the file.

PREVIEW A FILE

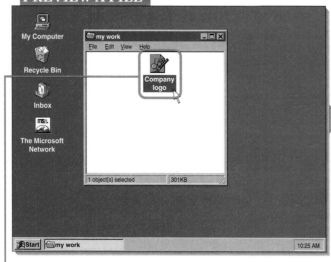

1 Click the file you want to preview.

2 Click **File**.

3 Click **Quick View**.

*Note: If **Quick View** is not available, either you cannot preview the type of file you selected or you must add the **Quick View** component. To add the component, which is found in the Accessories category on the Windows 95 CD-ROM, refer to page 186.*

72

TIP

**You can display an entire page
of your file in the Quick View window.**

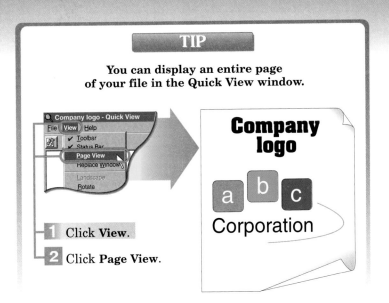

1 Click **View**.

2 Click **Page View**.

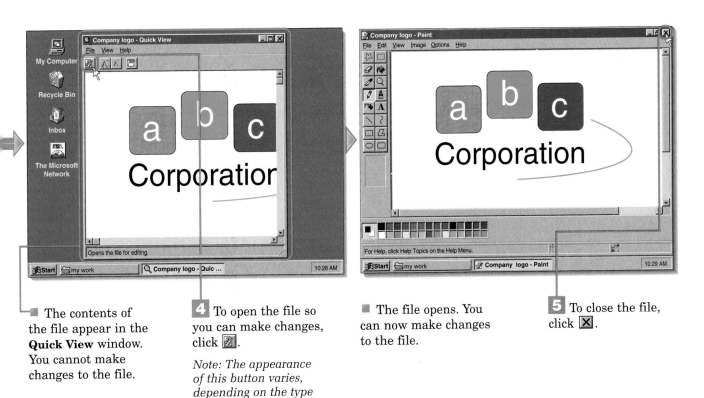

■ The contents of
the file appear in the
Quick View window.
You cannot make
changes to the file.

4 To open the file so
you can make changes,
click 🖾.

*Note: The appearance
of this button varies,
depending on the type
of file you are viewing.*

■ The file opens. You
can now make changes
to the file.

5 To close the file,
click ⊠.

PRINT A FILE

You can produce a paper copy of a file stored on your computer. Before printing, make sure your printer is turned on and contains paper.

PRINT A FILE

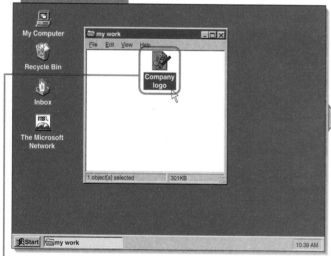

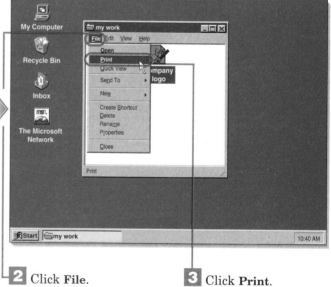

1 Click the file you want to print.

■ To print more than one file, select the files.

Note: To select multiple files, refer to page 61.

2 Click **File**.

3 Click **Print**.

You can view information about the files you send to the printer.

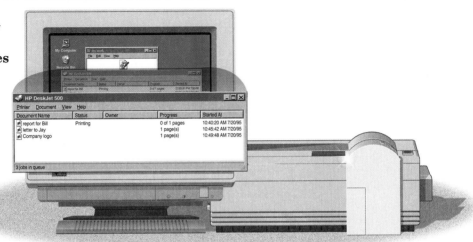

VIEW FILES SENT TO THE PRINTER

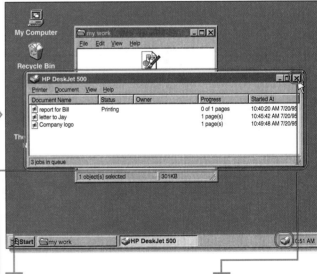

■ When you print a file, the printer icon ( ) appears in this area.

Note: The printer icon disappears when the file is finished printing.

1 To see how many files are waiting to print, position the mouse over the printer icon ( ).

■ A box appears, displaying the number of files.

2 To view information about the files waiting to print, double-click the printer icon ( ).

■ A window appears, displaying information about the files. The file at the top of the list will print first.

3 To close the window, click ☒.

PAUSE THE PRINTER

You can pause your printer and then resume printing at any time. This is useful when you want to change the type of paper in the printer.

PAUSE THE PRINTER

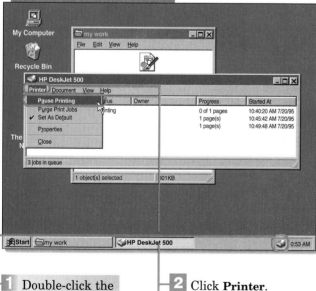

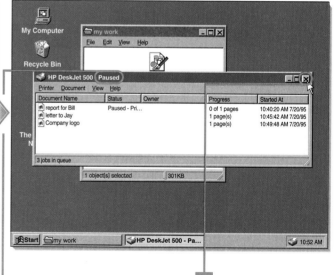

1 Double-click the printer icon (🖨️).

■ A window appears, displaying information about the files waiting to print.

2 Click **Printer**.

3 Click **Pause Printing**.

■ The word **Paused** appears at the top of the window.

4 To resume printing, repeat steps **2** and **3**.

5 To close the window, click ☒.

You can cancel the
printing of a file if
you forgot to make
last-minute changes.

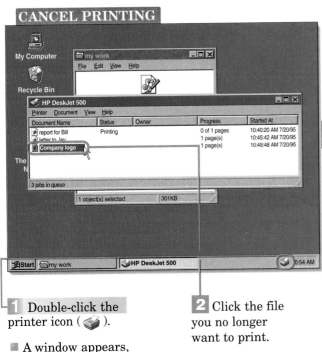

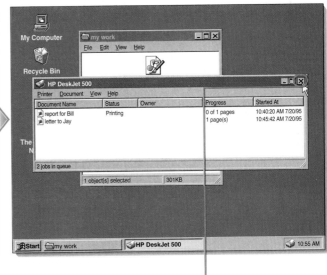

1 Double-click the
printer icon (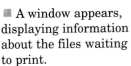).

■ A window appears,
displaying information
about the files waiting
to print.

2 Click the file
you no longer
want to print.

3 Press `Delete` on
your keyboard and
the file disappears
from the list.

4 To close the
window, click ⊠.

DELETE A FILE

You can delete a file you no longer need.

DELETE A FILE

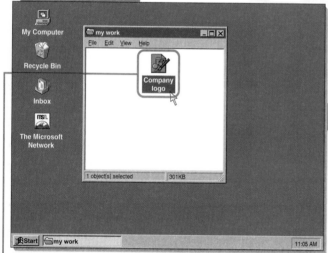

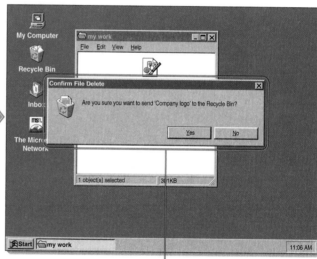

1 Click the file you want to delete.

■ To delete more than one file, select the files.

Note: To select multiple files, refer to page 61.

2 Press Delete on your keyboard.

■ The **Confirm File Delete** dialog box appears.

78

TIP

You can restore a file you have
deleted.

*Note: For more information,
refer to page 80.*

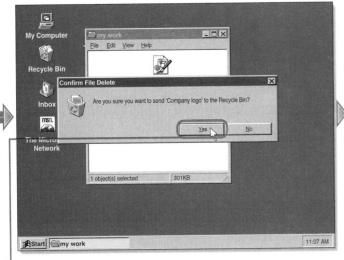

3 To delete the file,
click **Yes**.

■ The file disappears.

 **DELETE A FOLDER**

**You can delete a folder
and all the files it contains.**

1 Click the folder you
want to delete.

2 Perform steps **2** and **3**
starting on page 78.

RESTORE A DELETED FILE

The Recycle Bin
stores all the files
you have deleted.
You can easily
restore any of
these files.

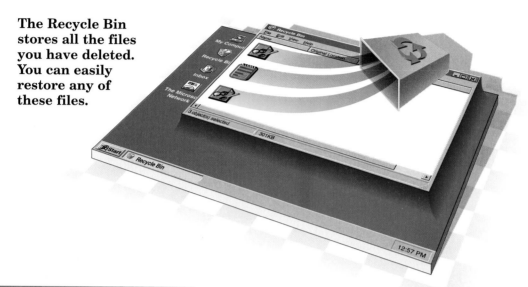

RESTORE A DELETED FILE

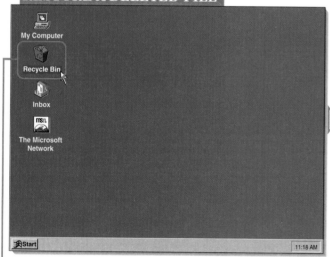

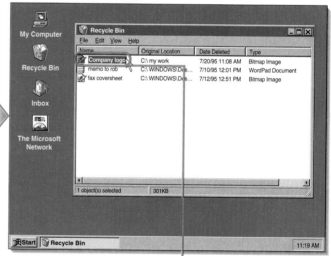

1 To display all the files
you have deleted, double-
click **Recycle Bin**.

■ The **Recycle Bin**
window appears,
listing all the files
you have deleted.

2 Click the file you
want to restore.

■ To restore more than
one file, select the files.

*Note: To select multiple
files, refer to page 61.*

80

The appearance of the Recycle Bin indicates whether or not the bin contains deleted files.

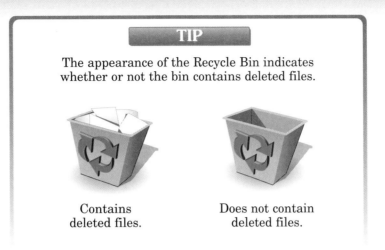

Contains
deleted files.

Does not contain
deleted files.

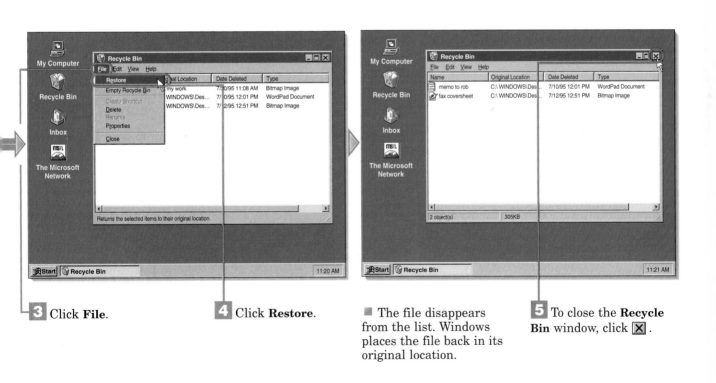

3 Click **File**.

4 Click **Restore**.

■ The file disappears from the list. Windows places the file back in its original location.

5 To close the **Recycle Bin** window, click ☒.

EMPTY THE RECYCLE BIN

You can create more space on your computer by permanently removing all the files from the Recycle Bin.

EMPTY THE RECYCLE BIN

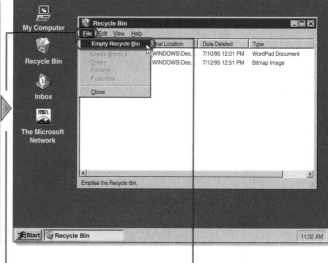

1 To display all the files you have deleted, double-click **Recycle Bin**.

■ The **Recycle Bin** window appears, listing all the files you have deleted.

2 Click **File**.

3 Click **Empty Recycle Bin**.

IMPORTANT

Before emptying the Recycle Bin, make sure it does not contain files you may need in the future.

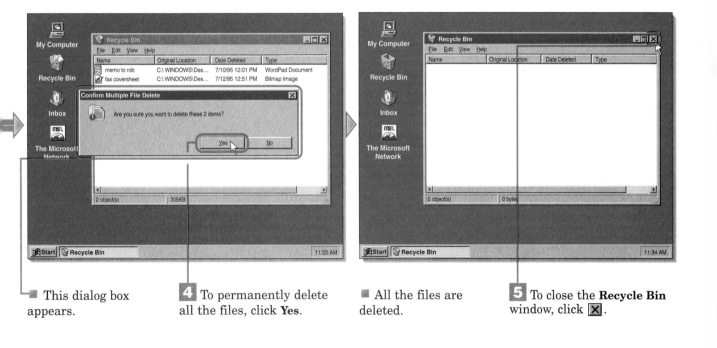

■ This dialog box appears.

4 To permanently delete all the files, click **Yes**.

■ All the files are deleted.

5 To close the **Recycle Bin** window, click ✕.

START WINDOWS EXPLORER

Like a map, Windows Explorer shows the location of every folder and file on your computer.

START WINDOWS EXPLORER

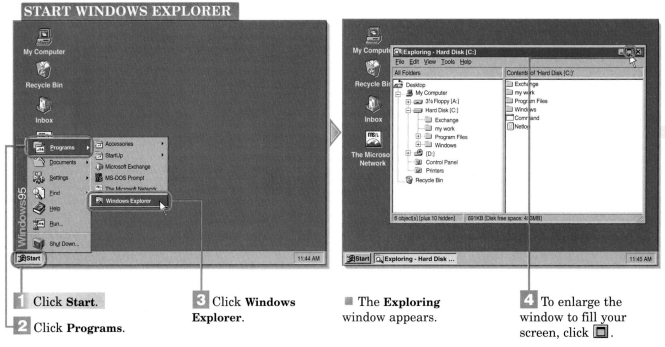

1 Click **Start**.

2 Click **Programs**.

3 Click **Windows Explorer**.

■ The **Exploring** window appears.

4 To enlarge the window to fill your screen, click ▢.

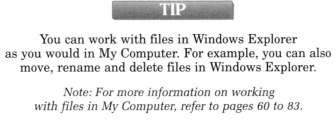

TIP

You can work with files in Windows Explorer
as you would in My Computer. For example, you can also
move, rename and delete files in Windows Explorer.

*Note: For more information on working
with files in My Computer, refer to pages 60 to 83.*

Windows Explorer   **My Computer**

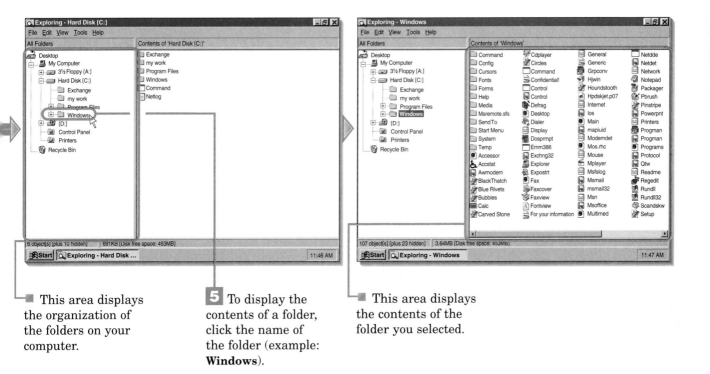

■ This area displays
the organization of
the folders on your
computer.

5 To display the
contents of a folder,
click the name of
the folder (example:
Windows).

■ This area displays
the contents of the
folder you selected.

DISPLAY OR HIDE FOLDERS

A folder may contain other folders. You can easily display or hide these folders at any time.

DISPLAY HIDDEN FOLDERS

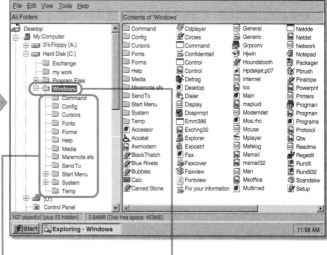

You can display hidden folders to view more of the contents of your computer.

■1 To display the hidden folders within a folder, click the plus sign (⊞) beside the folder.

■ The hidden folders appear.

■ The plus sign (⊞) beside the folder changes to a minus sign (⊟). This indicates that all the folders within the folder are now displayed.

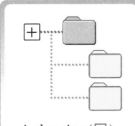

A plus sign (⊞) beside a folder indicates that all the folders it contains are hidden.

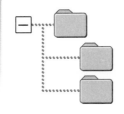

A minus sign (⊟) beside a folder indicates that all the folders it contains are displayed.

No sign beside a folder indicates that the folder does not contain any folders, although it may contain files.

HIDE FOLDERS

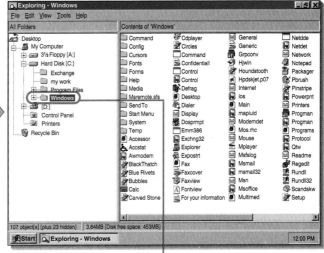

You can hide folders to reduce the amount of information on your screen.

1 To hide the folders within a folder, click the minus sign (⊟) beside the folder.

■ The folders are hidden.

■ The minus sign (⊟) beside the folder changes to a plus sign (⊞). This indicates that all the folders within the folder are now hidden.

87

**In this chapter you will learn
how to use several Windows features
that will save you time.**

CHAPTER 6: TIME-SAVING FEATURES

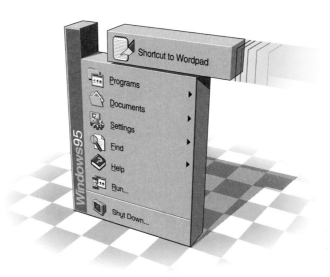

FIND A FILE

If you cannot remember the name or location of a file you want to work with, you can have Windows search for the file.

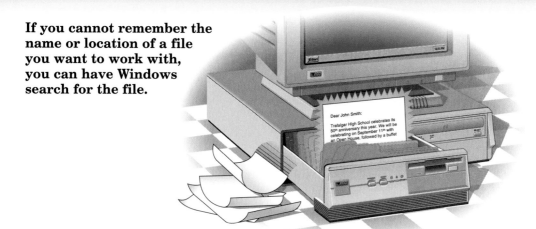

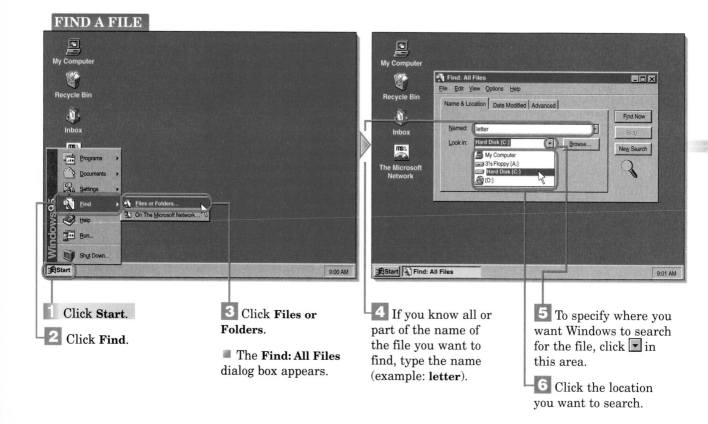

FIND A FILE

1 Click **Start**.

2 Click **Find**.

3 Click **Files or Folders**.

■ The **Find: All Files** dialog box appears.

4 If you know all or part of the name of the file you want to find, type the name (example: **letter**).

5 To specify where you want Windows to search for the file, click ▼ in this area.

6 Click the location you want to search.

TIP

You can search for a specific type of file, such as an application.

Note: An application is a program that lets you perform tasks (example: WordPad).

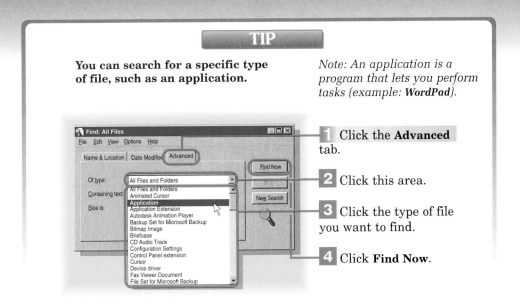

1 Click the **Advanced** tab.

2 Click this area.

3 Click the type of file you want to find.

4 Click **Find Now**.

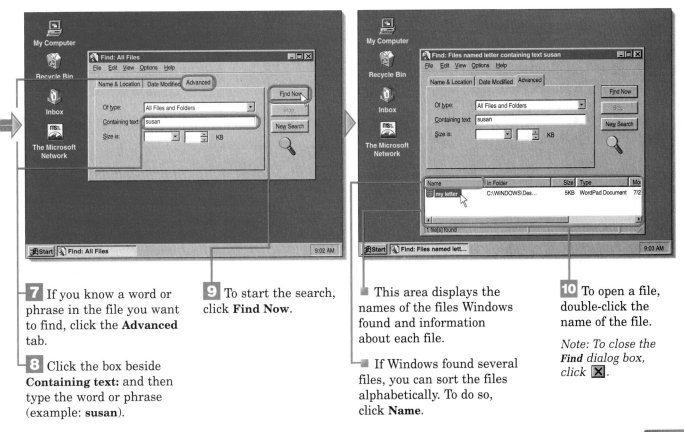

7 If you know a word or phrase in the file you want to find, click the **Advanced** tab.

8 Click the box beside **Containing text:** and then type the word or phrase (example: **susan**).

9 To start the search, click **Find Now**.

■ This area displays the names of the files Windows found and information about each file.

■ If Windows found several files, you can sort the files alphabetically. To do so, click **Name**.

10 To open a file, double-click the name of the file.

Note: To close the **Find** *dialog box, click* ⊠.

ADD A SHORTCUT TO THE DESKTOP

You can add a shortcut to
the desktop to provide a
quick way of opening a
file you use regularly.

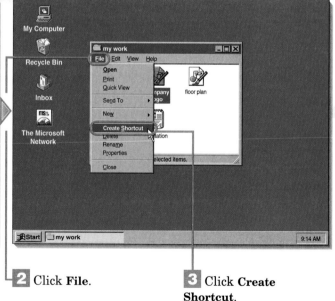

1 Click the file you want
to create a shortcut to.

2 Click **File**.

3 Click **Create
Shortcut**.

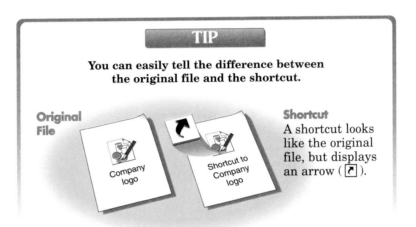

TIP

You can easily tell the difference between the original file and the shortcut.

Original File

Shortcut
A shortcut looks like the original file, but displays an arrow (↗).

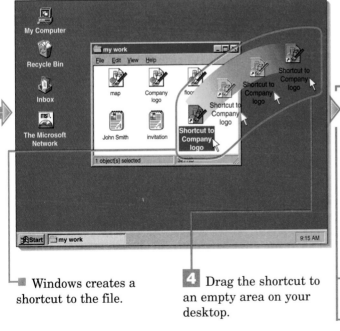

■ Windows creates a shortcut to the file.

4 Drag the shortcut to an empty area on your desktop.

■ The shortcut appears on the desktop.

■ To open the file and display its contents on your screen, double-click the shortcut.

Note: When you add a shortcut to the desktop, the original file does not move. The original file remains in the same place on your hard disk.

PUT PART OF A DOCUMENT ON THE DESKTOP

You can place frequently used information on your desktop. This gives you quick access to the information.

■ Information you place on the desktop is called a scrap.

PUT PART OF A DOCUMENT ON THE DESKTOP

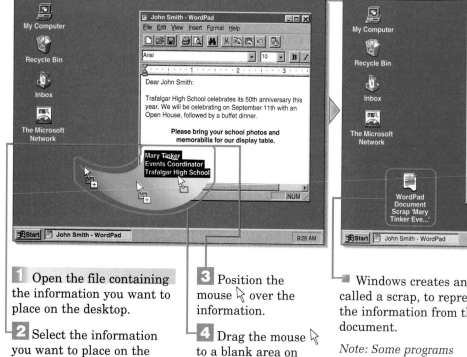

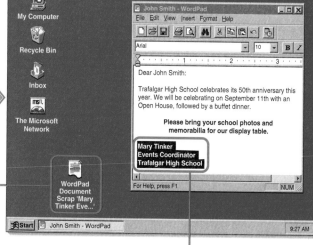

1 Open the file containing the information you want to place on the desktop.

2 Select the information you want to place on the desktop.

3 Position the mouse ⍟ over the information.

4 Drag the mouse ⍟ to a blank area on your desktop.

■ Windows creates an icon, called a scrap, to represent the information from the document.

Note: Some programs cannot create scraps.

■ The information does not move from the document.

TIP

You can create scraps for information
you frequently use in documents, such as your
name and address or company logo.

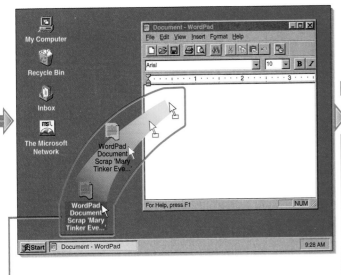

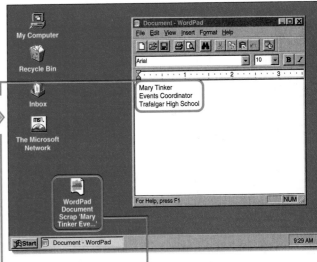

USING SCRAPS

1 To use a scrap in a
document, drag the scrap
to where you want the
information to appear.

■ The information
appears in the
document.

■ The scrap remains on your
desktop. This lets you place
the information in as many
documents as you wish.

*Note: You can delete a scrap
from your screen as you would
delete any file. To delete a file,
refer to page 78.*

ADD A PROGRAM TO THE START MENU

You can add your favorite programs to the Start menu so you can quickly open them.

ADD A PROGRAM TO THE START MENU

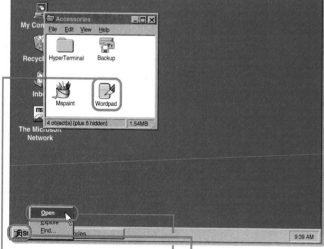

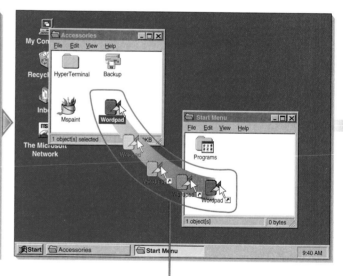

1 Locate a program you want to add to the Start menu.

Note: To find a program, refer to the Tip on page 91.

2 Click **Start** using the **right** button. A menu appears.

3 Click **Open**.

■ The **Start Menu** window appears.

4 To place a copy of the program in the **Start Menu** window, drag the program to a blank area in the **Start Menu** window.

If you no longer want a program to appear on the Start menu, delete the program from the **Start Menu** window as you would delete any file.

Note: To delete a file, refer to page 78.

Removing a program from the **Start Menu** window does not delete the program from your hard disk.

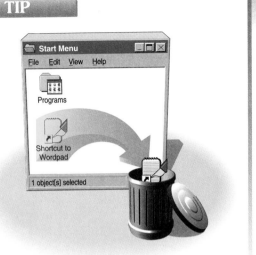

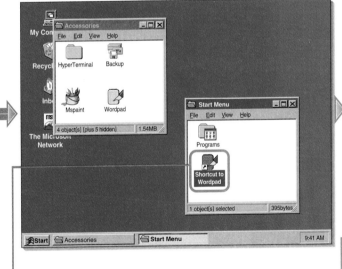

■ A copy of the program appears in the **Start Menu** window.

■ When you copy a program to the **Start Menu** window, you do not change the location of the program on your hard disk.

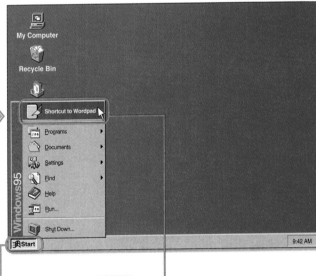

START THE PROGRAM

1 Click **Start**.

■ The program you added to the Start menu appears at the top of the menu.

2 To start the program, click the name of the program.

97

HAVE A PROGRAM START AUTOMATICALLY

If you use the same program every day, you can have the program start automatically every time you turn on your computer.

> Click

HAVE A PROGRAM START AUTOMATICALLY

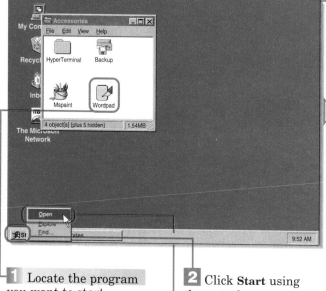

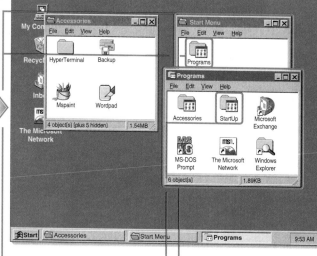

1 Locate the program you want to start automatically.

Note: To find a program, refer to the Tip on page 91.

2 Click **Start** using the **right** button. A menu appears.

3 Click **Open**.

■ The **Start Menu** window appears.

4 To display the contents of the **Programs** folder, double-click the folder.

■ The **Programs** window appears.

■ The **StartUp** folder contains all the programs that start automatically when you turn on your computer.

The items in the Programs menu match the items in the Programs window.

If you add or remove items in the Programs window, the Programs menu will display the changes.

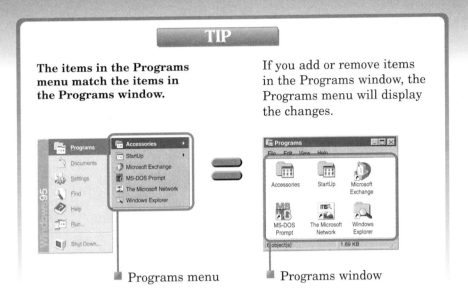

■ Programs menu   ■ Programs window

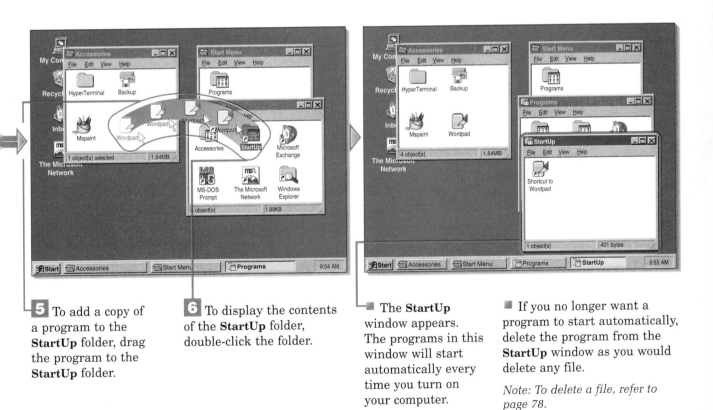

5 To add a copy of a program to the **StartUp** folder, drag the program to the **StartUp** folder.

6 To display the contents of the **StartUp** folder, double-click the folder.

■ The **StartUp** window appears. The programs in this window will start automatically every time you turn on your computer.

■ If you no longer want a program to start automatically, delete the program from the **StartUp** window as you would delete any file.

Note: To delete a file, refer to page 78.

**In this chapter you will learn
how to change Windows settings
to suit your needs.**

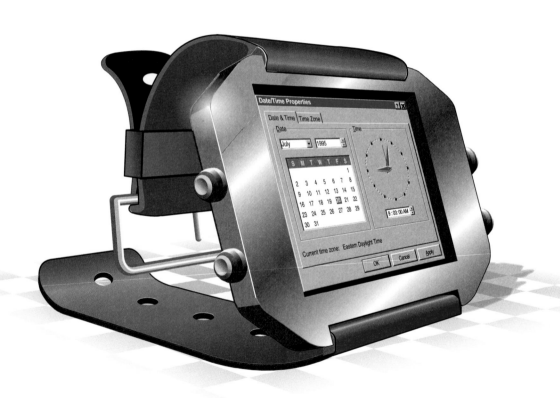

CHAPTER 7: PERSONALIZE WINDOWS

CHANGE THE DATE AND TIME

It is important to have the correct date and time set in your computer. Windows uses this information to identify each document you create or update.

CHANGE THE DATE AND TIME

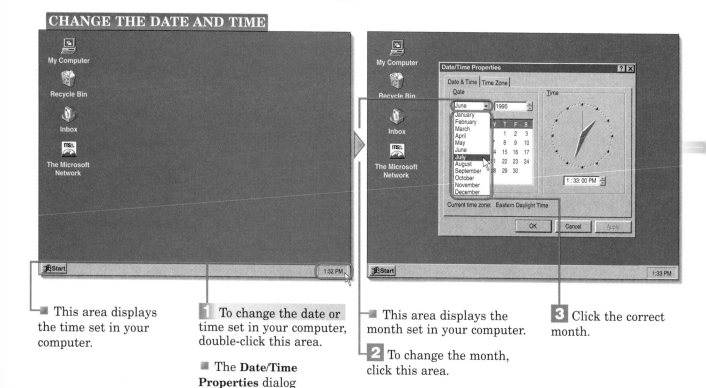

■ This area displays the time set in your computer.

1 To change the date or time set in your computer, double-click this area.

■ The **Date/Time Properties** dialog box appears.

■ This area displays the month set in your computer.

2 To change the month, click this area.

3 Click the correct month.

TIP

Your computer has a built-in clock that keeps track of the date and time even when you turn off the computer.

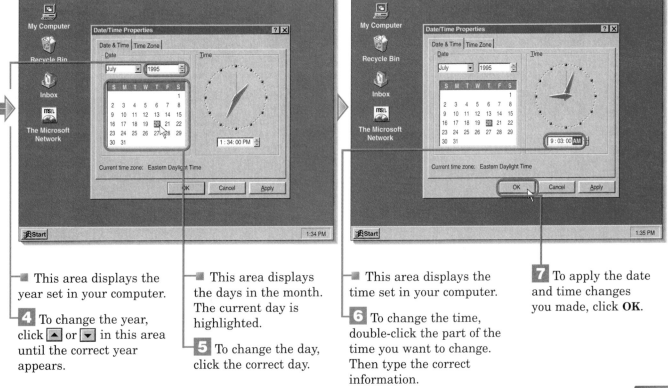

■ This area displays the year set in your computer.

4 To change the year, click ▲ or ▼ in this area until the correct year appears.

■ This area displays the days in the month. The current day is highlighted.

5 To change the day, click the correct day.

■ This area displays the time set in your computer.

6 To change the time, double-click the part of the time you want to change. Then type the correct information.

7 To apply the date and time changes you made, click **OK**.

ADD WALLPAPER

You can decorate
your screen by
adding wallpaper.

ADD WALLPAPER

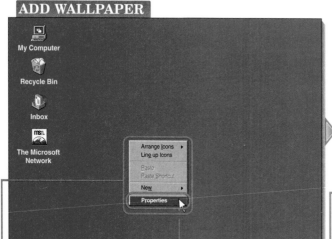

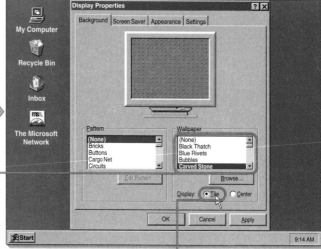

1 Click a blank area
on your screen using
the **right** button. A
menu appears.

2 Click **Properties**.

■ The **Display Properties**
dialog box appears.

3 Click the wallpaper
you want to display.

*Note: To view all the
available wallpapers,
use the scroll bar. For
more information, refer
to page 24.*

4 To cover your entire
screen with the wallpaper
you selected, click **Tile**
(○ changes to ◉).

*Note: To place a small
wallpaper image in the
middle of your screen,
click **Center**.*

These are a few of the available wallpapers.

Straw Mat

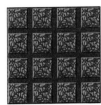
Tiles

Triangles

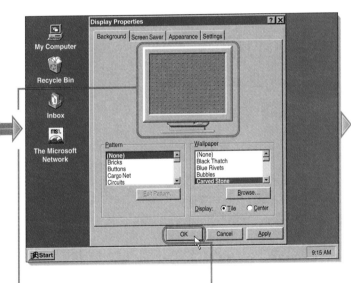

■ This area displays how the wallpaper you selected will look on your screen.

5 To display the wallpaper on your screen, click **OK**.

■ Your screen displays the wallpaper you selected.

*Note: To remove wallpaper from your screen, perform steps 1 to 3, selecting (**None**) in step 3. Then perform step 5.*

CHANGE SCREEN COLORS

You can change the colors displayed on your screen to suit your preferences.

CHANGE SCREEN COLORS

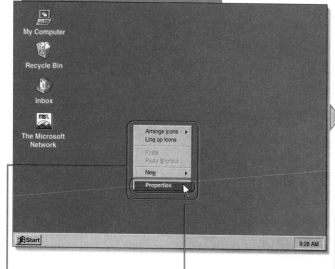

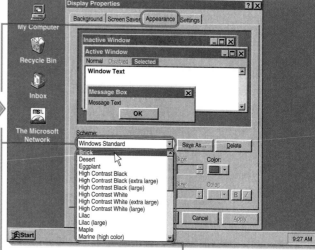

1 Click a blank area on your screen using the **right** button. A menu appears.

2 Click **Properties**.

■ The **Display Properties** dialog box appears.

3 Click the **Appearance** tab.

4 To display a list of the available color schemes, click this area.

5 Click the color scheme you want to use.

Note: To view all the available color schemes, use the scroll bar. For more information, refer to page 24.

106

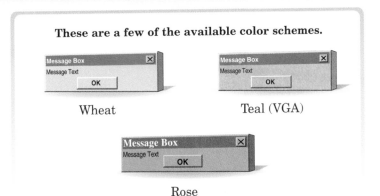

These are a few of the available color schemes.

Wheat

Teal (VGA)

Rose

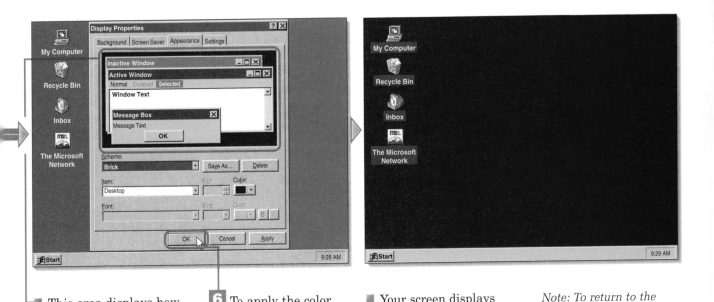

■ This area displays how your screen will look with the color scheme you selected.

6 To apply the color scheme, click **OK**.

■ Your screen displays the color scheme you selected.

Note: To return to the original color scheme, repeat steps 1 to 6, selecting **Windows Standard** *in step 5.*

SET UP A SCREEN SAVER

A screen saver is a moving picture or pattern that appears on the screen when you do not use your computer for a period of time.

SET UP A SCREEN SAVER

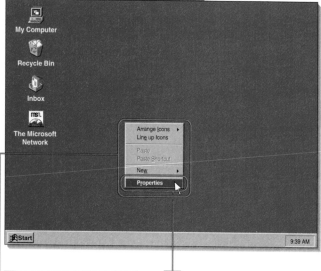

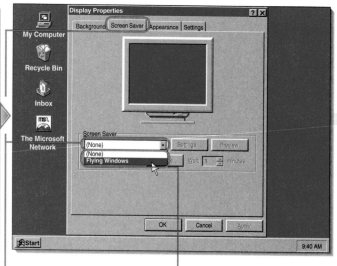

1 Click a blank area on your screen using the **right** button. A menu appears.

2 Click **Properties**.

■ The **Display Properties** dialog box appears.

3 Click the **Screen Saver** tab.

4 To display a list of the available screen savers, click this area.

5 Click the screen saver you want to use.

Note: To install additional screen savers that come with Windows, refer to page 186.

Screen savers were originally designed to prevent screen burn, which occurs when an image appears in a fixed position for a period of time.

Today's monitors are better designed to prevent screen burn, but people still use screen savers for entertainment.

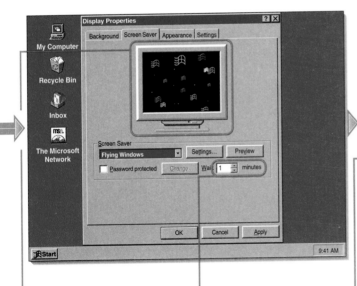

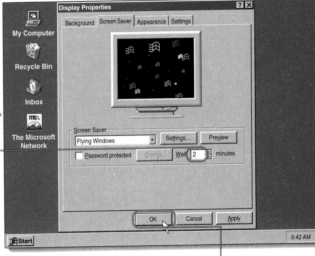

■ This area displays how the screen saver will look on your screen.

■ The screen saver will appear when you do not use your computer for the amount of time displayed in this area.

6 To change the amount of time, click this area.

7 Press **◆Backspace** or **Delete** on your keyboard to remove the existing number. Then type a new number.

8 Click **OK**.

CHANGE MOUSE SETTINGS

You can change
the way your
mouse works to
suit your needs.

CHANGE MOUSE SETTINGS

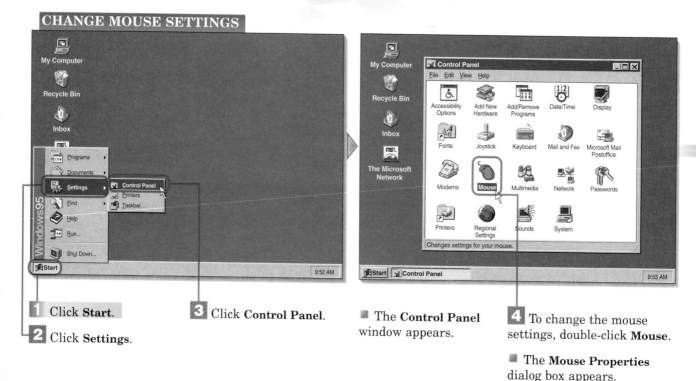

1 Click **Start**.

2 Click **Settings**.

3 Click **Control Panel**.

■ The **Control Panel** window appears.

4 To change the mouse settings, double-click **Mouse**.

■ The **Mouse Properties** dialog box appears.

TIP

A mouse pad provides a smooth surface for moving the mouse on your desk. You can buy mouse pads displaying interesting designs or pictures at most computer stores.

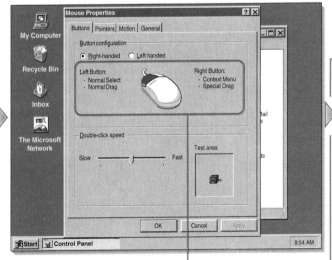

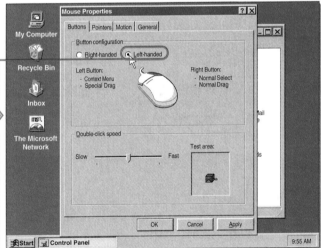

SWITCH BUTTONS

If you are left-handed, you can switch the functions of the left and right mouse buttons to make the mouse easier to use.

◾ This area describes the current functions of the left and right mouse buttons.

1 To switch the functions of the buttons, click this option (○ changes to ●).

Note: This change will not take effect until you confirm the changes. To do so, refer to page 113.

CONTINUED

CHANGE MOUSE SETTINGS

You can personalize your
mouse by changing the
double-click speed and
the way the mouse
pointer moves on
your screen.

CHANGE MOUSE SETTINGS (CONTINUED)

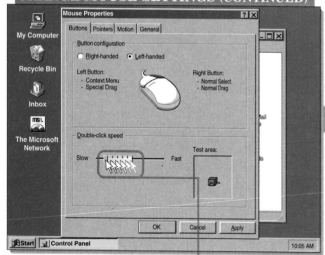

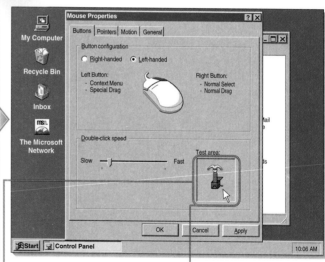

DOUBLE-CLICK SPEED

You can change the
amount of time that can
pass between two clicks
of the mouse button for
Windows to recognize a
double-click.

1 To change the
double-click speed,
drag the slider (⬇)
to a new position.

2 To test the double-
click speed, double-click
this area.

■ The jack-in-the-box
appears if you clicked
at the correct speed.

*Note: If you are an
inexperienced mouse
user, you may find a
slower speed easier
to use.*

Displaying mouse trails can help you follow the movement of the mouse on your screen. This is especially useful on portable computer screens, where the mouse can be difficult to follow.

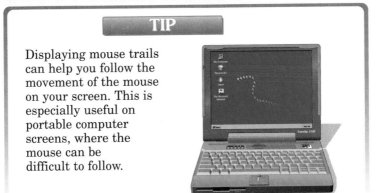

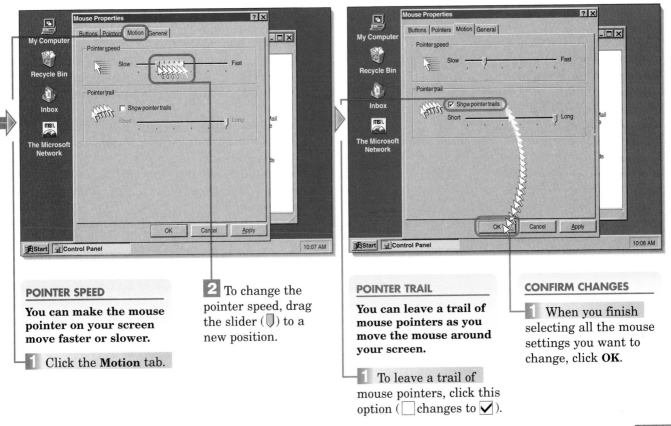

POINTER SPEED

You can make the mouse pointer on your screen move faster or slower.

1 Click the **Motion** tab.

2 To change the pointer speed, drag the slider ( ) to a new position.

POINTER TRAIL

You can leave a trail of mouse pointers as you move the mouse around your screen.

1 To leave a trail of mouse pointers, click this option (changes to ✓).

CONFIRM CHANGES

1 When you finish selecting all the mouse settings you want to change, click **OK**.

MOVE THE TASKBAR

You can move the taskbar to a more convenient location on your screen.

MOVE THE TASKBAR

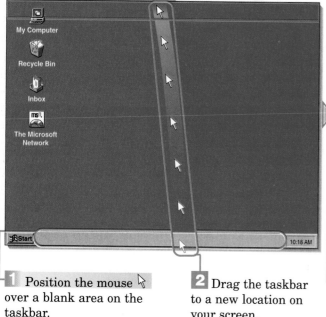

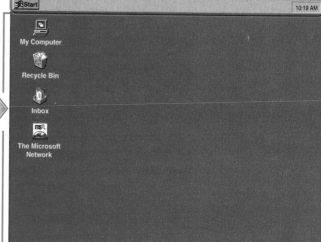

1 Position the mouse ⌖ over a blank area on the taskbar.

2 Drag the taskbar to a new location on your screen.

■ The taskbar moves to the new location.

Note: You can move the taskbar to the top, bottom, left or right side of your screen.

You can change the size of the taskbar so it can display more information.

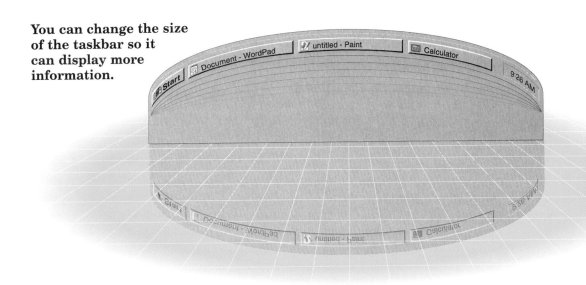

SIZE THE TASKBAR

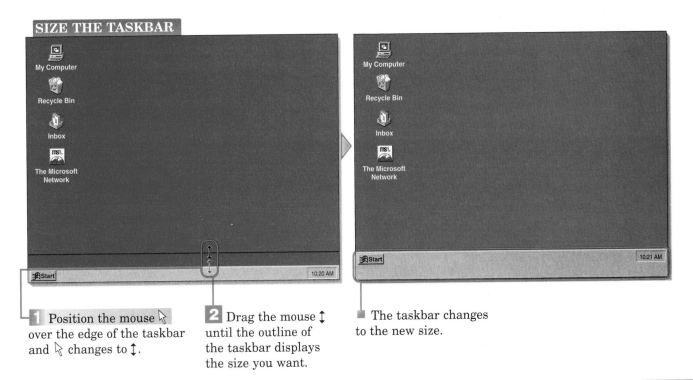

1 Position the mouse ⬉ over the edge of the taskbar and ⬉ changes to ↕.

2 Drag the mouse ↕ until the outline of the taskbar displays the size you want.

■ The taskbar changes to the new size.

HIDE THE TASKBAR

You can hide the taskbar to give you more room on the screen to accomplish your tasks.

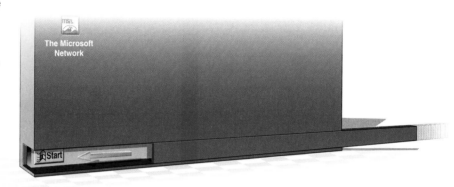

HIDE THE TASKBAR

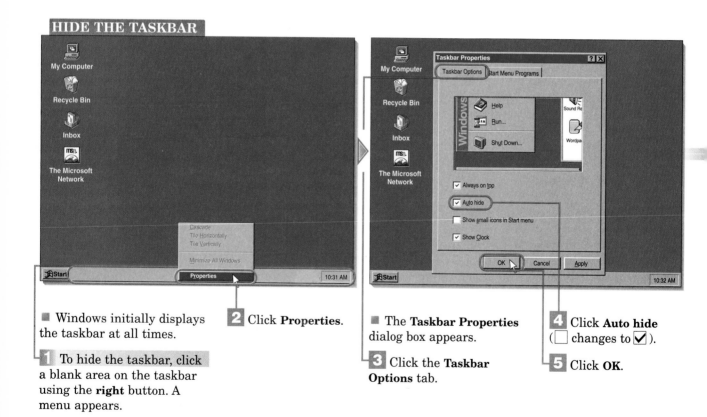

■ Windows initially displays the taskbar at all times.

1 To hide the taskbar, click a blank area on the taskbar using the **right** button. A menu appears.

2 Click **Properties**.

■ The **Taskbar Properties** dialog box appears.

3 Click the **Taskbar Options** tab.

4 Click **Auto hide** (☐ changes to ☑).

5 Click **OK**.

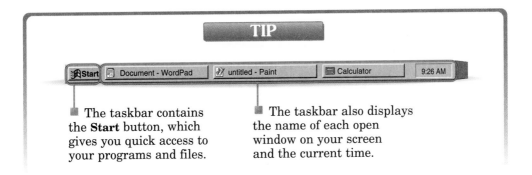

■ The taskbar contains the **Start** button, which gives you quick access to your programs and files.

■ The taskbar also displays the name of each open window on your screen and the current time.

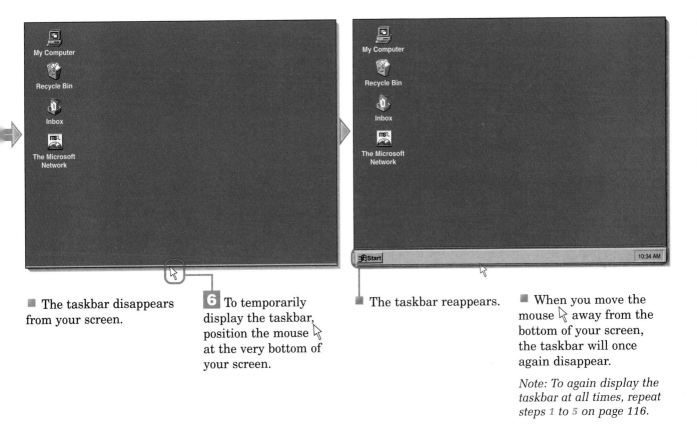

■ The taskbar disappears from your screen.

6 To temporarily display the taskbar, position the mouse ⬐ at the very bottom of your screen.

■ The taskbar reappears.

■ When you move the mouse ⬐ away from the bottom of your screen, the taskbar will once again disappear.

Note: To again display the taskbar at all times, repeat steps 1 to 5 on page 116.

CHANGE SCREEN RESOLUTION

You can change the amount of information that can fit on your screen.

You cannot change the screen resolution for some monitors.

640 x 480
Lower resolutions display larger images on the screen. This lets you see information more clearly.

CHANGE SCREEN RESOLUTION

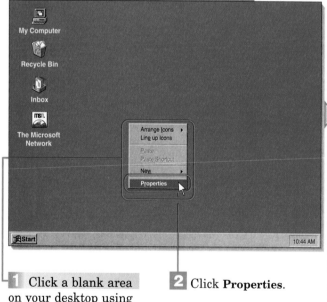

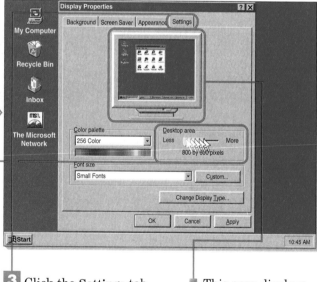

1 Click a blank area on your desktop using the **right** button. A menu appears.

2 Click **Properties**.

■ The **Display Properties** dialog box appears.

3 Click the **Settings** tab.

4 To change the resolution, drag the slider (⬇) until you select the resolution you want to use.

■ This area displays how your screen will look at the new resolution.

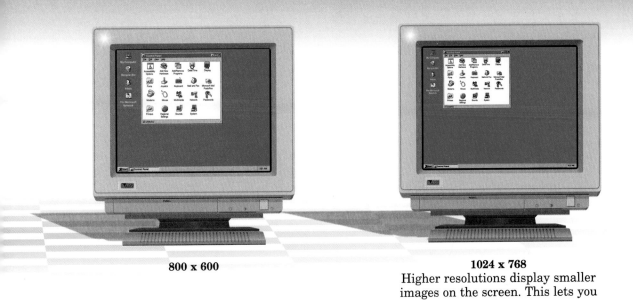

800 x 600

1024 x 768
Higher resolutions display smaller images on the screen. This lets you display more information at once.

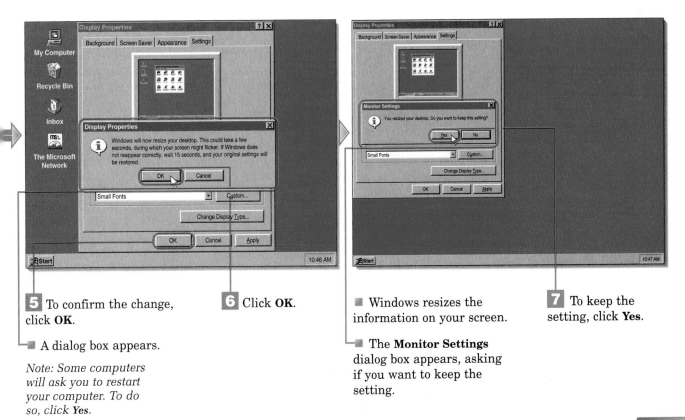

5 To confirm the change, click **OK**.

6 Click **OK**.

■ A dialog box appears.

Note: Some computers will ask you to restart your computer. To do so, click Yes.

■ Windows resizes the information on your screen.

■ The **Monitor Settings** dialog box appears, asking if you want to keep the setting.

7 To keep the setting, click **Yes**.

CHANGE COLOR DEPTH

You can change the number of colors displayed on your screen. More colors result in more realistic images.

16 Color
Choppy-looking images.

256 Color
Ideal for most home and business applications.

CHANGE COLOR DEPTH

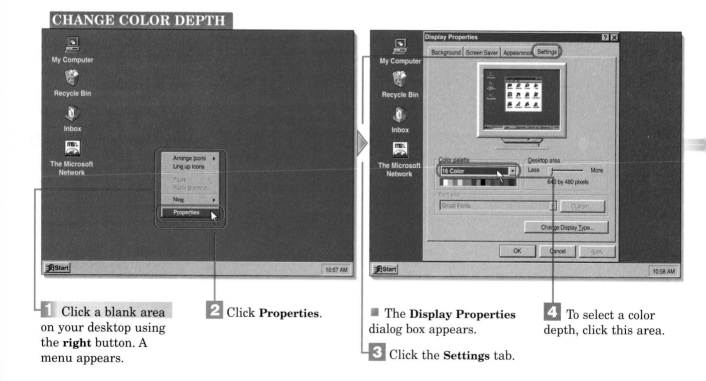

1 Click a blank area on your desktop using the **right** button. A menu appears.

2 Click **Properties**.

■ The **Display Properties** dialog box appears.

3 Click the **Settings** tab.

4 To select a color depth, click this area.

High Color
Ideal for video and
desktop publishing.

True Color
Ideal for high-end graphics
programs and photo-retouching.

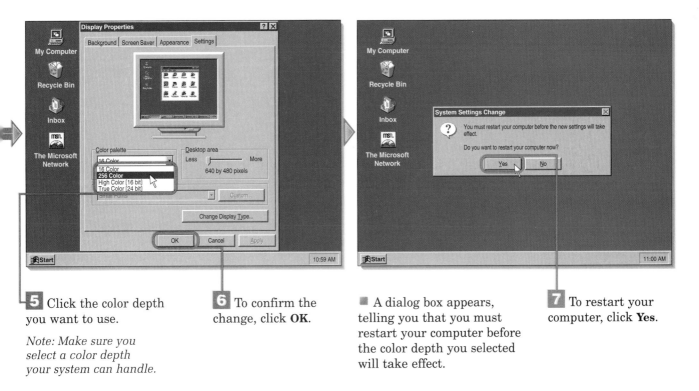

5 Click the color depth
you want to use.

*Note: Make sure you
select a color depth
your system can handle.*

6 To confirm the
change, click **OK**.

■ A dialog box appears,
telling you that you must
restart your computer before
the color depth you selected
will take effect.

7 To restart your
computer, click **Yes**.

**In this chapter you will learn
how to view videos and hear and record
sounds on your computer.**

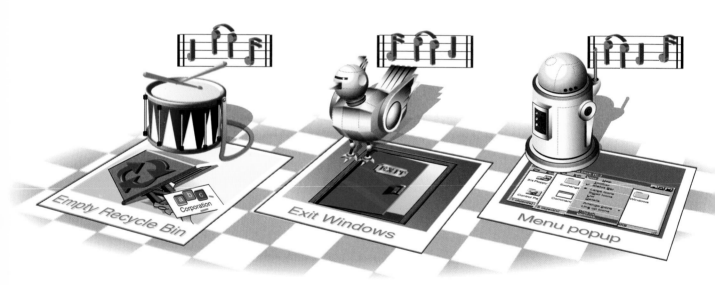

CHAPTER 8: ENTERTAINING FEATURES

PLAY A MUSIC CD

You can use your computer to play music CDs while you work.

You need a CD-ROM drive, a sound card and speakers to play music CDs.

PLAY A MUSIC CD

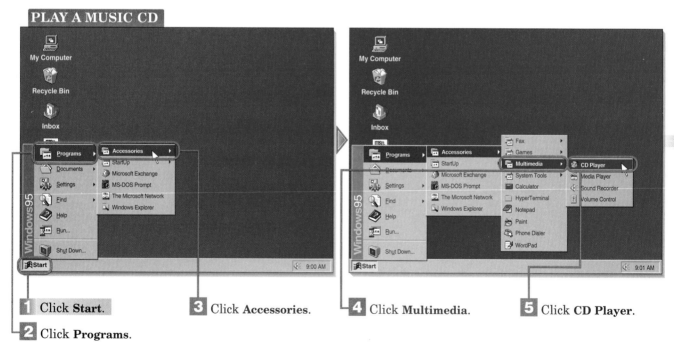

1 Click **Start**.

2 Click **Programs**.

3 Click **Accessories**.

4 Click **Multimedia**.

5 Click **CD Player**.

TIP

You can also listen to music privately by plugging a headset into your CD-ROM drive.

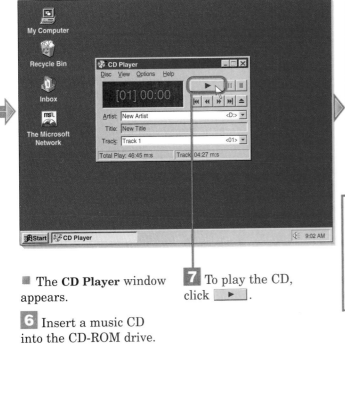

■ The **CD Player** window appears.

6 Insert a music CD into the CD-ROM drive.

7 To play the CD, click ► .

PLAY ANOTHER SONG

1 To play another song on the CD, click one of the following buttons.

|◄◄| Plays previous song.

|►►| Plays next song.

CONTINUED

PLAY A MUSIC CD

You can have Windows pause or stop the music at any time and play songs in random order.

PLAY A MUSIC CD (CONTINUED)

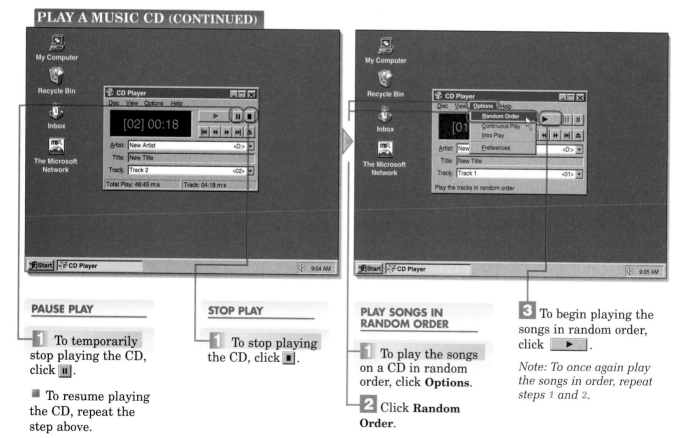

PAUSE PLAY

1 To temporarily stop playing the CD, click ▐▐.

▪ To resume playing the CD, repeat the step above.

STOP PLAY

1 To stop playing the CD, click ▪.

PLAY SONGS IN RANDOM ORDER

1 To play the songs on a CD in random order, click **Options**.

2 Click **Random Order**.

3 To begin playing the songs in random order, click ► .

Note: To once again play the songs in order, repeat steps 1 and 2.

ADJUST THE VOLUME

You can easily adjust the volume of sound coming from your speakers.

ADJUST THE VOLUME

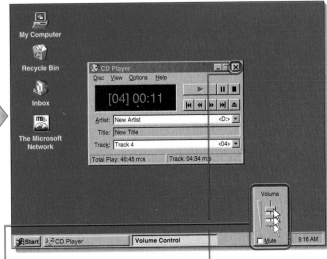

1 To display the **Volume** control box, click 🔊.

2 Drag the slider (▭) up or down to increase or decrease the volume.

3 To hide the **Volume** control box, click outside the box.

■ To close the **CD Player** window, click ☒.

ASSIGN SOUNDS TO PROGRAM EVENTS

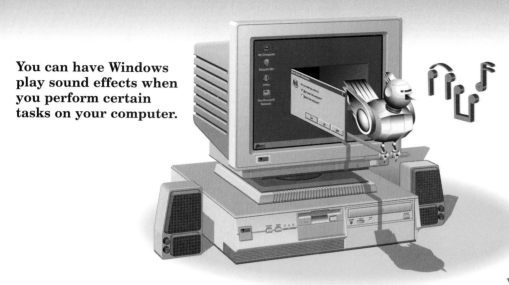

You can have Windows play sound effects when you perform certain tasks on your computer.

For example, you can hear a bird chirp when you close a program or a musical melody when you exit Windows.

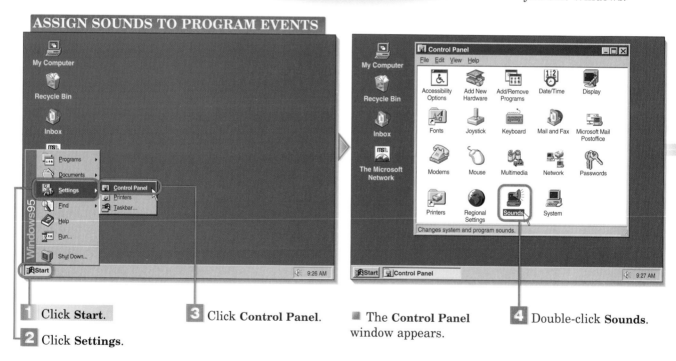

ASSIGN SOUNDS TO PROGRAM EVENTS

1 Click **Start**.

2 Click **Settings**.

3 Click **Control Panel**.

■ The **Control Panel** window appears.

4 Double-click **Sounds**.

IMPORTANT

When you first set up Windows, not all the sound schemes that come with Windows are added to your computer. The schemes you can add later include:

Jungle **Musica** **Robotz** **Utopia**

To add one or more sound schemes to your computer, refer to page 186. You can find these schemes in the Multimedia category.

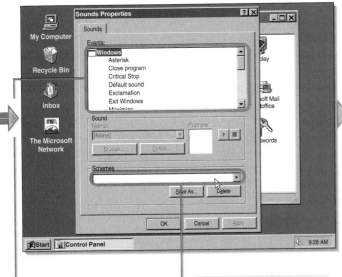

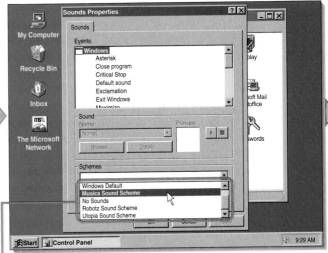

■ The **Sounds Properties** dialog box appears.

■ This area displays the events you can assign sounds to.

ASSIGN SOUNDS TO ALL EVENTS

1 To have Windows assign sounds to all program events at once, click this area.

Note: To assign a sound to only one event, refer to page 130.

2 Click the sound scheme you want to use.

Note: The available sound schemes depend on the schemes you have installed on your computer. For more information, refer to the top of this page.

CONTINUED

ASSIGN SOUNDS TO PROGRAM EVENTS

Assigning sounds to events can make Windows more fun and entertaining.

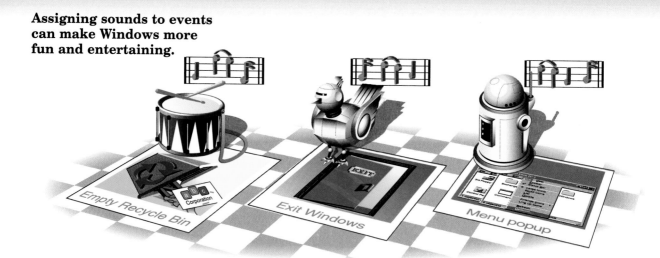

ASSIGN SOUNDS (CONTINUED)

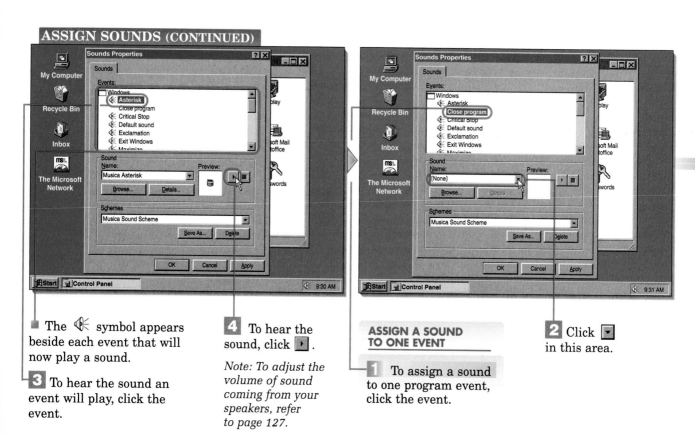

■ The 🔊 symbol appears beside each event that will now play a sound.

3 To hear the sound an event will play, click the event.

4 To hear the sound, click ▶.

Note: To adjust the volume of sound coming from your speakers, refer to page 127.

ASSIGN A SOUND TO ONE EVENT

1 To assign a sound to one program event, click the event.

2 Click ▼ in this area.

TIP

You need a sound card
and speakers to hear
sounds on your computer.

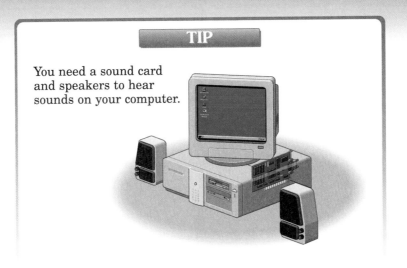

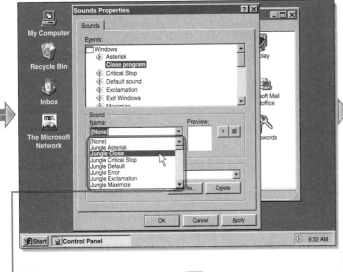

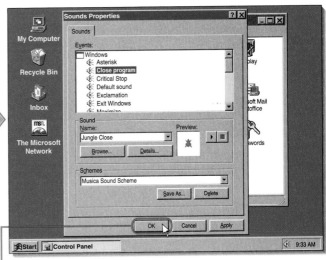

3 Click the sound you
want to hear every time
the event occurs.

4 To assign sounds
to other events, repeat
steps 1 to 3 starting on
page 130 for each event.

5 To confirm the choices
you have made, click **OK**.

RECORD SOUNDS

You can record your own sounds.

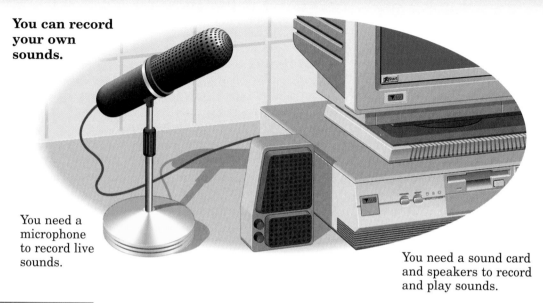

You need a microphone to record live sounds.

You need a sound card and speakers to record and play sounds.

RECORD SOUNDS

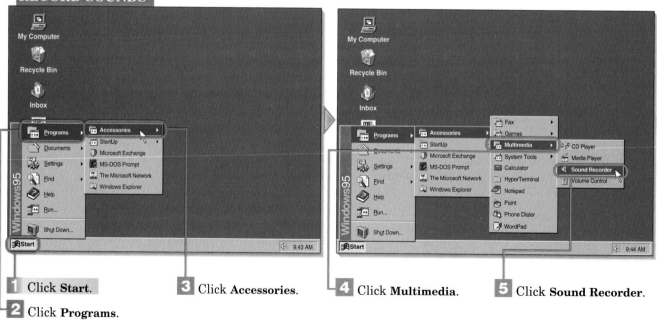

1 Click **Start**.

2 Click **Programs**.

3 Click **Accessories**.

4 Click **Multimedia**.

5 Click **Sound Recorder**.

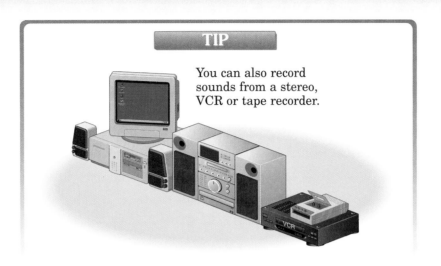

TIP

You can also record
sounds from a stereo,
VCR or tape recorder.

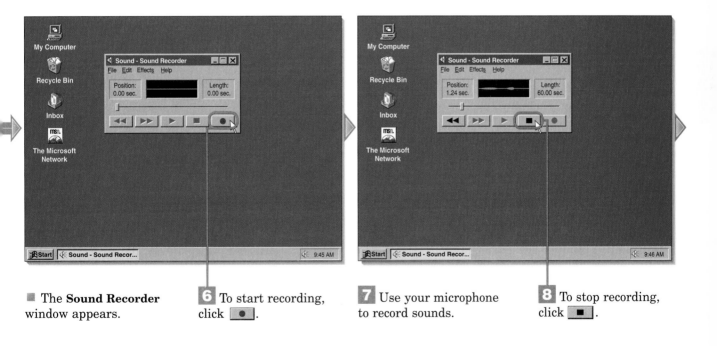

■ The **Sound Recorder** window appears.

6 To start recording, click ●.

7 Use your microphone to record sounds.

8 To stop recording, click ■.

CONTINUED

RECORD SOUNDS

You can store sounds you record and listen to them later.

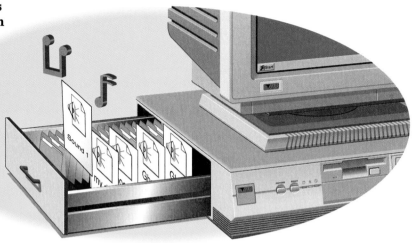

RECORD SOUNDS (CONTINUED)

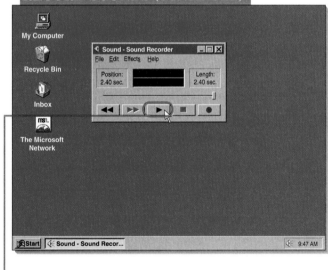

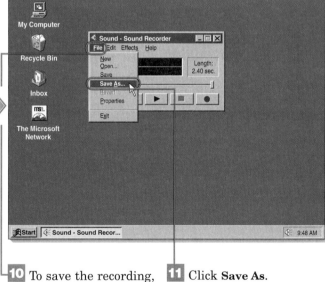

9 To play your recording, click .

10 To save the recording, click **File**.

11 Click **Save As**.

■ The **Save As** dialog box appears.

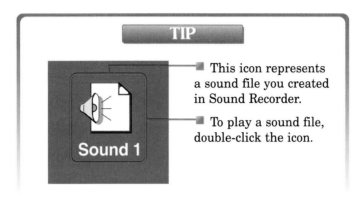

■ This icon represents
a sound file you created
in Sound Recorder.

■ To play a sound file,
double-click the icon.

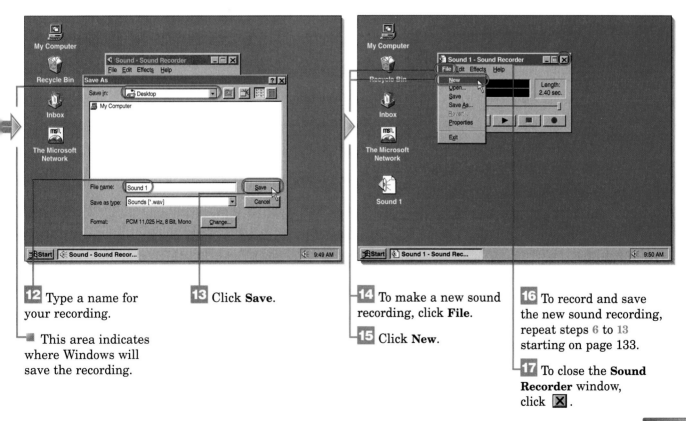

12 Type a name for
your recording.

■ This area indicates
where Windows will
save the recording.

13 Click **Save**.

14 To make a new sound
recording, click **File**.

15 Click **New**.

16 To record and save
the new sound recording,
repeat steps 6 to 13
starting on page 133.

17 To close the **Sound
Recorder** window,
click ☒.

USING MEDIA PLAYER

Media Player lets you play sound, video and animation files.

USING MEDIA PLAYER

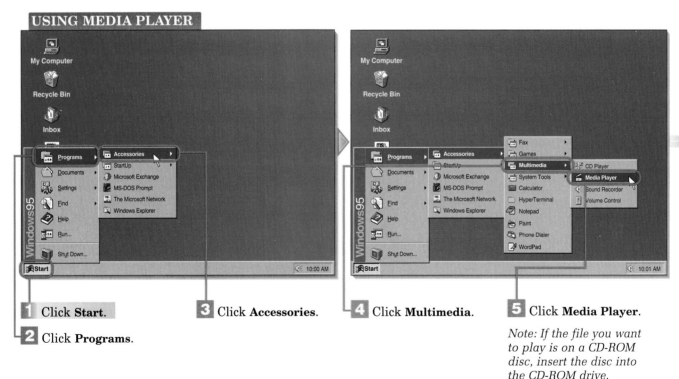

1 Click **Start**.

2 Click **Programs**.

3 Click **Accessories**.

4 Click **Multimedia**.

5 Click **Media Player**.

Note: If the file you want to play is on a CD-ROM disc, insert the disc into the CD-ROM drive.

TIP

The Windows 95 CD-ROM disc includes several video files you can play.

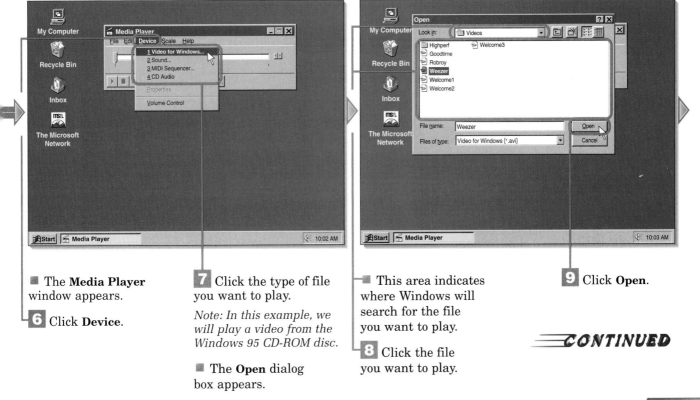

■ The **Media Player** window appears.

6 Click **Device**.

7 Click the type of file you want to play.

Note: In this example, we will play a video from the Windows 95 CD-ROM disc.

■ The **Open** dialog box appears.

■ This area indicates where Windows will search for the file you want to play.

8 Click the file you want to play.

9 Click **Open**.

CONTINUED

USING MEDIA PLAYER

You can use Media
Player to play files
you get from
the Internet.

USING MEDIA PLAYER (CONTINUED)

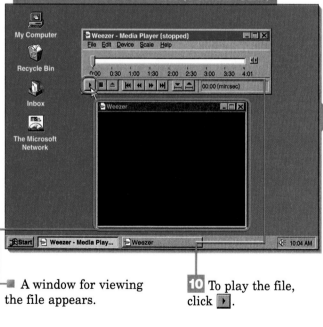

■ A window for viewing
the file appears.

10 To play the file,
click .

11 To fast forward or
rewind the file, drag
the slider (▯) to a
new location.

TIP

Media Player can play animation, video,
sound and MIDI files. You can tell the type of file
by the three letters at the end of the file name.
For example, **music.wav** is a sound file.

Animation (.flc, .fli, .aas)
Video (.avi)

Sound (.wav)
MIDI (.mid, .rmi)

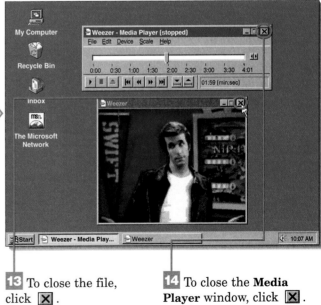

12 To stop playing
the file, click ■.

13 To close the file,
click ☒ .

14 To close the **Media
Player** window, click ☒ .

**In this chapter you will learn
how to exchange information
between documents.**

CHAPTER 9: OBJECT LINKING AND EMBEDDING

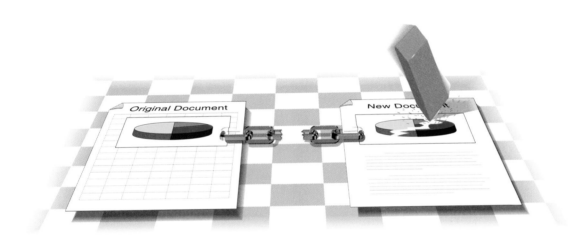

EMBED OR LINK INFORMATION

You can easily exchange information between documents.

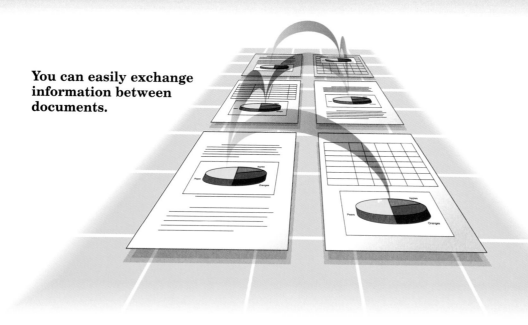

EMBED OR LINK INFORMATION

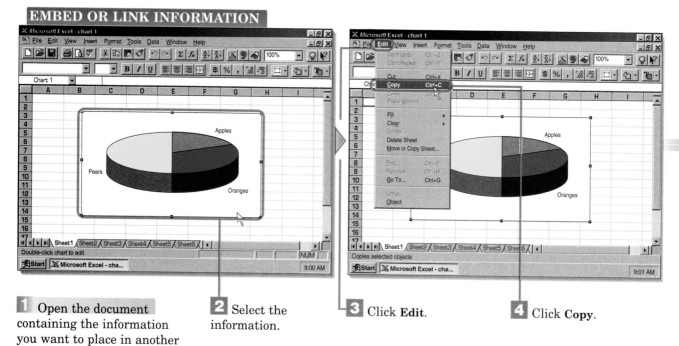

1 Open the document containing the information you want to place in another document.

2 Select the information.

3 Click **Edit**.

4 Click **Copy**.

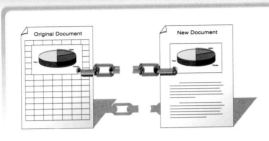

EMBED INFORMATION

When you embed information, the information becomes part of the new document.

The original document is no longer needed, since the new document now contains the information.

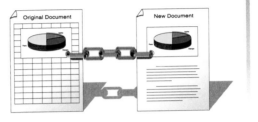

LINK INFORMATION

When you link information, the new document receives a "screen image" of the information. The information remains in the original document.

Since the new document only contains a "screen image" of the information, a connection exists between the two documents.

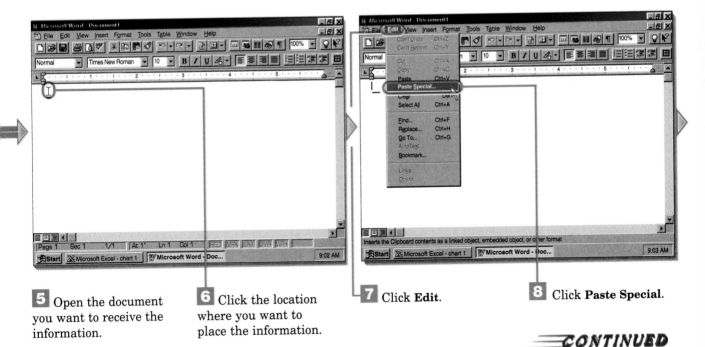

5 Open the document you want to receive the information.

Note: In this example, we opened a Word document using the Start button.

6 Click the location where you want to place the information.

7 Click **Edit**.

8 Click **Paste Special**.

CONTINUED

EMBED OR LINK INFORMATION

You can exchange pictures, charts, text, slides and spreadsheets between documents.

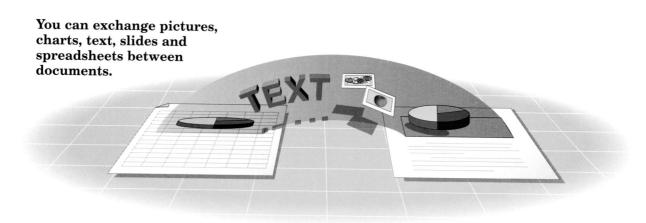

EMBED OR LINK INFORMATION (CONTINUED)

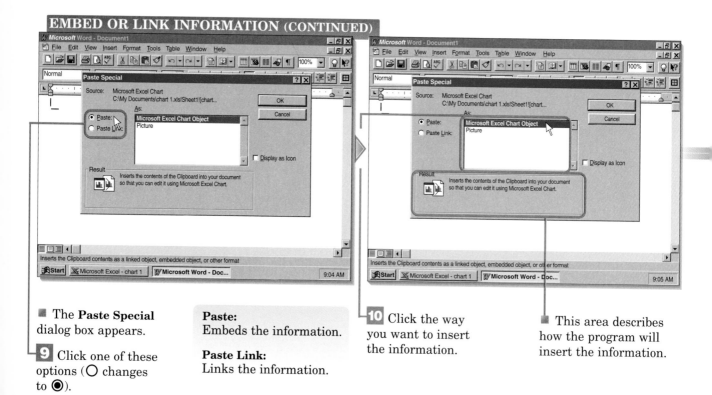

■ The **Paste Special** dialog box appears.

9 Click one of these options (○ changes to ◉).

Paste:
Embeds the information.

Paste Link:
Links the information.

10 Click the way you want to insert the information.

■ This area describes how the program will insert the information.

TIP

A document containing embedded information takes up more space on your computer than a document containing linked information.

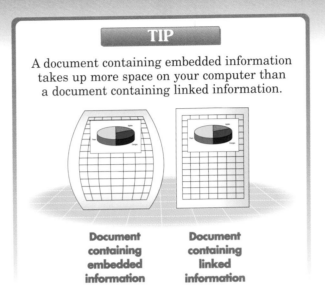

Document containing embedded information

Document containing linked information

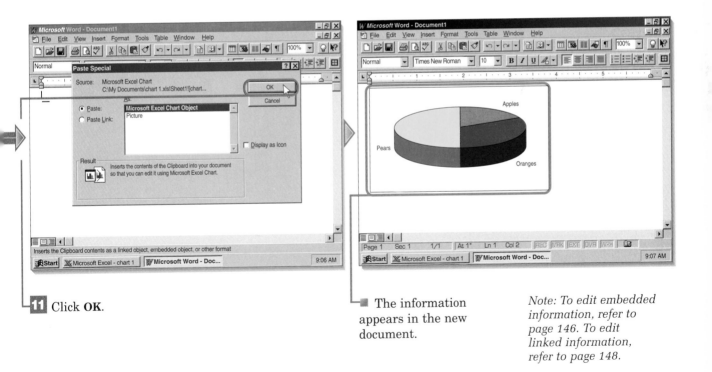

11 Click **OK**.

■ The information appears in the new document.

Note: To edit embedded information, refer to page 146. To edit linked information, refer to page 148.

EDIT EMBEDDED INFORMATION

When you change embedded information, the original document does not change.

EDIT EMBEDDED INFORMATION

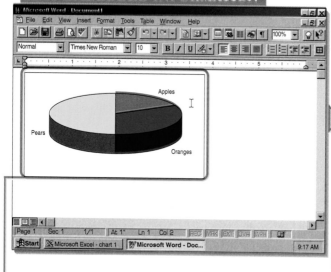

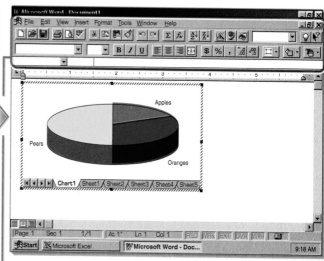

1 Double-click the embedded information you want to change.

The toolbars and menus from the program you used to create the information appear. This lets you access all the commands you need to make the necessary changes.

TIP

A program that can link and embed information
supports OLE—Object Linking and Embedding.

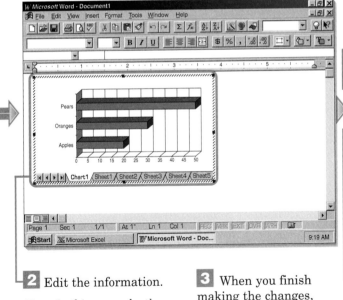

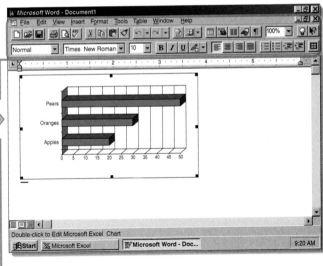

2 Edit the information.

Note: In this example, the pie chart is changed to a bar chart.

3 When you finish making the changes, click anywhere outside the information.

■ The original toolbars and menus reappear.

147

EDIT LINKED INFORMATION

When you change linked information, the original and new documents both display the changes.

EDIT LINKED INFORMATION

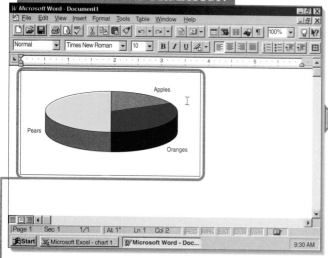

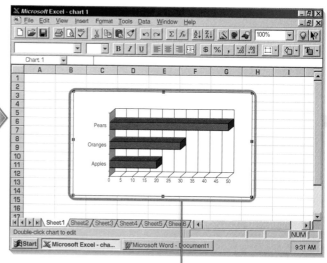

1 Double-click the linked information you want to change.

■ The program you used to create the information opens. This lets you access all the commands you need to make the necessary changes.

2 Edit the information.

Note: In this example, the pie chart is changed to a bar chart.

You can link information to several documents.

When you change linked information, the information changes in all linked documents. This is useful when you want several documents to display the same, up-to-date information.

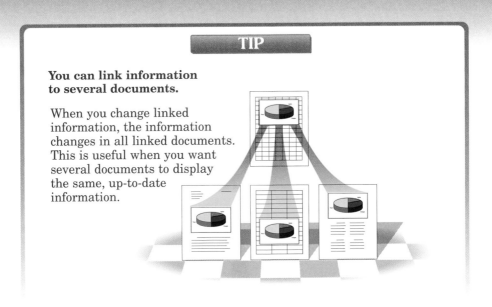

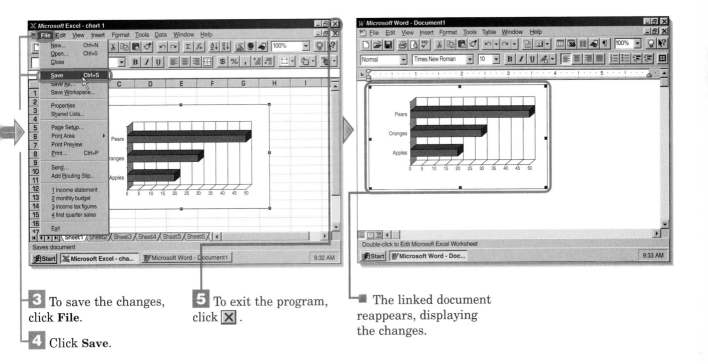

3 To save the changes, click **File**.

4 Click **Save**.

5 To exit the program, click ⊠.

■ The linked document reappears, displaying the changes.

149

**In this chapter you will learn
how to send and receive faxes
on your computer.**

CHAPTER 10: FAXING

START MICROSOFT EXCHANGE

Microsoft Exchange lets you send and receive faxes and electronic mail (e-mail).

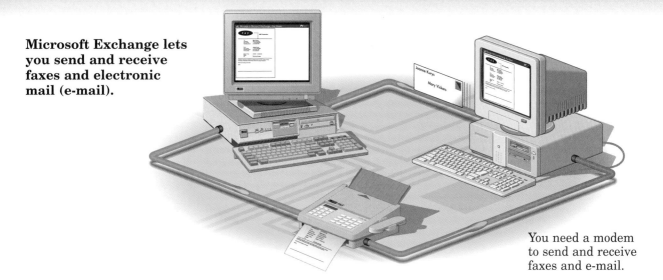

You need a modem to send and receive faxes and e-mail.

START MICROSOFT EXCHANGE

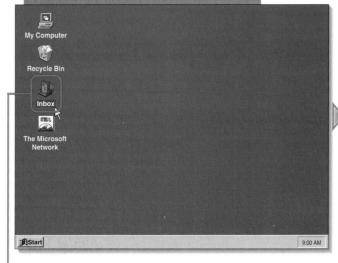

1 Double-click **Inbox**.

*Note: If your screen does not display **Inbox**, you must install the Microsoft Exchange and Microsoft Fax programs to continue.*

■ The **Microsoft Exchange** window appears.

2 To display the folders that store your messages, click .

A fax displays this icon.

An e-mail message displays this icon.

Note: For information on e-mail, refer to the Electronic Mail chapter starting on page 166.

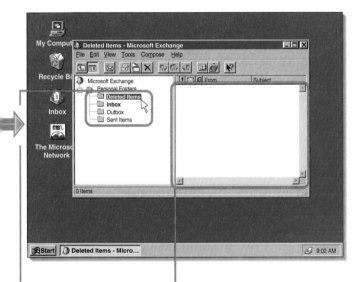

Microsoft Exchange provides four folders to store your messages.

DELETED ITEMS
Stores messages you have deleted.

INBOX
Stores messages sent to you.

OUTBOX
Temporarily stores messages you have sent until they are delivered.

SENT ITEMS
Stores copies of messages you have sent.

■ The folders appear.

3 To display the contents of a folder, click the folder.

■ This area displays the contents of the folder you selected. You can only display the contents of one folder at a time.

*Note: In this example, there are no messages in the **Deleted Items** folder.*

SEND A FAX

You can easily send a fax to a colleague across the city or around the world.

SEND A FAX

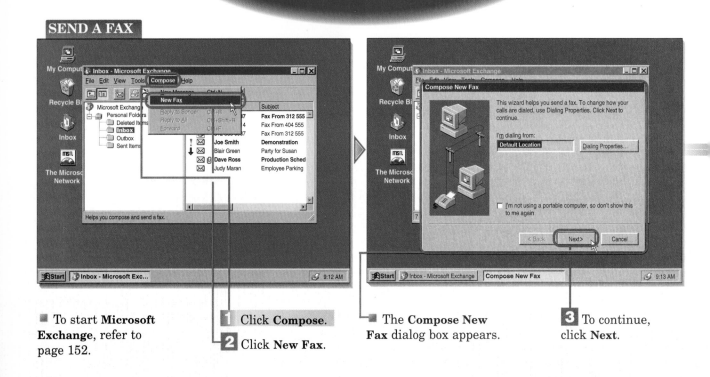

■ To start **Microsoft Exchange**, refer to page 152.

1 Click **Compose**.

2 Click **New Fax**.

■ The **Compose New Fax** dialog box appears.

3 To continue, click **Next**.

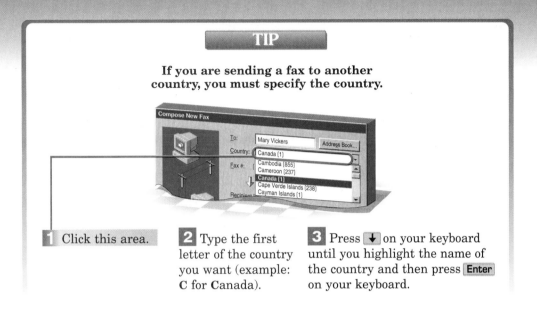

TIP

If you are sending a fax to another country, you must specify the country.

1 Click this area.

2 Type the first letter of the country you want (example: **C** for **C**anada).

3 Press ↓ on your keyboard until you highlight the name of the country and then press **Enter** on your keyboard.

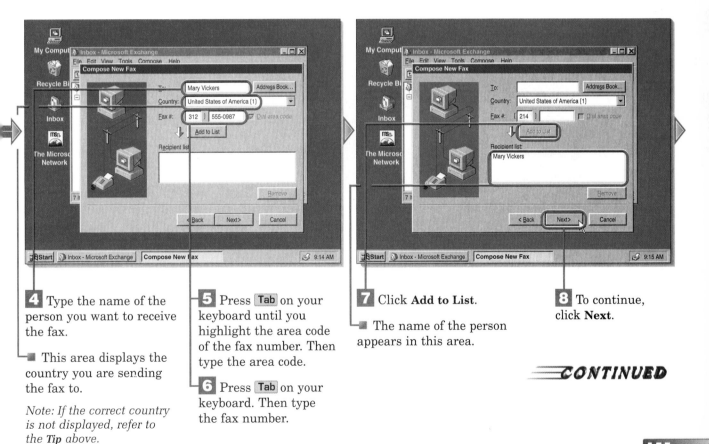

4 Type the name of the person you want to receive the fax.

◼ This area displays the country you are sending the fax to.

Note: If the correct country is not displayed, refer to the **Tip** *above.*

5 Press **Tab** on your keyboard until you highlight the area code of the fax number. Then type the area code.

6 Press **Tab** on your keyboard. Then type the fax number.

7 Click **Add to List**.

◼ The name of the person appears in this area.

8 To continue, click **Next**.

CONTINUED

SEND A FAX

Microsoft Exchange offers four types of cover pages you can include with your fax.

SEND A FAX (CONTINUED)

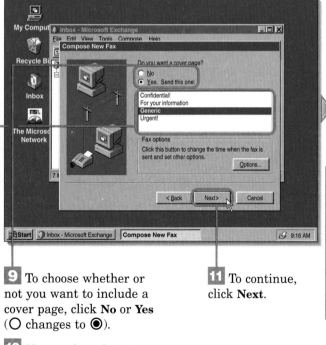

9 To choose whether or not you want to include a cover page, click **No** or **Yes** (○ changes to ●).

10 If you selected **Yes** in step **9**, click the type of cover page you want.

11 To continue, click **Next**.

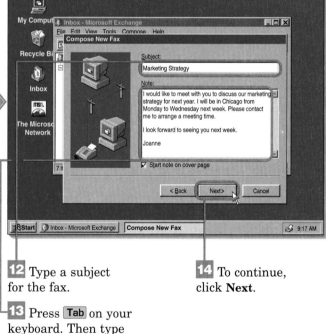

12 Type a subject for the fax.

13 Press **Tab** on your keyboard. Then type your message.

14 To continue, click **Next**.

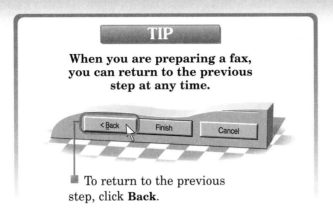

TIP

When you are preparing a fax, you can return to the previous step at any time.

■ To return to the previous step, click **Back**.

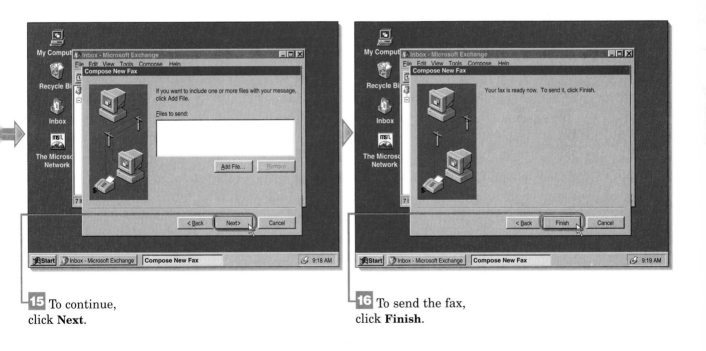

15 To continue, click **Next**.

16 To send the fax, click **Finish**.

CHANGE HOW MODEM ANSWERS FAXES

You can instruct your
modem to answer
incoming faxes
in the way
that is most
convenient
for you.

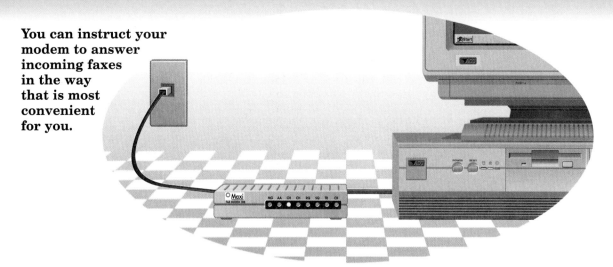

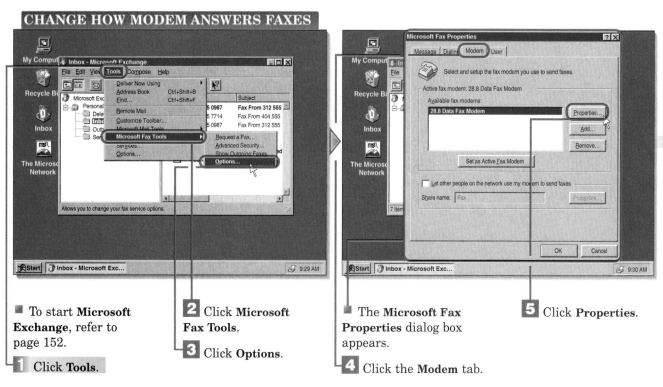

■ To start **Microsoft
Exchange**, refer to
page 152.

1 Click **Tools**.

2 Click **Microsoft
Fax Tools**.

3 Click **Options**.

■ The **Microsoft Fax
Properties** dialog box
appears.

4 Click the **Modem** tab.

5 Click **Properties**.

ANSWER AFTER

The modem will answer all incoming faxes after the number of rings you specify. Select this option if you use the telephone line primarily for faxing.

MANUAL

The modem will only answer incoming faxes when you instruct it to. Select this option if you use the telephone line primarily for voice calls.

Note: A dialog box appears when someone is sending you a fax. To answer the fax, click Yes.

DON'T ANSWER

The modem will not answer incoming faxes.

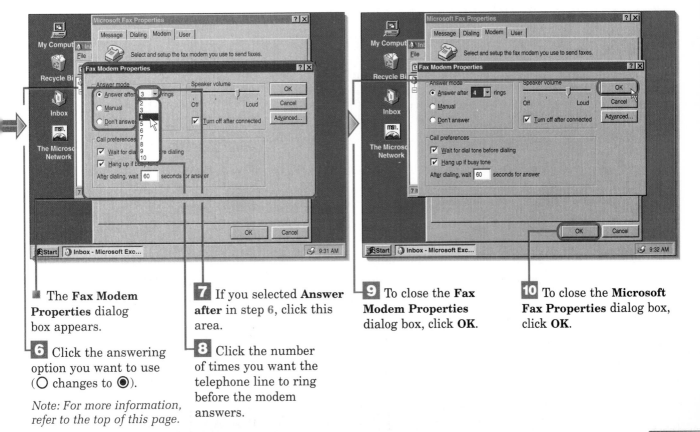

■ The **Fax Modem Properties** dialog box appears.

6 Click the answering option you want to use (○ changes to ●).

Note: For more information, refer to the top of this page.

7 If you selected **Answer after** in step **6**, click this area.

8 Click the number of times you want the telephone line to ring before the modem answers.

9 To close the **Fax Modem Properties** dialog box, click **OK**.

10 To close the **Microsoft Fax Properties** dialog box, click **OK**.

VIEW A FAX

You can display a fax on your screen so you can read the message.

VIEW A FAX

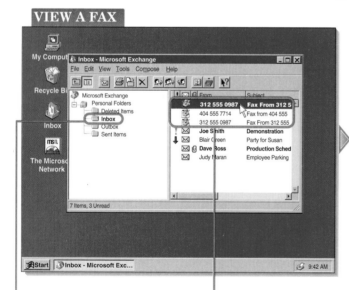

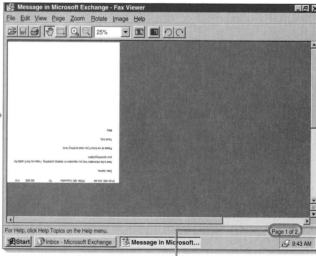

■ To start **Microsoft Exchange**, refer to page 152.

1 To display the faxes sent to you, click the **Inbox** folder.

2 Double-click the fax you want to view.

Note: A fax displays the ⚡ icon.

■ The **Fax Viewer** window appears, displaying the first page of the fax.

Note: To enlarge the window to fill your screen, refer to page 13.

■ This area indicates which page is displayed and the total number of pages in the fax.

TIP

You can magnify or reduce a page displayed on your screen.

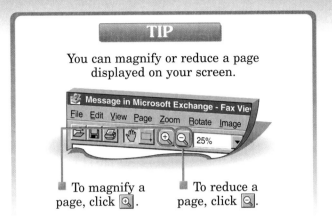

■ To magnify a page, click 🔍.

■ To reduce a page, click 🔍.

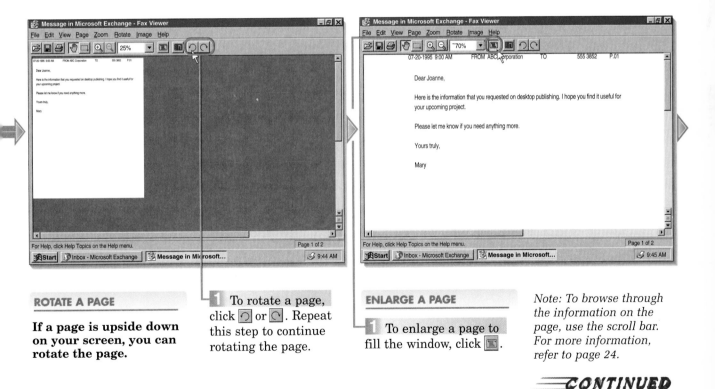

ROTATE A PAGE

If a page is upside down on your screen, you can rotate the page.

■ To rotate a page, click ↺ or ↻. Repeat this step to continue rotating the page.

ENLARGE A PAGE

■ To enlarge a page to fill the window, click 🔳.

Note: To browse through the information on the page, use the scroll bar. For more information, refer to page 24.

CONTINUED

VIEW A FAX

The Fax Viewer
window lets you
easily flip through
the pages in your
fax.

VIEW A FAX (CONTINUED)

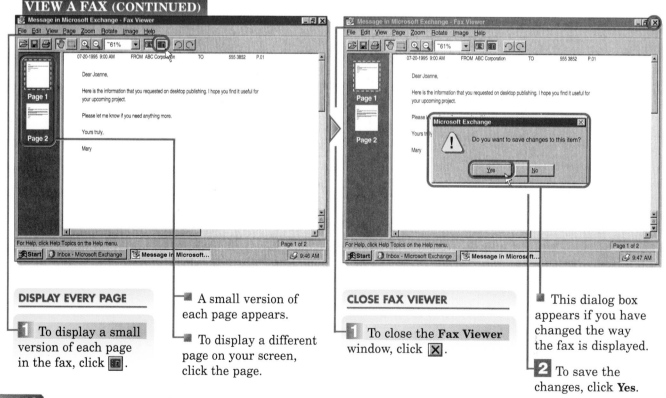

DISPLAY EVERY PAGE

1 To display a small
version of each page
in the fax, click 🔢.

■ A small version of
each page appears.

■ To display a different
page on your screen,
click the page.

CLOSE FAX VIEWER

1 To close the **Fax Viewer**
window, click ☒.

■ This dialog box
appears if you have
changed the way
the fax is displayed.

2 To save the
changes, click **Yes**.

PRINT A FAX

You can easily produce a paper copy of a fax you received.

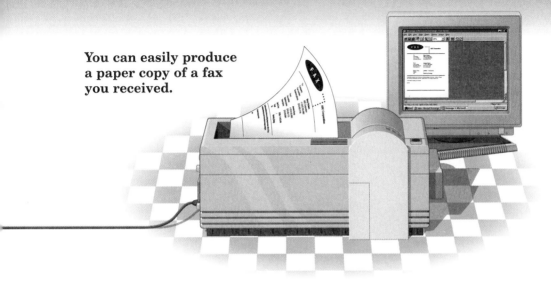

PRINT A FAX

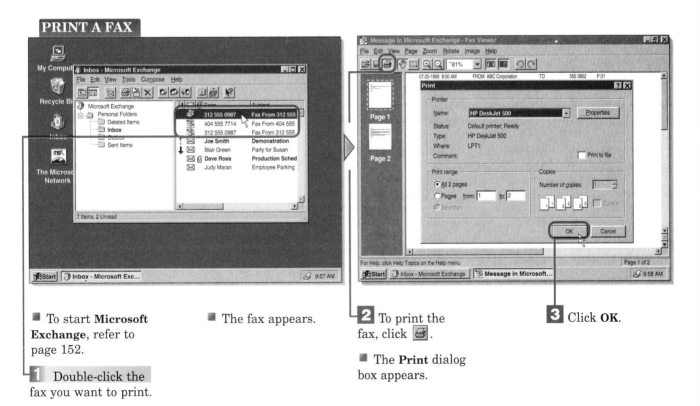

■ To start **Microsoft Exchange**, refer to page 152.

1 Double-click the fax you want to print.

■ The fax appears.

2 To print the fax, click 🖨.

■ The **Print** dialog box appears.

3 Click **OK**.

**In this chapter you will learn
how to send and receive electronic mail.**

CHAPTER 11: ELECTRONIC MAIL

ADD A NAME TO THE ADDRESS BOOK

Microsoft Exchange provides
a personal address book
where you can store the
names and addresses of
people you frequently
send messages to.

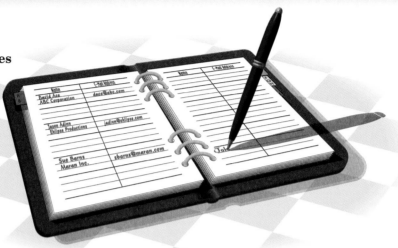

ADD A NAME TO THE ADDRESS BOOK

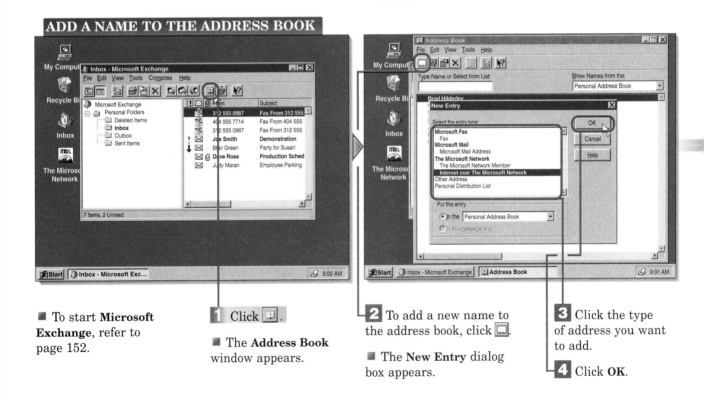

■ To start **Microsoft
Exchange**, refer to
page 152.

1 Click 📖.

■ The **Address Book**
window appears.

2 To add a new name to
the address book, click ▭.

■ The **New Entry** dialog
box appears.

3 Click the type
of address you want
to add.

4 Click **OK**.

TIP

An Internet address consists of two parts, separated by the @ symbol.

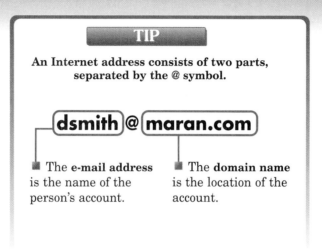

■ The **e-mail address** is the name of the person's account.

■ The **domain name** is the location of the account.

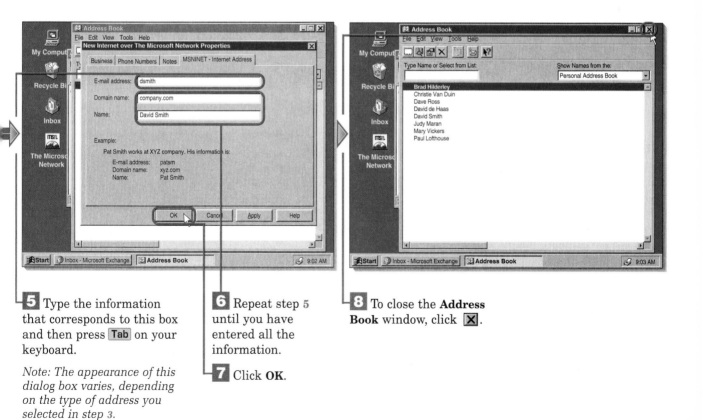

5 Type the information that corresponds to this box and then press **Tab** on your keyboard.

Note: The appearance of this dialog box varies, depending on the type of address you selected in step 3.

6 Repeat step 5 until you have entered all the information.

7 Click **OK**.

8 To close the **Address Book** window, click **X**.

167

SEND A MESSAGE

You can send a
message to another
person to exchange
ideas or request
information.

SEND A MESSAGE

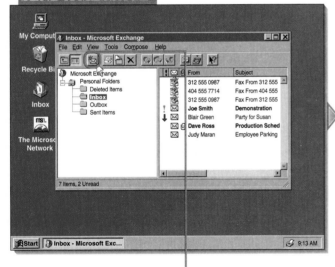

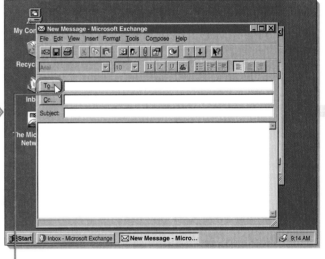

■ To start **Microsoft
Exchange**, refer to
page 152.

1 Click 🖾.

■ The **New Message**
window appears.

2 To send the
message to a
person listed in
an address book,
click **To**.

*Note: You can also type the e-mail
address of the person you want to
receive the message in the **To** box
(example: **dsmith@company.com**).
This lets you skip steps 2 to 7.*

■ The **Address Book** dialog box
appears.

Microsoft Exchange provides several address books to help you quickly find the person you want to send a message to.

Personal Address Book

Lists the address of each person you frequently send messages to.

Note: To add a name to the Personal Address Book, refer to page 166.

Microsoft Network

Lists the address of each person connected to The Microsoft Network.

Postoffice Address List

Lists the address of each person connected to the network at your office.

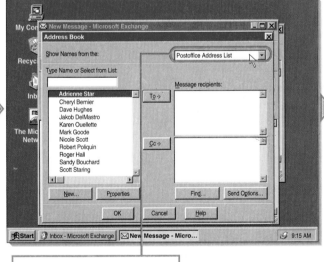

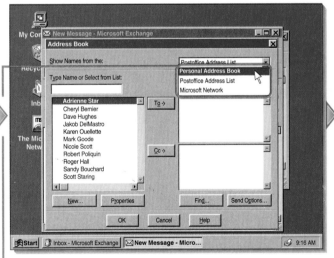

■ This area displays the name of the address book currently displayed.

*Note: For information on address books, refer to the **Tip** above.*

3 To display the names from a different address book, click this area.

4 Click the name of the address book you want to display.

CONTINUED

SEND A MESSAGE

When sending a message, you should enter a subject that will help the reader quickly identify the contents of your message.

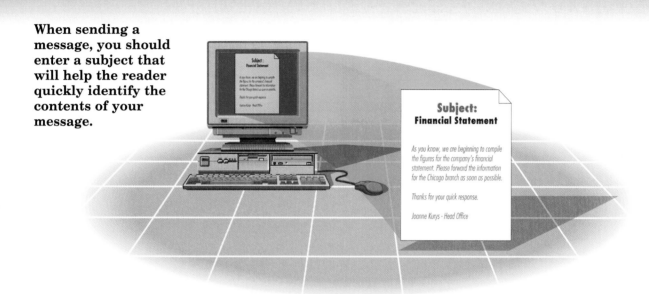

**Subject:
Financial Statement**

As you know, we are beginning to compile the figures for the company's financial statement. Please forward the information for the Chicago branch as soon as possible.

Thanks for your quick response.

Joanne Kurys - Head Office

SEND A MESSAGE (CONTINUED)

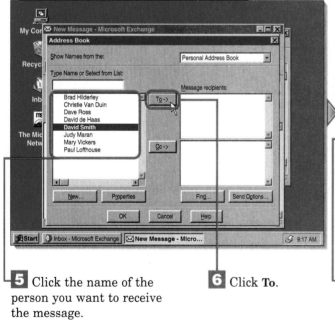

5 Click the name of the person you want to receive the message.

6 Click **To**.

■ This area displays the name of the person you selected.

Note: To send the message to more than one person, repeat steps 5 and 6 for each person.

7 Click **OK**.

TIP

You can use Microsoft Exchange to send messages to co-workers, other members of The Microsoft Network, members of other online services and anyone using the Internet.

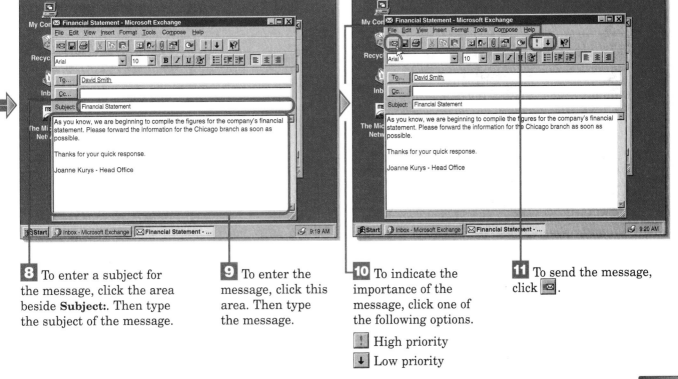

8 To enter a subject for the message, click the area beside **Subject:**. Then type the subject of the message.

9 To enter the message, click this area. Then type the message.

10 To indicate the importance of the message, click one of the following options.

High priority

Low priority

11 To send the message, click ⊞⊠.

171

INSERT A FILE IN A MESSAGE

You can insert a file in a
message. This is useful
when you want to include
additional information.

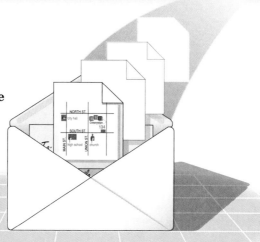

INSERT A FILE IN A MESSAGE

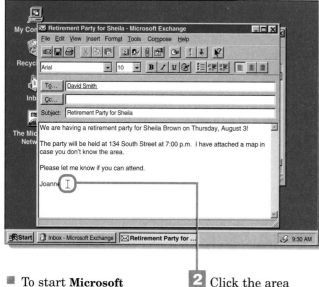

■ To start **Microsoft
Exchange**, refer to
page 152.

1 To create a message,
perform steps 1 to 10
starting on page 168.

2 Click the area
where you want to
insert the file.

3 Click 🔘.

■ The **Insert File**
dialog box appears.

To display the contents of a
file in a message, double-click
the file's icon.

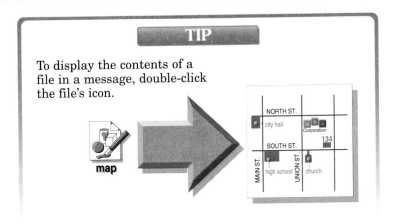

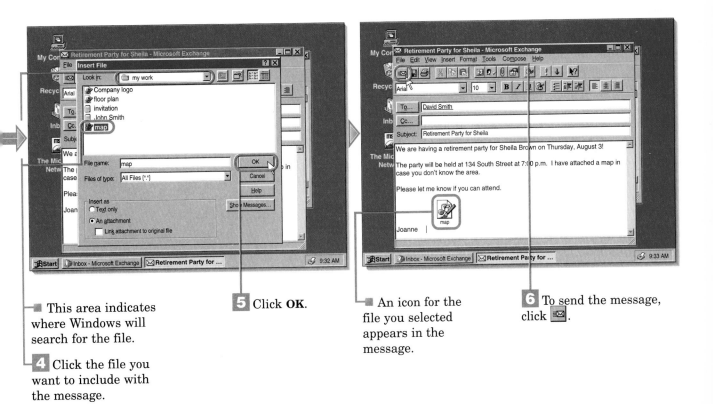

■ This area indicates
where Windows will
search for the file.

4 Click the file you
want to include with
the message.

5 Click **OK**.

■ An icon for the
file you selected
appears in the
message.

6 To send the message,
click 🖾.

READ A MESSAGE

You can easily display
a message sent to you.
Each message displays
a symbol to provide
additional information.

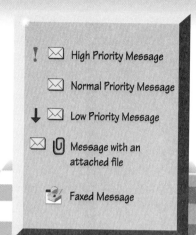

! ⊠ High Priority Message

⊠ Normal Priority Message

↓ ⊠ Low Priority Message

⊠ 🔘 Message with an
attached file

📠 Faxed Message

READ A MESSAGE

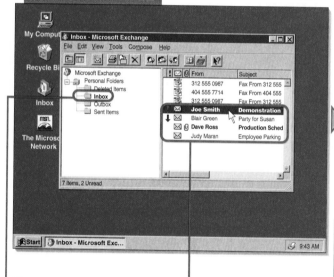

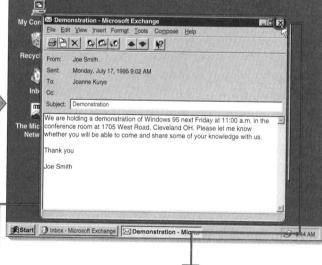

■ To start **Microsoft Exchange**, refer to page 152.

1 Click the **Inbox** folder.

■ This area displays a list of all your messages. Messages you have not read appear in **bold** type.

2 To read a message, double-click the message.

■ The message appears.

3 When you finish reading the message, click ⊠.

You can delete
a message you
no longer need.

DELETE A MESSAGE

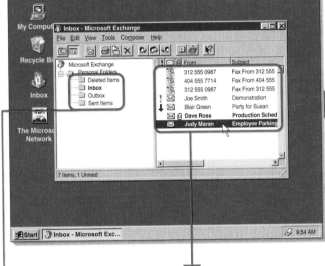

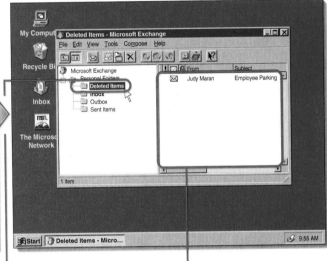

■ To start **Microsoft Exchange**, refer to page 152.

1 Click the folder containing the message you want to delete (example: **Inbox**).

2 Click the message you want to delete.

3 Press Delete on your keyboard and Microsoft Exchange places the message in the **Deleted Items** folder.

4 To view all the messages you have deleted, click the **Deleted Items** folder.

■ This area displays the messages you have deleted.

*Note: Deleting a message from the **Deleted Items** folder will permanently remove the message from your computer.*

REPLY TO A MESSAGE

After reading a message, you can send a reply. This lets you comment on the message or answer questions.

REPLY TO A MESSAGE

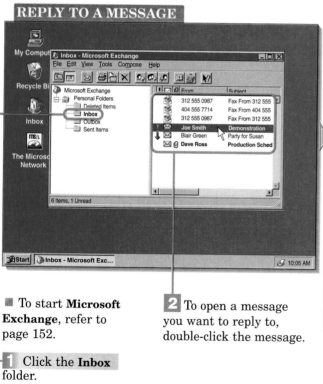

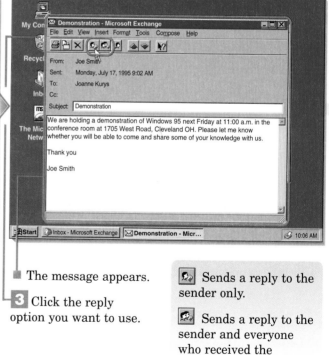

■ To start **Microsoft Exchange**, refer to page 152.

1 Click the **Inbox** folder.

2 To open a message you want to reply to, double-click the message.

■ The message appears.

3 Click the reply option you want to use.

[icon] Sends a reply to the sender only.

[icon] Sends a reply to the sender and everyone who received the original message.

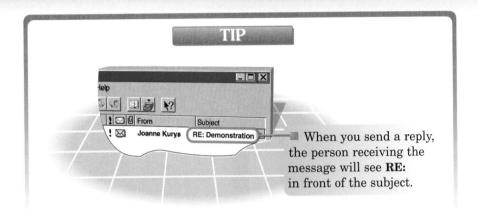

When you send a reply, the person receiving the message will see **RE:** in front of the subject.

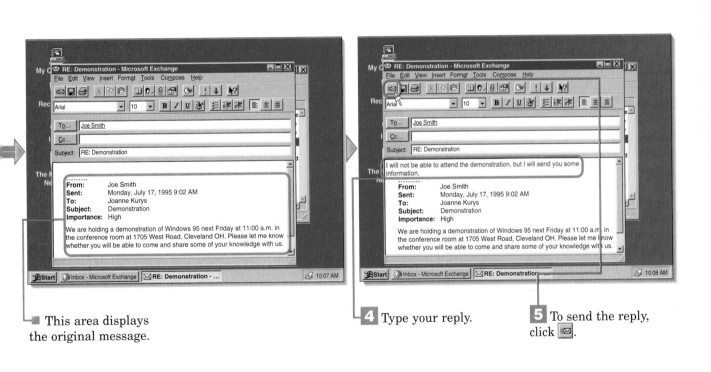

■ This area displays the original message.

4 Type your reply.

5 To send the reply, click ⊠.

177

FORWARD A MESSAGE

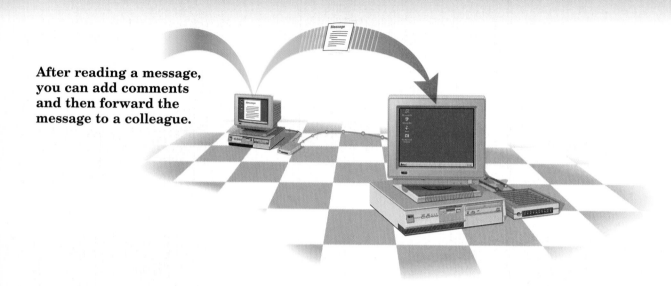

After reading a message, you can add comments and then forward the message to a colleague.

FORWARD A MESSAGE

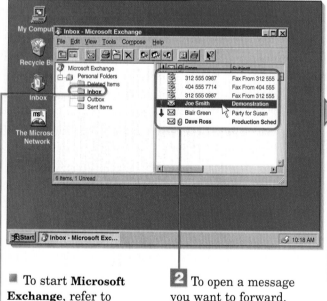

■ To start **Microsoft Exchange**, refer to page 152.

1 Click the **Inbox** folder.

2 To open a message you want to forward, double-click the message.

■ The message appears.

3 To forward the message, click [icon].

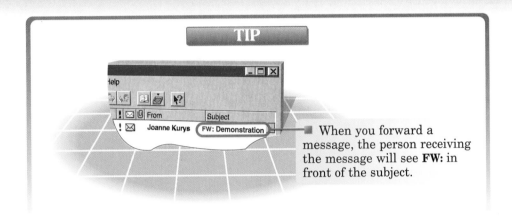

When you forward a message, the person receiving the message will see **FW:** in front of the subject.

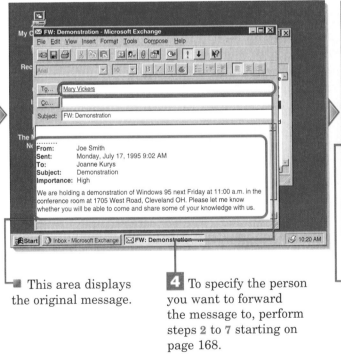

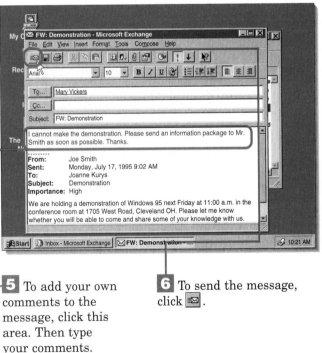

■ This area displays the original message.

4 To specify the person you want to forward the message to, perform steps 2 to 7 starting on page 168.

5 To add your own comments to the message, click this area. Then type your comments.

6 To send the message, click 🖾.

**In this chapter you will learn
how to add new fonts, Windows components,
programs and hardware to your computer.**

CHAPTER 12: ADD HARDWARE AND SOFTWARE

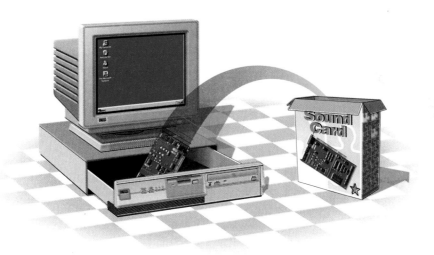

ADD FONTS

You can add fonts to
your computer to give
you more choices when
creating documents.

ADD FONTS

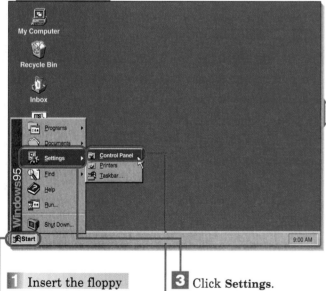

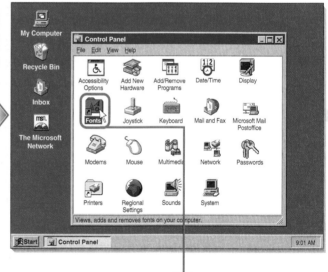

1 Insert the floppy
disk containing the
fonts into a drive.

2 Click **Start**.

3 Click **Settings**.

4 Click **Control Panel**.

■ The **Control Panel**
window appears.

5 To view the fonts
stored on your computer,
double-click **Fonts**.

TIP

You can buy fonts to add
to your computer at most
computer stores.

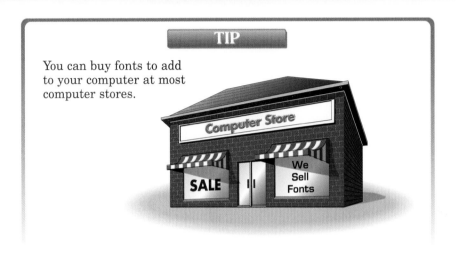

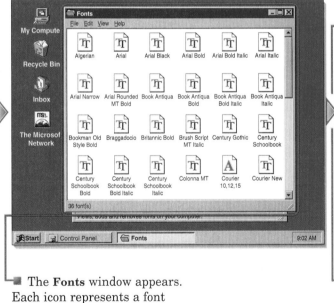

The **Fonts** window appears.
Each icon represents a font
stored on your computer.

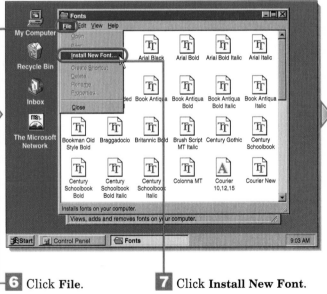

6 Click **File**.

7 Click **Install New Font**.

CONTINUED

ADD FONTS

When you add fonts to your computer, the fonts will be available for use in all your programs.

Bell MT   Mistral

ADD FONTS (CONTINUED)

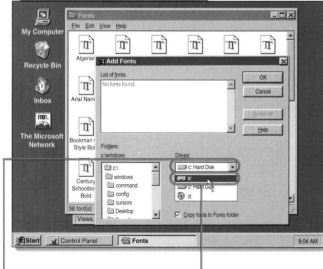

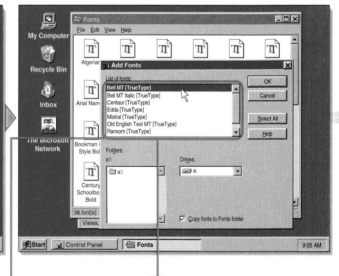

■ The **Add Fonts** dialog box appears.

8 To view the fonts stored on the floppy disk, click this area.

9 Click the drive containing the floppy disk.

■ This area now displays the fonts stored on the floppy disk.

10 To select a font you want to add to your computer, click the font.

TIP

Fonts take up space
on your hard drive.
If you do not use fonts
you added to your computer,
delete them as you would any
file. Do not delete fonts that
come with Windows.

*Note: To delete a file,
refer to page 78.*

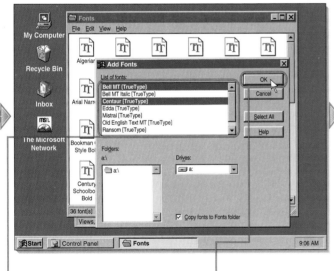

11 To select additional fonts,
press and hold down **Ctrl** on
your keyboard as you repeat
step 10 for each font.

*Note: To select all the fonts
stored on the floppy disk,
click* Select All *.*

12 To add the fonts
to your computer,
click **OK**.

■ Windows copies the
fonts to your computer.

■ The fonts now appear
in the **Fonts** window.

185

ADD WINDOWS COMPONENTS

You can add components to your computer that you did not add when you first set up Windows.

When setting up Windows, most people do not install all the components that come with the program. This avoids taking up storage space with components they do not plan to use.

ADD WINDOWS COMPONENTS

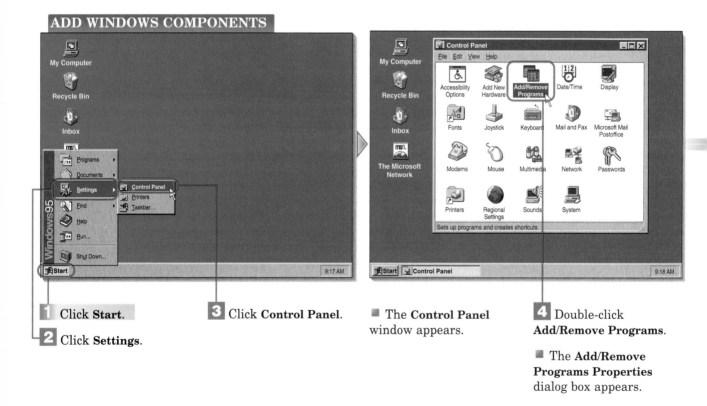

1 Click **Start**.

2 Click **Settings**.

3 Click **Control Panel**.

■ The **Control Panel** window appears.

4 Double-click **Add/Remove Programs**.

■ The **Add/Remove Programs Properties** dialog box appears.

TIP

**Here are some Windows components
you can add to your computer.**

Games   Microsoft   Microsoft   Screen
               Exchange   Fax   Savers

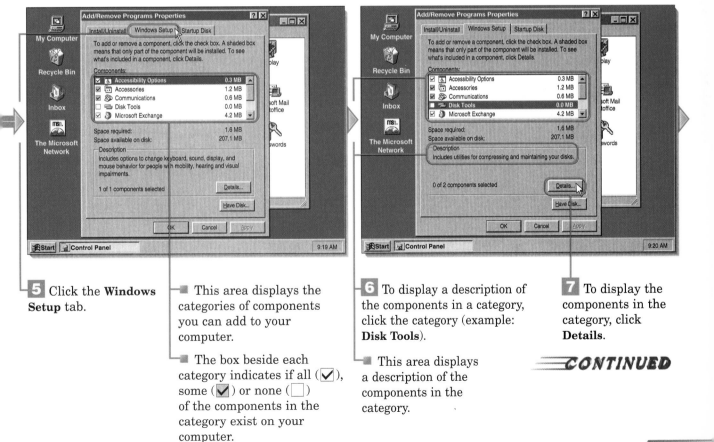

5 Click the **Windows
Setup** tab.

■ This area displays the
categories of components
you can add to your
computer.

■ The box beside each
category indicates if all (☑),
some (☑) or none (☐)
of the components in the
category exist on your
computer.

6 To display a description of
the components in a category,
click the category (example:
Disk Tools).

■ This area displays
a description of the
components in the
category.

7 To display the
components in the
category, click
Details.

CONTINUED

ADD WINDOWS COMPONENTS

When adding Windows components, you must insert the installation CD-ROM disc or floppy disks that come with Windows.

Some components, such as CD Player and Quick View, are available on the Windows CD-ROM disc but not on the Windows floppy disks.

ADD WINDOWS COMPONENTS (CONTINUED)

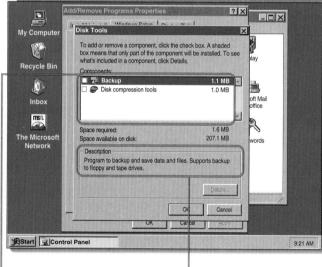

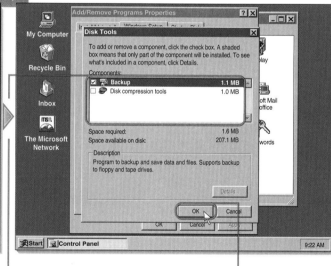

■ The components in the category appear. The box beside each component indicates if the component exists (✓) or does not exist (☐) on your computer.

■ This area displays a description of the highlighted component.

8 To select a component, click the box (☐) beside the component (☐ changes to ✓).

9 Repeat step **8** for each component in the category you want to add to your computer.

10 Click **OK**.

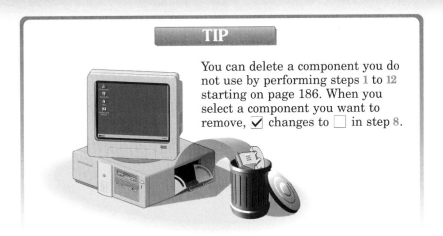

You can delete a component you do not use by performing steps **1** to **12** starting on page 186. When you select a component you want to remove, ✔ changes to ☐ in step **8**.

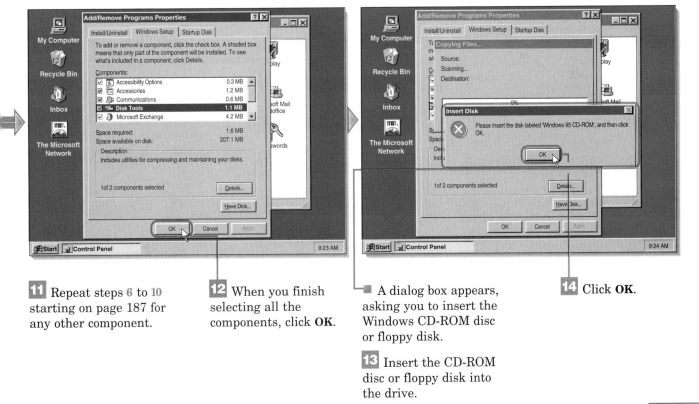

11 Repeat steps **6** to **10** starting on page 187 for any other component.

12 When you finish selecting all the components, click **OK**.

■ A dialog box appears, asking you to insert the Windows CD-ROM disc or floppy disk.

13 Insert the CD-ROM disc or floppy disk into the drive.

14 Click **OK**.

ADD A NEW PROGRAM

MAIN TYPES OF PROGRAMS

WORD PROCESSORS

A word processor helps you create documents quickly and efficiently. Popular word processors include Word and WordPerfect.

SPREADSHEETS

A spreadsheet program helps you manage, analyze and present financial information. Popular spreadsheet programs include Excel and Lotus 1-2-3.

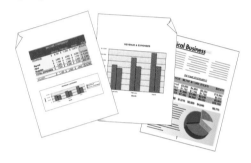

DATABASES

A database helps you manage large collections of information. Popular databases include Access and dBASE.

DESKTOP PUBLISHING

A desktop publishing program helps you create sophisticated documents by combining text and graphics on a page. Popular desktop publishing programs include PageMaker and QuarkXPress.

GAMES

There are thousands of games to entertain you. Popular games include Doom and Golf.

GRAPHICS

A graphics program helps you create and manipulate illustrations. Popular graphics programs include CorelDRAW! and Adobe Illustrator.

You can easily add a new program to your computer.

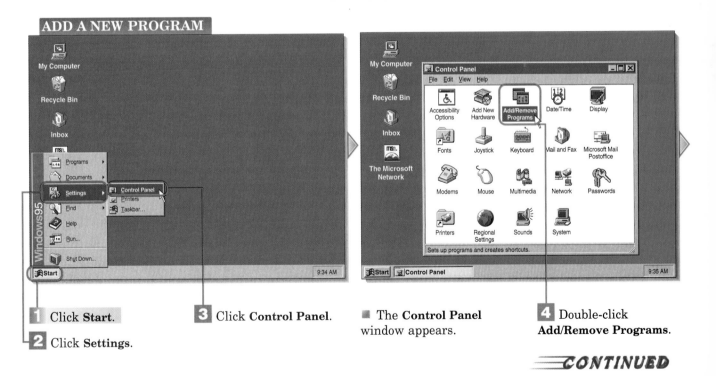

1 Click **Start**.

2 Click **Settings**.

3 Click **Control Panel**.

■ The **Control Panel** window appears.

4 Double-click **Add/Remove Programs**.

CONTINUED

ADD A NEW PROGRAM

Programs come on either a CD-ROM disc or floppy disks.

When you finish installing a program, make sure you keep the CD-ROM disc or floppy disks in a safe place. If your computer fails or if you accidentally erase the program files, you may need to install the program again.

ADD A NEW PROGRAM (CONTINUED)

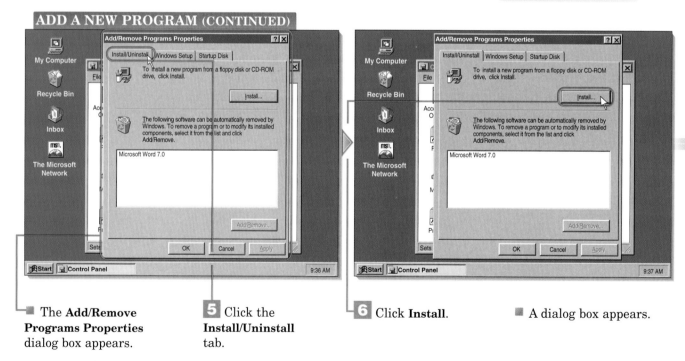

■ The **Add/Remove Programs Properties** dialog box appears.

5 Click the **Install/Uninstall** tab.

6 Click **Install**.

■ A dialog box appears.

TIP

You can often select the way you want to install a program. Common options include:

Typical—Installs the program as recommended for most people.

Custom—Lets you customize the program to suit your specific needs.

Minimum—Installs the minimum amount of the program needed. This is ideal for portable computers or computers with limited disk space.

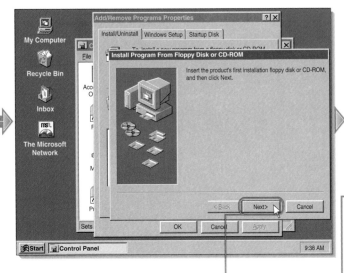

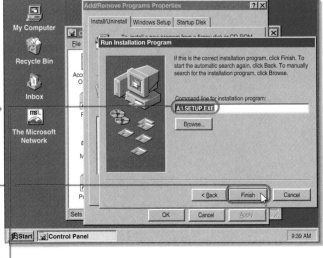

7 Insert the CD-ROM disc or the floppy disk labeled **Disk 1** into a drive.

8 To continue, click **Next**.

■ Windows locates the file needed to install the program.

9 To install the program, click **Finish**.

10 Follow the instructions on your screen. Every program sets itself up differently.

SET UP NEW HARDWARE

You can easily add
new hardware to
your computer.

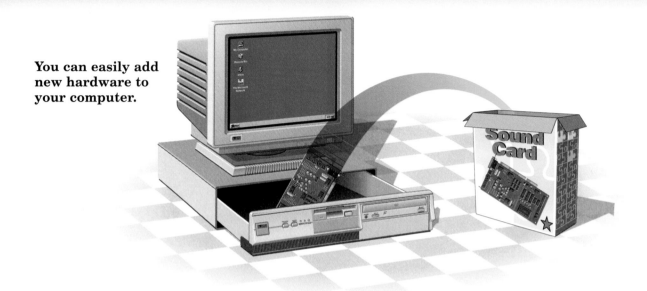

SET UP NEW HARDWARE

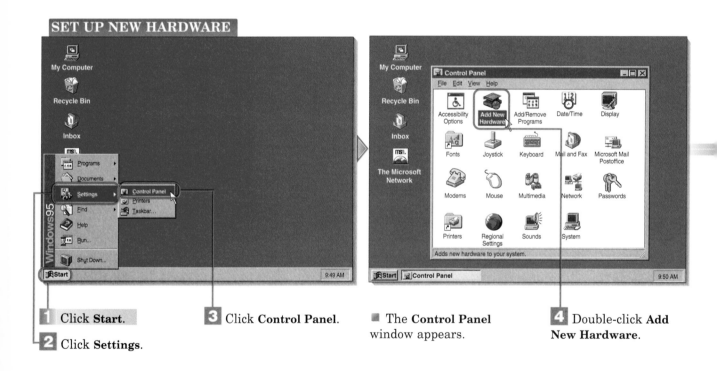

1 Click **Start**.

2 Click **Settings**.

3 Click **Control Panel**.

■ The **Control Panel** window appears.

4 Double-click **Add New Hardware**.

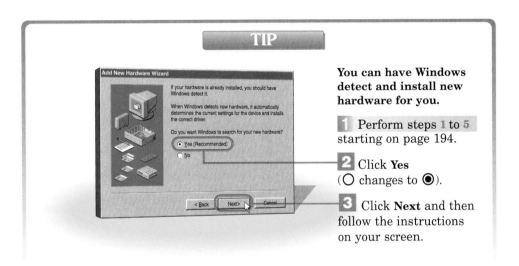

You can have Windows detect and install new hardware for you.

1 Perform steps 1 to 5 starting on page 194.

2 Click **Yes** (○ changes to ●).

3 Click **Next** and then follow the instructions on your screen.

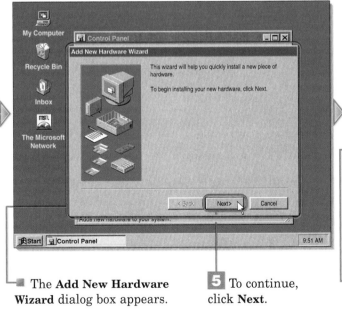

■ The **Add New Hardware Wizard** dialog box appears.

5 To continue, click **Next**.

6 If you know the details about the hardware, click **No** (○ changes to ●).

*Note: If you do not know the details about the hardware, refer to the **Tip** above.*

7 Click **Next**.

CONTINUED

SET UP NEW HARDWARE

When adding new hardware, you must specify the manufacturer and model of the hardware.

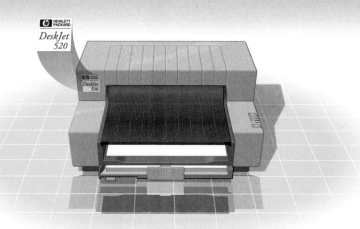

SET UP NEW HARDWARE (CONTINUED)

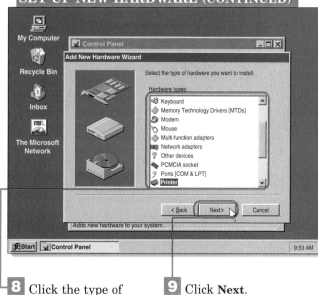

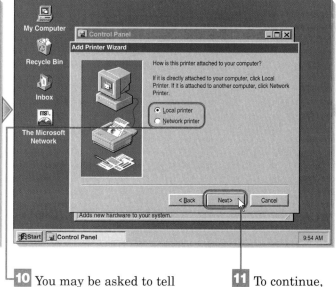

8 Click the type of hardware you want to install.

9 Click **Next**.

■ The remaining steps depend on the type of hardware you selected in step 8. In this example, we install a new printer.

10 You may be asked to tell Windows how the printer connects to your computer. To do so, click one of the following options (○ changes to ◉).

Local printer
Printer connects directly to your computer.

Network printer
Printer connects to another computer.

11 To continue, click **Next**.

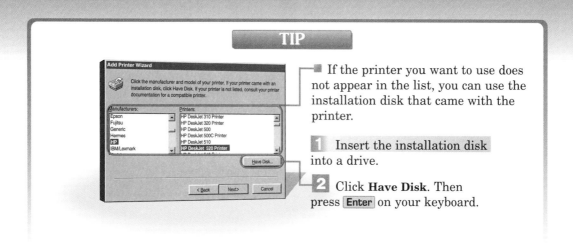

If the printer you want to use does not appear in the list, you can use the installation disk that came with the printer.

1 Insert the installation disk into a drive.

2 Click **Have Disk**. Then press **Enter** on your keyboard.

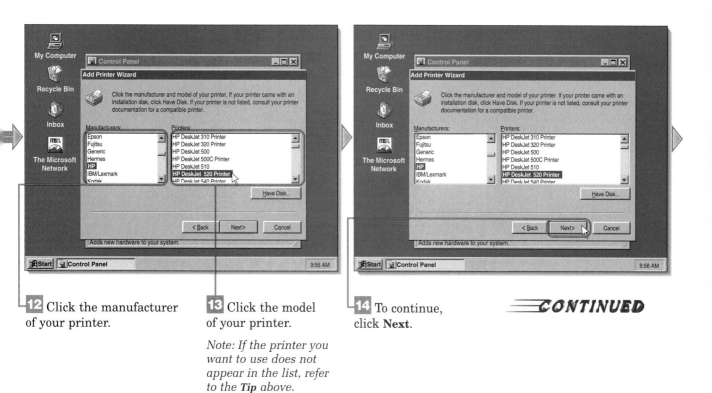

12 Click the manufacturer of your printer.

13 Click the model of your printer.

*Note: If the printer you want to use does not appear in the list, refer to the **Tip** above.*

14 To continue, click **Next**.

CONTINUED

SET UP NEW HARDWARE

Windows asks you questions about the new hardware. This helps Windows set up the hardware to suit your specific needs.

SET UP NEW HARDWARE (CONTINUED)

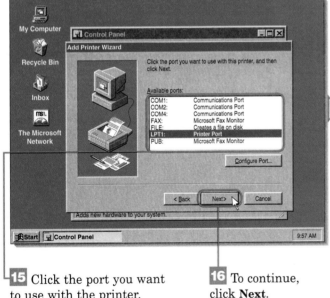

15 Click the port you want to use with the printer.

Note: A port is a socket at the back of a computer where you plug in a device. LPT1 is the most commonly used port for printers.

16 To continue, click **Next**.

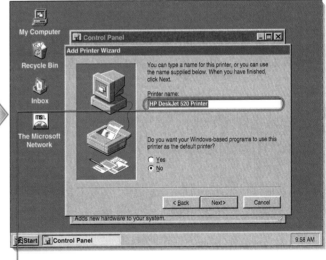

17 Type a name for the printer.

Note: To use the name supplied by Windows, do not type a name.

Windows 95 supports Plug and Play. Before Plug and Play, adding new features to a computer was difficult and frustrating. Plug and Play lets you quickly and easily add new features to your computer.

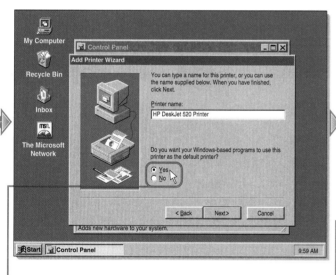

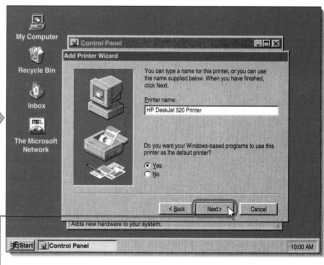

18 To specify if you want to use the printer as the default printer, click one of these options (○ changes to ◉).

Yes - Documents will always print to this printer.

No - Documents will print to this printer only when you select the printer.

19 To continue, click **Next**.

CONTINUED

SET UP NEW HARDWARE

To complete the installation, Windows will ask you to insert the Windows 95 installation CD-ROM disc or floppy disks.

SET UP NEW HARDWARE (CONTINUED)

20 To specify if you want to print a test page, click **Yes** or **No**. A test page will confirm that your printer is set up properly.

21 To complete the installation, click **Finish**.

For your computer to use new hardware, you have to install special software, called a **driver**. A driver is a program that helps the computer communicate with the hardware. Windows provides the most popular drivers and helps you install them.

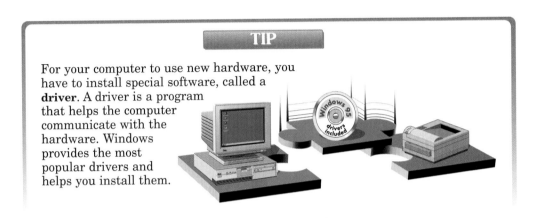

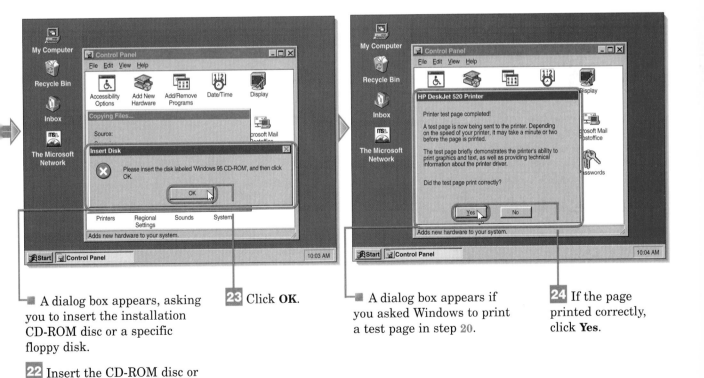

■ A dialog box appears, asking you to insert the installation CD-ROM disc or a specific floppy disk.

22 Insert the CD-ROM disc or floppy disk into a drive.

23 Click **OK**.

■ A dialog box appears if you asked Windows to print a test page in step 20.

24 If the page printed correctly, click **Yes**.

**In this chapter you will learn
how to format and copy disks and improve
the performance of your computer.**

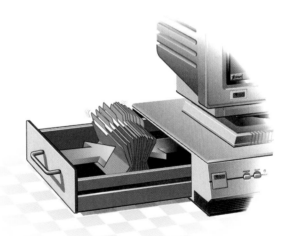

FORMAT A DISK

You must format a floppy
disk before you can use
it to store information.

FORMAT A DISK

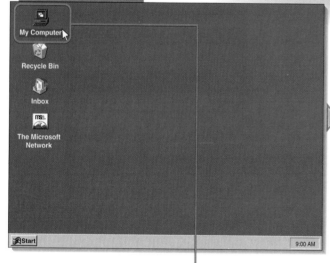

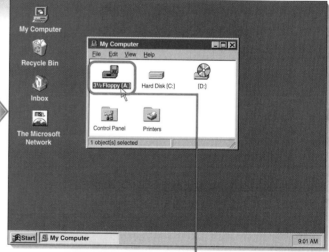

1 Insert the floppy disk
you want to format into a
drive.

2 Double-click **My
Computer**.

■ The **My Computer**
window appears.

3 Click the drive
containing the floppy
disk you want to
format (example: **A:**).

IMPORTANT

Before formatting a floppy disk, make sure the disk does not contain information you want to keep. Formatting will remove all the information on the disk.

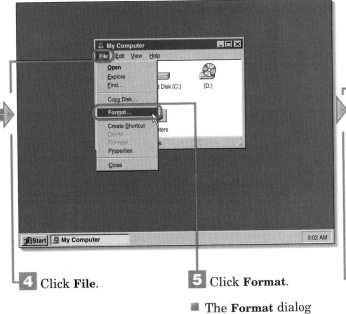

4 Click **File**.

5 Click **Format**.

■ The **Format** dialog box appears.

6 Click the type of format you want to perform (O changes to ◉).

Note: If the floppy disk has never been formatted, select the Full option.

Quick (erase)
Removes all files but does not scan the disk for damaged areas.

Full
Removes all files and scans the disk for damaged areas.

CONTINUED

FORMAT A DISK

When formatting a floppy disk, you must tell Windows how much information the disk can hold.

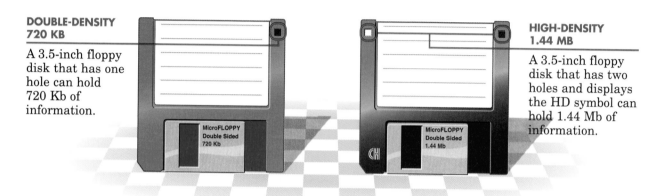

DOUBLE-DENSITY 720 KB

A 3.5-inch floppy disk that has one hole can hold 720 Kb of information.

HIGH-DENSITY 1.44 MB

A 3.5-inch floppy disk that has two holes and displays the HD symbol can hold 1.44 Mb of information.

FORMAT A DISK (CONTINUED)

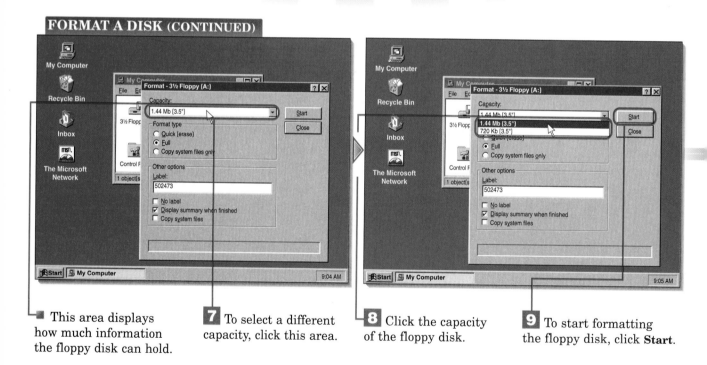

■ This area displays how much information the floppy disk can hold.

7 To select a different capacity, click this area.

8 Click the capacity of the floppy disk.

9 To start formatting the floppy disk, click **Start**.

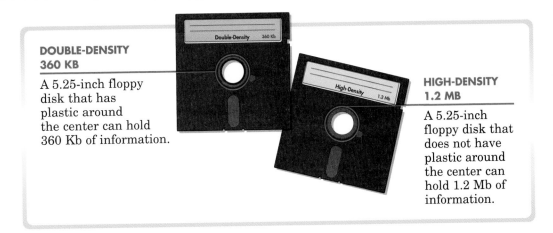

**DOUBLE-DENSITY
360 KB**

A 5.25-inch floppy
disk that has
plastic around
the center can hold
360 Kb of information.

**HIGH-DENSITY
1.2 MB**

A 5.25-inch
floppy disk that
does not have
plastic around
the center can
hold 1.2 Mb of
information.

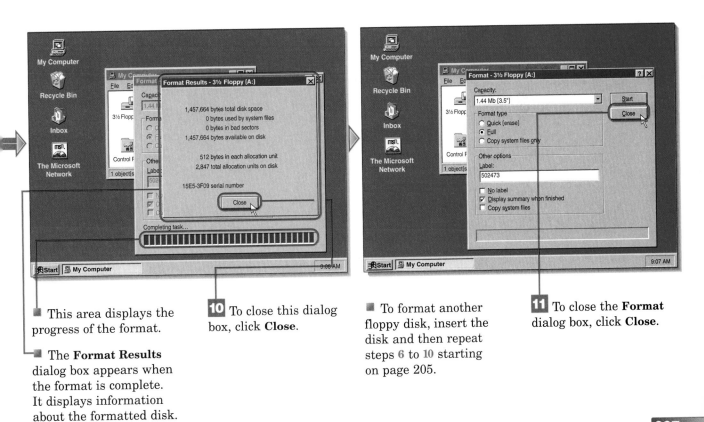

This area displays the
progress of the format.

The **Format Results**
dialog box appears when
the format is complete.
It displays information
about the formatted disk.

10 To close this dialog
box, click **Close**.

To format another
floppy disk, insert the
disk and then repeat
steps 6 to 10 starting
on page 205.

11 To close the **Format**
dialog box, click **Close**.

DETECT AND REPAIR DISK ERRORS

You can improve the performance
of your computer by using
ScanDisk to search for
and repair disk errors.

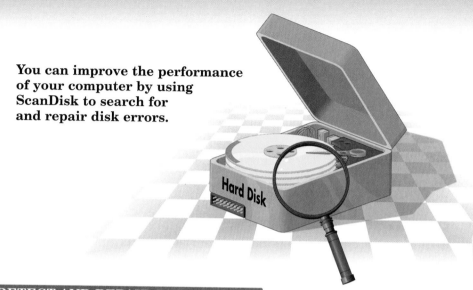

The hard disk is
the primary device
a computer uses to
store information.

DETECT AND REPAIR DISK ERRORS

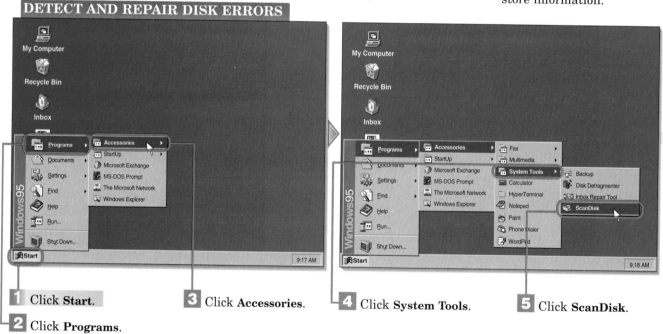

1 Click **Start**.

2 Click **Programs**.

3 Click **Accessories**.

4 Click **System Tools**.

5 Click **ScanDisk**.

You should check your hard disk for errors at least once a month.

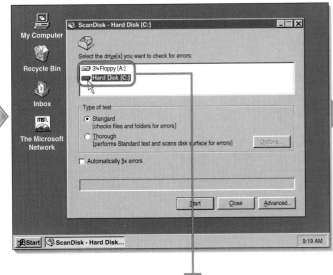

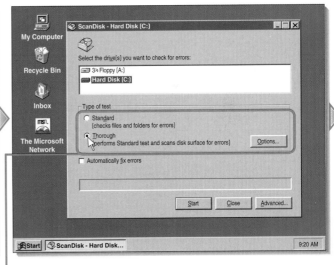

■ The **ScanDisk** dialog box appears.

6 Click the drive you want to check for errors (example: **C:**).

7 Click the type of test you want to perform (○ changes to ●).

Standard
Checks files and folders for errors.

Thorough
Checks files, folders and the disk surface for errors.

CONTINUED

DETECT AND REPAIR DISK ERRORS

You can have Windows automatically repair any disk errors it finds.

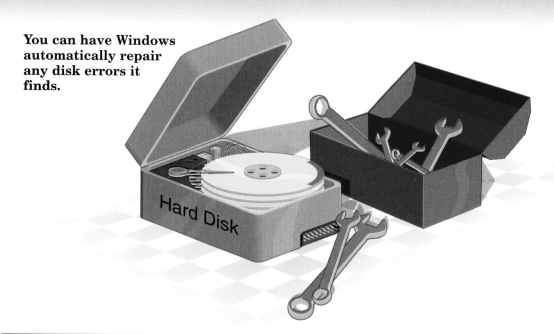

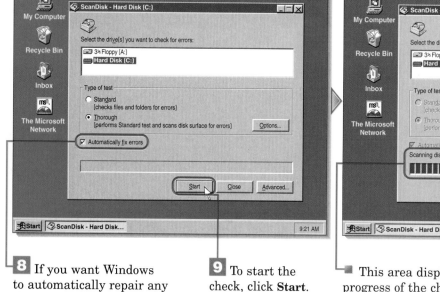

DETECT AND REPAIR DISK ERRORS (CONTINUED)

8 If you want Windows to automatically repair any disk errors it finds, click this option (changes to ☑).

9 To start the check, click **Start**.

■ This area displays the progress of the check.

**If you did not tell Windows to automatically
repair any disk errors it finds, this dialog box
will appear each time ScanDisk finds an error.**

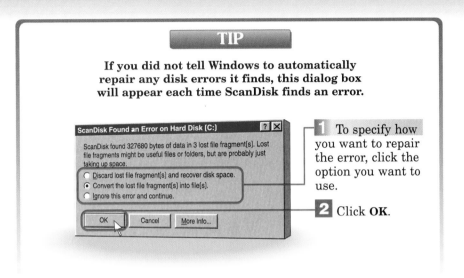

1 To specify how
you want to repair
the error, click the
option you want to
use.

2 Click **OK**.

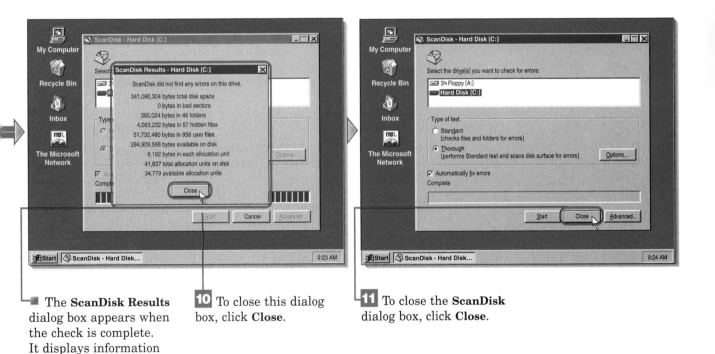

■ The **ScanDisk Results**
dialog box appears when
the check is complete.
It displays information
about the disk.

10 To close this dialog
box, click **Close**.

11 To close the **ScanDisk**
dialog box, click **Close**.

DEFRAGMENT A DISK

A fragmented hard disk stores parts of a file in many different locations. To retrieve a file, your computer must search many areas on the disk.

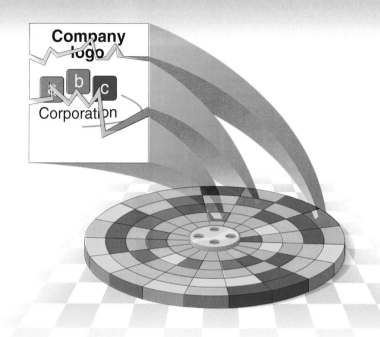

DEFRAGMENT A DISK

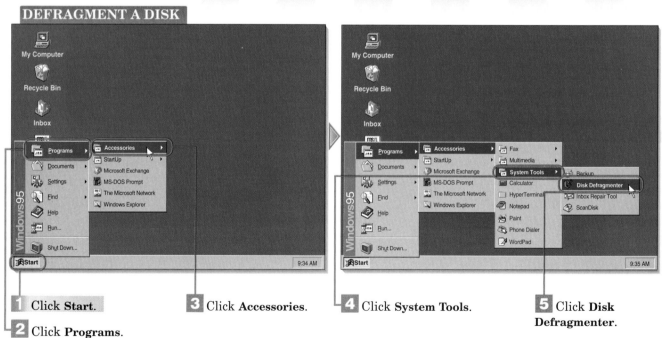

1 Click **Start**.

2 Click **Programs**.

3 Click **Accessories**.

4 Click **System Tools**.

5 Click **Disk Defragmenter**.

You can improve the
performance of your
computer by using
the **Disk Defragmenter**
program.

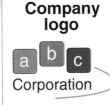
Company logo

a b c
Corporation

You can use the Disk
Defragmenter program to
place all the parts of a file
in one location. This reduces
the time your computer will
spend locating the file.

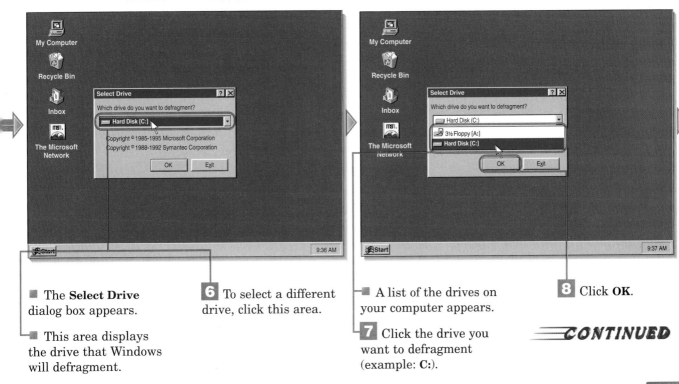

■ The **Select Drive**
dialog box appears.

■ This area displays
the drive that Windows
will defragment.

6 To select a different
drive, click this area.

■ A list of the drives on
your computer appears.

7 Click the drive you
want to defragment
(example: **C:**).

8 Click **OK**.

CONTINUED

DEFRAGMENT A DISK

You can perform other tasks on
your computer while Windows
defragments a disk, but your
computer will operate slower.

DEFRAGMENT A DISK (CONTINUED)

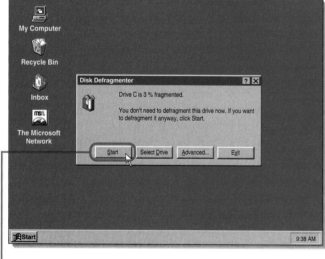

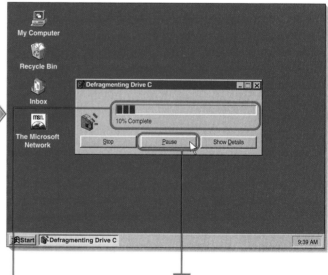

9 Click **Start**.

■ This area displays
the progress of the
defragmentation.

10 To temporarily stop
the defragmentation so
you can perform other
tasks at full speed,
click **Pause**.

You should defragment your hard disk at least once a month.

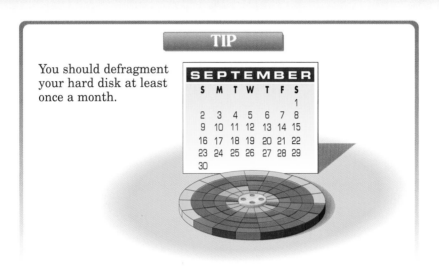

SEPTEMBER

S	M	T	W	T	F	S
						1
2	3	4	5	6	7	8
9	10	11	12	13	14	15
16	17	18	19	20	21	22
23	24	25	26	27	28	29
30						

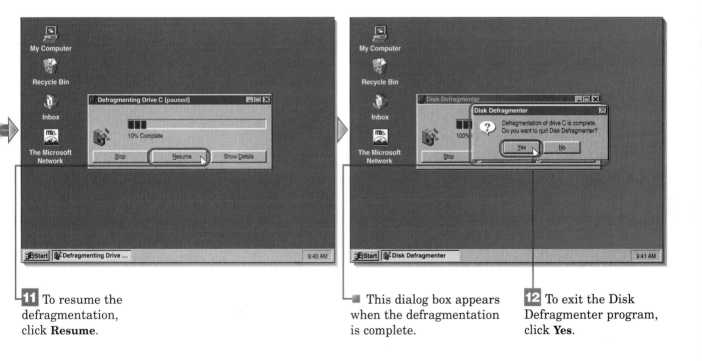

11 To resume the defragmentation, click **Resume**.

◼ This dialog box appears when the defragmentation is complete.

12 To exit the Disk Defragmenter program, click **Yes**.

COPY A FLOPPY DISK

You can make an exact copy of a floppy disk. This is ideal when you want to make a backup copy of an important disk.

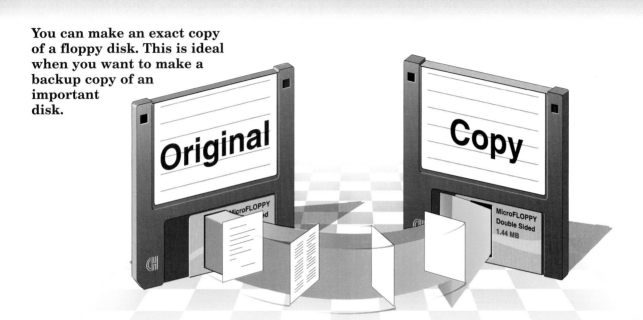

COPY A FLOPPY DISK

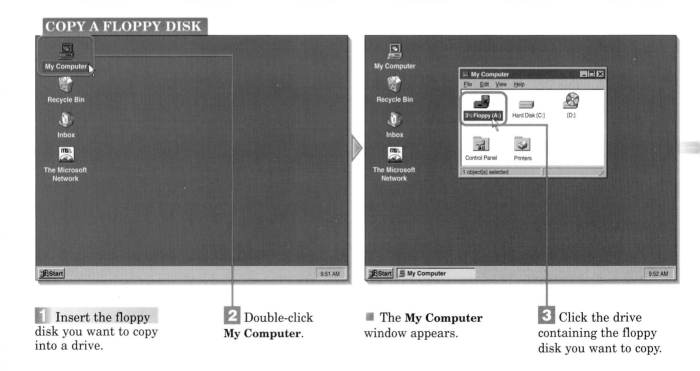

1 Insert the floppy disk you want to copy into a drive.

2 Double-click **My Computer**.

■ The **My Computer** window appears.

3 Click the drive containing the floppy disk you want to copy.

**The original floppy disk and the disk
that will receive the copy must be able to store
the same amount of information.**

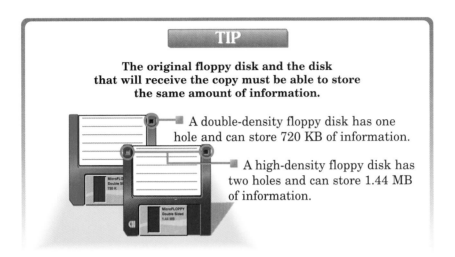

A double-density floppy disk has one
hole and can store 720 KB of information.

A high-density floppy disk has
two holes and can store 1.44 MB
of information.

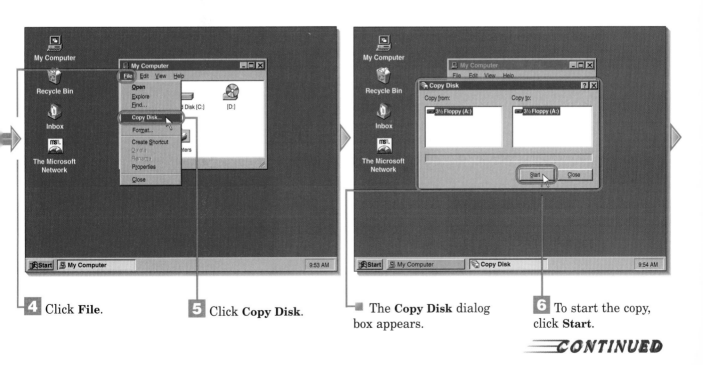

4 Click **File**.

5 Click **Copy Disk**.

■ The **Copy Disk** dialog
box appears.

6 To start the copy,
click **Start**.

CONTINUED

COPY A FLOPPY DISK

Make sure the floppy disk receiving the copy does not contain information you want to keep. Copying will remove all the old information from the disk.

COPY A FLOPPY DISK (CONTINUED)

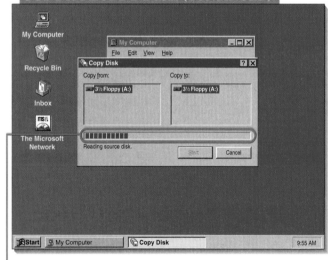

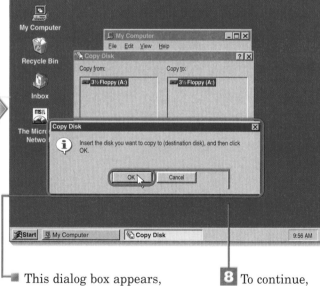

■ This area shows the progress of the copy.

■ This dialog box appears, telling you to insert the floppy disk you want to receive the copy.

7 Remove the floppy disk from the drive and then insert the disk you want to receive the copy.

8 To continue, click **OK**.

TIP

Keep floppy disks away
from magnets, which
can damage the
information stored
on the disks. Also
be careful not to
spill liquids, such
as coffee or soda,
on the disks.

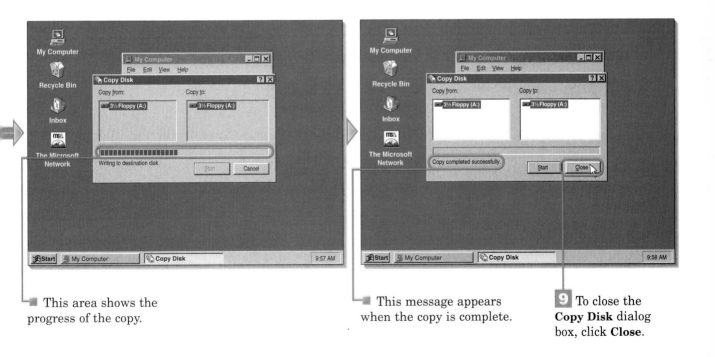

◾ This area shows the
progress of the copy.

◾ This message appears
when the copy is complete.

9 To close the
Copy Disk dialog
box, click **Close**.

COMPRESS A DISK

You can compress, or squeeze together, the information stored on your hard disk. This can double the amount of information the disk can store.

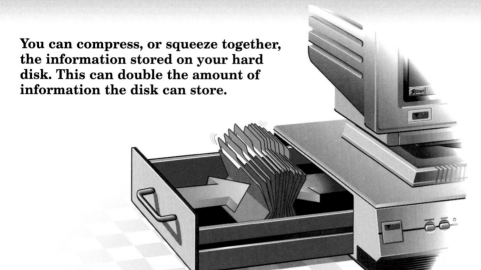

You can also compress floppy disks to store more information.

COMPRESS A DISK

Before compressing your hard disk, perform the following:

Exit all programs.

Back up the information on your hard disk.

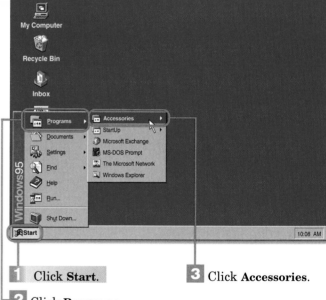

1 Click **Start**.

2 Click **Programs**.

3 Click **Accessories**.

IMPORTANT

You should only compress your hard disk if:

■ The hard disk is running out of space to store new information.

■ You have tried all other ways of increasing the available storage space, such as deleting all files you no longer need.

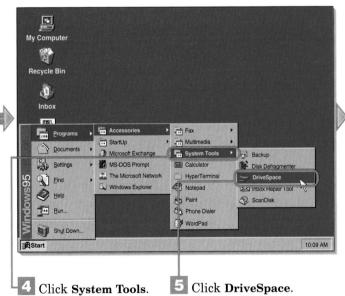

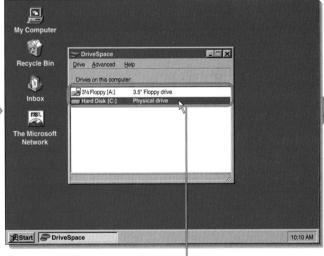

4 Click **System Tools**.

5 Click **DriveSpace**.

Note: If DriveSpace is not available, you must add the Windows component called Disk compression tools. This component is found in the Disk Tools category. To add Windows components, refer to page 186.

■ The **DriveSpace** window appears.

6 Click the disk you want to compress.

CONTINUED

COMPRESS A DISK

Compressing your hard disk can take several hours. During this time, you cannot use your computer.

Compress your hard disk when you will not need your computer, such as after work.

COMPRESS A DISK (CONTINUED)

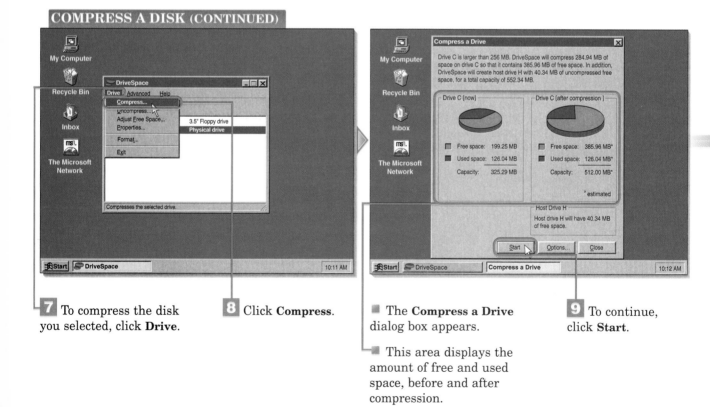

7 To compress the disk you selected, click **Drive**.

8 Click **Compress**.

■ The **Compress a Drive** dialog box appears.

■ This area displays the amount of free and used space, before and after compression.

9 To continue, click **Start**.

TIP

Before Windows compresses
your disk, it uses ScanDisk
to search for and repair
any disk errors.

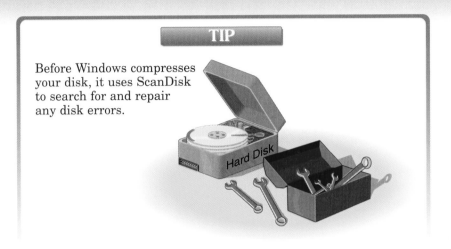

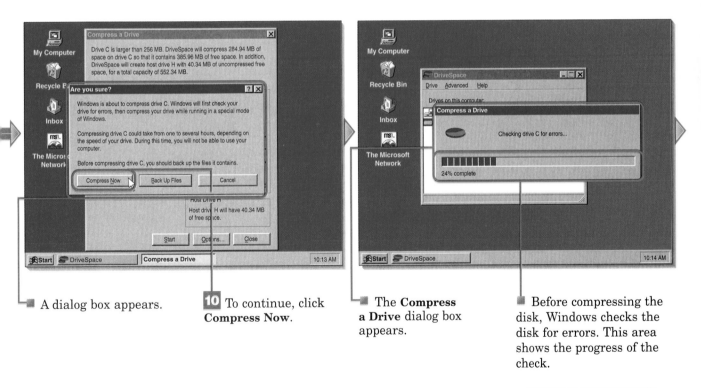

A dialog box appears.

10 To continue, click
Compress Now.

The **Compress
a Drive** dialog box
appears.

Before compressing the
disk, Windows checks the
disk for errors. This area
shows the progress of the
check.

CONTINUED

223

COMPRESS A DISK

When finished, Windows shows you the results of the compression.

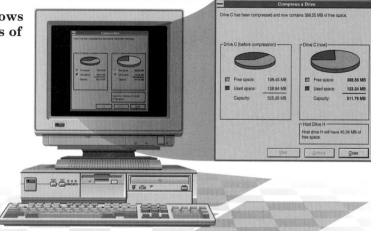

COMPRESS A DISK (CONTINUED)

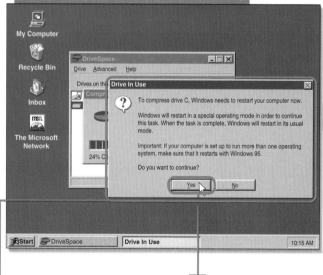

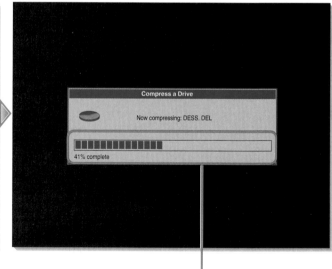

■ This dialog box appears if Windows needs to restart your computer before compressing the disk.

11 To continue, click **Yes**.

■ Windows restarts your computer and then begins compressing your disk.

■ This area displays the progress of the compression.

**After you compress your hard disk,
the amount of free space added to your computer
depends on the type of information stored the disk.**

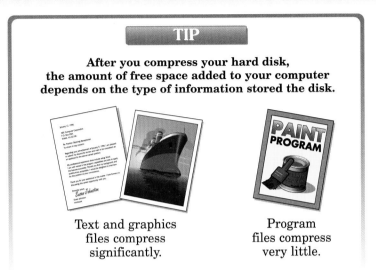

Text and graphics
files compress
significantly.

Program
files compress
very little.

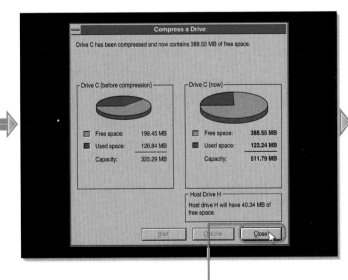

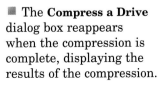

■ The **Compress a Drive**
dialog box reappears
when the compression is
complete, displaying the
results of the compression.

12 To close the dialog
box, click **Close**.

■ Windows restarts
your computer.

■ You can now use your
computer as usual.

**In this chapter you will learn
how to make backup copies of files
stored on your computer.**

CHAPTER 14: BACK UP YOUR FILES

INTRODUCTION

You should regularly make backup copies of the files stored on your computer to protect them from theft, computer failure and viruses.

BACKUP DEVICES

Floppy Disks

You can use floppy disks to back up important files stored on your computer.

Tape Cartridges

You can use tape cartridges to back up large amounts of information, such as all the files on your hard drive.

Note: You must have a tape drive to use tape cartridges.

Back up your work frequently.
Consider how much work you can
afford to lose. If you cannot afford
to lose the work accomplished in
one day, back up once a day.
If your work does not change
much during the week,
back up once a week.

Create and then strictly follow a
backup schedule. Hard drive
disasters always seem to
happen right after you
miss a scheduled
backup.

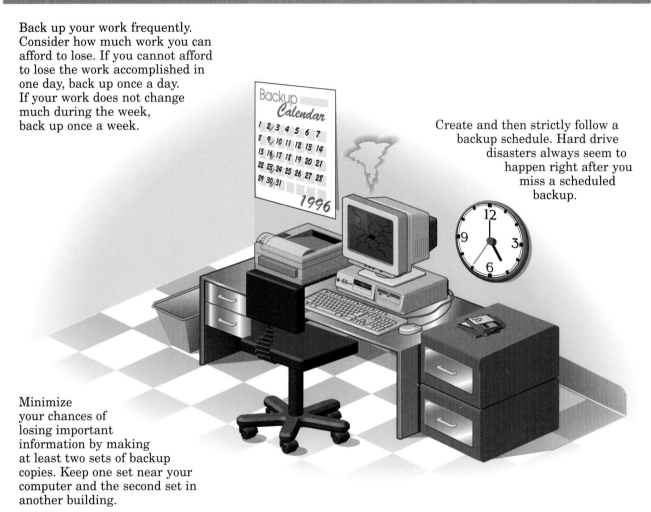

Minimize
your chances of
losing important
information by making
at least two sets of backup
copies. Keep one set near your
computer and the second set in
another building.

Store backup copies in a cool,
dry place, away from electrical
equipment and magnetic devices.

START MICROSOFT BACKUP

Microsoft Backup helps you copy important information stored on your computer to floppy disks.

You can also copy files to tape cartridges. You must have a tape drive to use tape cartridges.

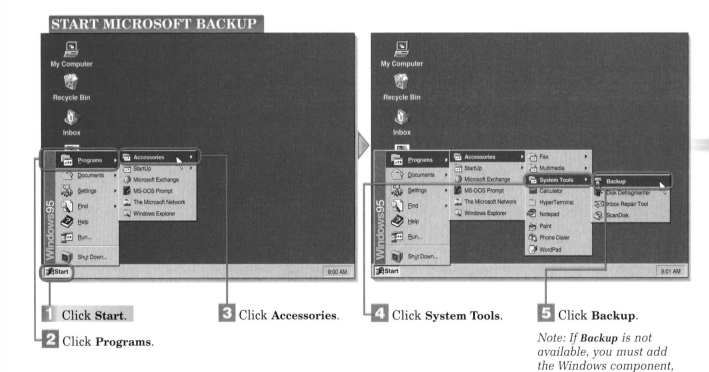

START MICROSOFT BACKUP

1 Click **Start**.

2 Click **Programs**.

3 Click **Accessories**.

4 Click **System Tools**.

5 Click **Backup**.

*Note: If **Backup** is not available, you must add the Windows component, which is found in the Disk Tools category. To do so, refer to page 186.*

TIP

You can also use Microsoft Backup to copy files you rarely use to floppy disks. You can then remove these files from your hard drive to create more storage space on your computer.

Note: To avoid losing the information, you should make two copies of these files and store the copies in different locations.

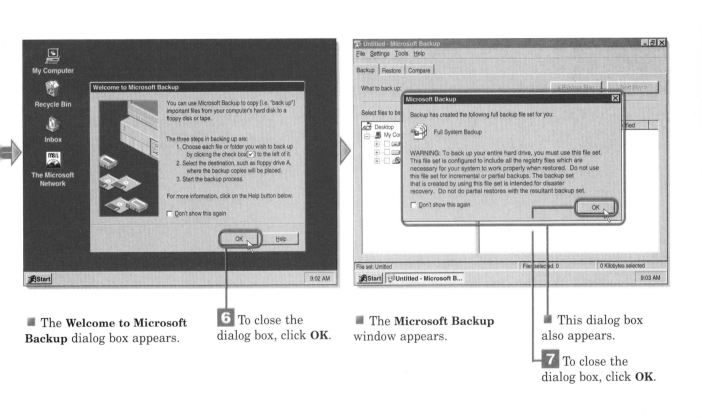

■ The **Welcome to Microsoft Backup** dialog box appears.

6 To close the dialog box, click **OK**.

■ The **Microsoft Backup** window appears.

■ This dialog box also appears.

7 To close the dialog box, click **OK**.

BACK UP SELECTED FILES

To perform a backup, you must select the files you want to back up.

BACKUP BASKET

BACK UP SELECTED FILES

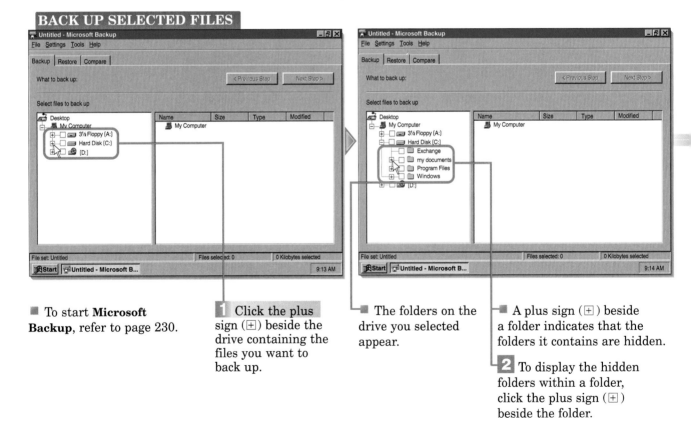

■ To start **Microsoft Backup**, refer to page 230.

1 Click the plus sign (⊞) beside the drive containing the files you want to back up.

■ The folders on the drive you selected appear.

■ A plus sign (⊞) beside a folder indicates that the folders it contains are hidden.

2 To display the hidden folders within a folder, click the plus sign (⊞) beside the folder.

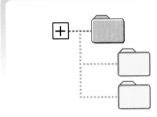

A plus sign (⊞) beside a folder indicates that all the folders it contains are hidden.

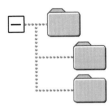

A minus sign (⊟) beside a folder indicates that all the folders it contains are displayed.

No sign beside a folder indicates that the folder does not contain any folders, although it may contain files.

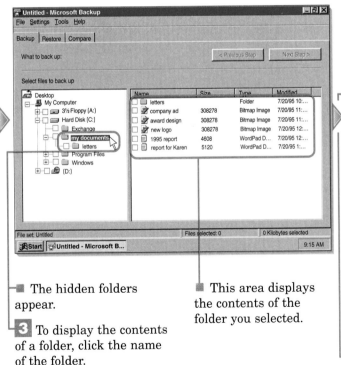

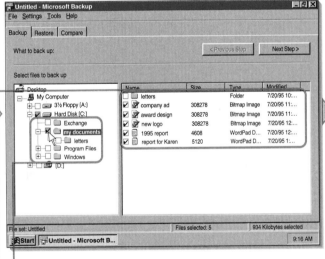

■ The hidden folders appear.

3 To display the contents of a folder, click the name of the folder.

■ This area displays the contents of the folder you selected.

 To back up the files in a folder, click the box (☐) beside the folder (☐ changes to ✔).

■ To back up a specific file, click the box (☐) beside the file. Repeat this for each file you want to back up.

5 Repeat steps 2 to 4 until you have selected all the files you want to back up.

CONTINUED

233

BACK UP SELECTED FILES

If you often back up the same files, you can assign a name to the group of files. This saves you time in future backups.

BACK UP SELECTED FILES (CONTINUED)

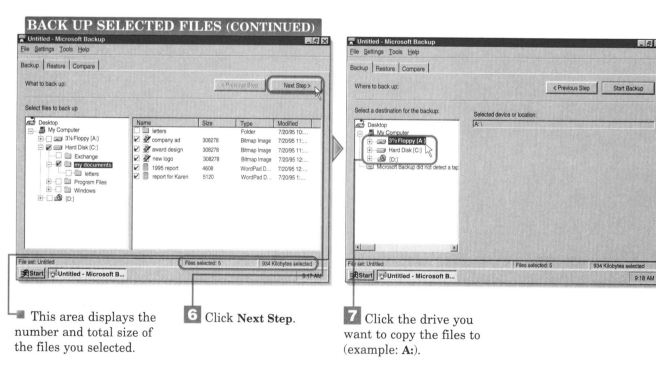

■ This area displays the number and total size of the files you selected.

6 Click **Next Step**.

7 Click the drive you want to copy the files to (example: **A:**).

TIP

Bytes are used to measure the size of files.

One byte equals one
character.

*Note: A character can
be a number, letter or
symbol.*

One kilobyte equals approximately
one thousand characters,
or one page of double-
spaced text.

*Note: If your files
total more than 5000
kilobytes, you should use a
tape cartridge to back up the files.*

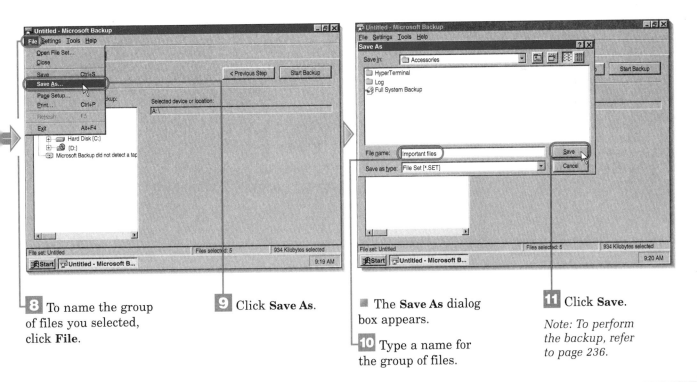

8 To name the group
of files you selected,
click **File**.

9 Click **Save As**.

■ The **Save As** dialog
box appears.

10 Type a name for
the group of files.

11 Click **Save**.

*Note: To perform
the backup, refer
to page 236.*

PERFORM THE BACKUP

After you have selected the files you want to back up, you can have Windows copy the files to floppy disks.

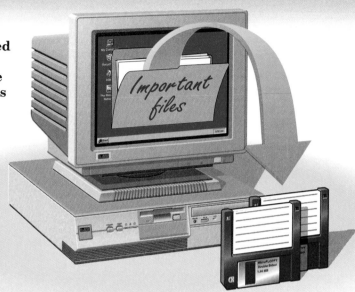

PERFORM THE BACKUP

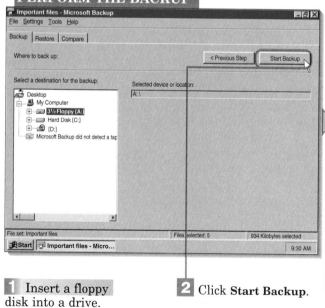

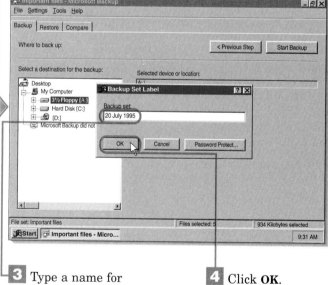

1 Insert a floppy disk into a drive.

2 Click **Start Backup**.

3 Type a name for the backup.

Note: To make it easier to identify the backup later, you can name the backup with the current date.

4 Click **OK**.

**If the backup requires more than one floppy disk,
this dialog box will appear when a disk is full.**

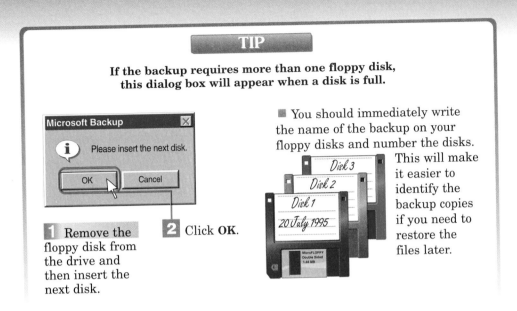

1 Remove the floppy disk from the drive and then insert the next disk.

2 Click **OK**.

■ You should immediately write the name of the backup on your floppy disks and number the disks.

This will make it easier to identify the backup copies if you need to restore the files later.

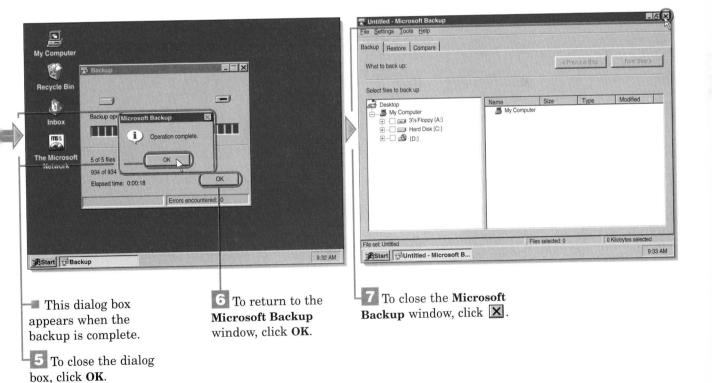

■ This dialog box appears when the backup is complete.

5 To close the dialog box, click **OK**.

6 To return to the **Microsoft Backup** window, click **OK**.

7 To close the **Microsoft Backup** window, click ⊠.

237

BACK UP NAMED FILES

If you assigned a name to a group of files in a previous backup, Windows can save you time by selecting those files for you.

BACK UP NAMED FILES

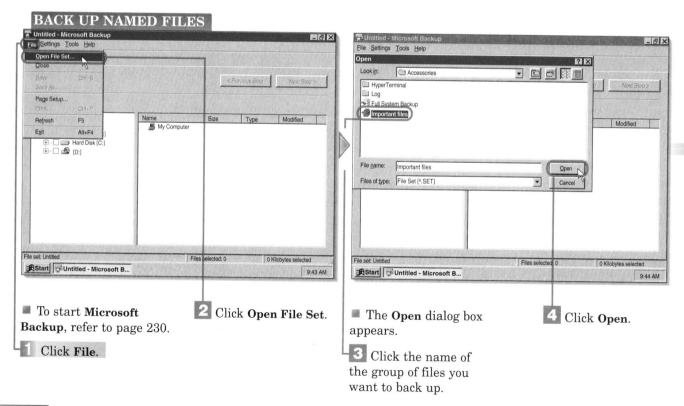

■ To start **Microsoft Backup**, refer to page 230.

1 Click **File**.

2 Click **Open File Set**.

■ The **Open** dialog box appears.

3 Click the name of the group of files you want to back up.

4 Click **Open**.

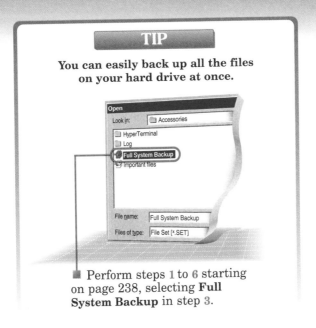

TIP

**You can easily back up all the files
on your hard drive at once.**

■ Perform steps **1** to **6** starting
on page 238, selecting **Full
System Backup** in step **3**.

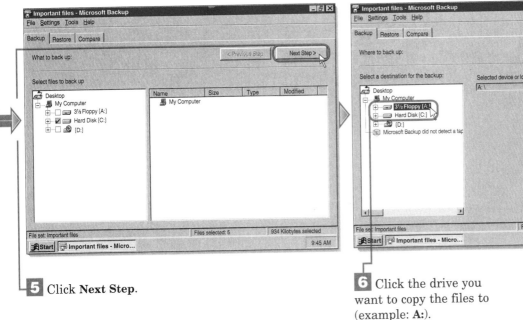

5 Click **Next Step**.

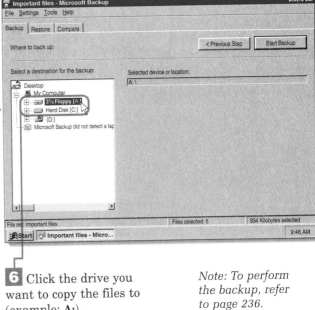

6 Click the drive you
want to copy the files to
(example: **A:**).

*Note: To perform
the backup, refer
to page 236.*

RESTORE FILES

If files on your computer are lost or damaged, you can use your backup copies to restore the files.

RESTORE FILES

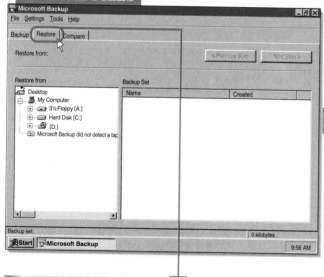

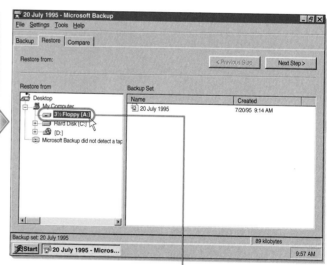

1 Start **Microsoft Backup**.

*Note: To start **Microsoft Backup**, refer to page 230.*

2 Click the **Restore** tab.

3 Insert the floppy disk containing the files you want to restore into a drive.

4 Click the drive containing the floppy disk (example: **A:**).

IMPORTANT

If your backup copies are stored on
more than one floppy disk, you must
insert the **last** disk
into a drive in step 3
on page 240.

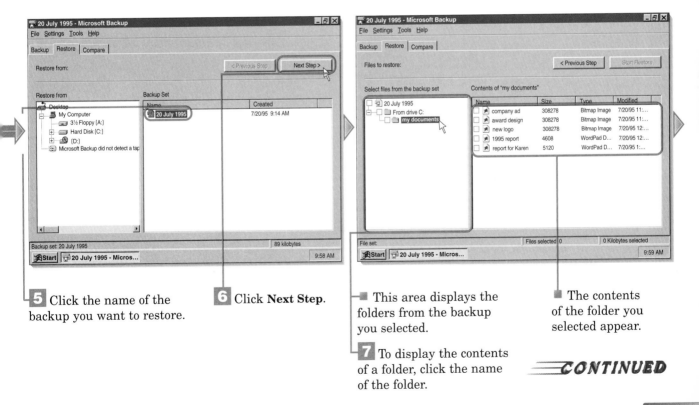

5 Click the name of the
backup you want to restore.

6 Click **Next Step**.

■ This area displays the
folders from the backup
you selected.

7 To display the contents
of a folder, click the name
of the folder.

■ The contents
of the folder you
selected appear.

CONTINUED

RESTORE FILES

If you do not need to restore all the files you backed up, you can select only the files you want to restore.

RESTORE FILES (CONTINUED)

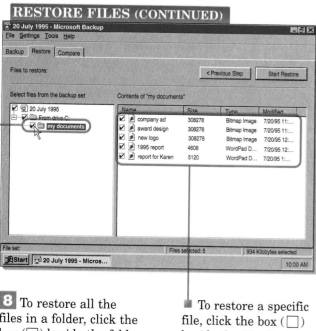

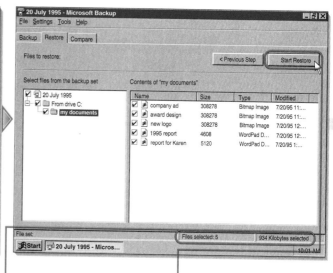

8 To restore all the files in a folder, click the box (☐) beside the folder (☐ changes to ✔).

■ To restore a specific file, click the box (☐) beside the file. Repeat this for each file you want to restore.

9 Repeat steps 7 and 8 starting on page 241 until you have selected all the files you want to restore.

■ This area displays the number and total size of the files you selected.

Note: If your backup copies are stored on more than one floppy disk, insert the first disk into the drive.

10 Click **Start Restore**.

242

If the files you want to restore are on more than one floppy disk, this dialog box appears when Windows wants you to insert the next disk.

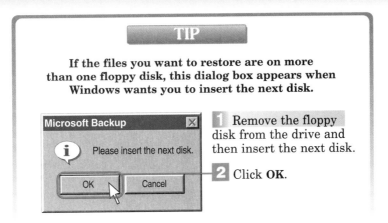

1 Remove the floppy disk from the drive and then insert the next disk.

2 Click **OK**.

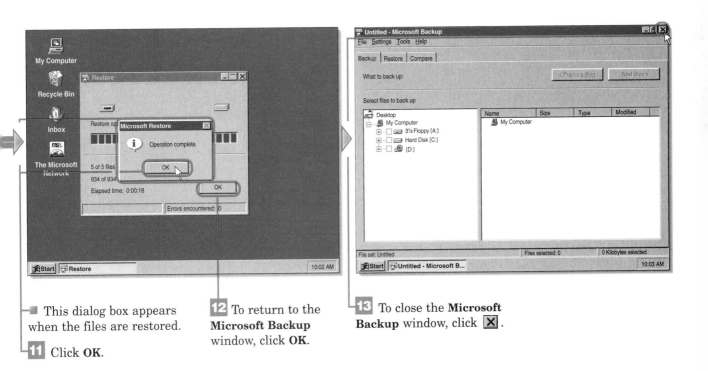

■ This dialog box appears when the files are restored.

11 Click **OK**.

12 To return to the **Microsoft Backup** window, click **OK**.

13 To close the **Microsoft Backup** window, click ⊠.

**In this chapter you will learn
how to use many of the accessories offered
by Windows 95.**

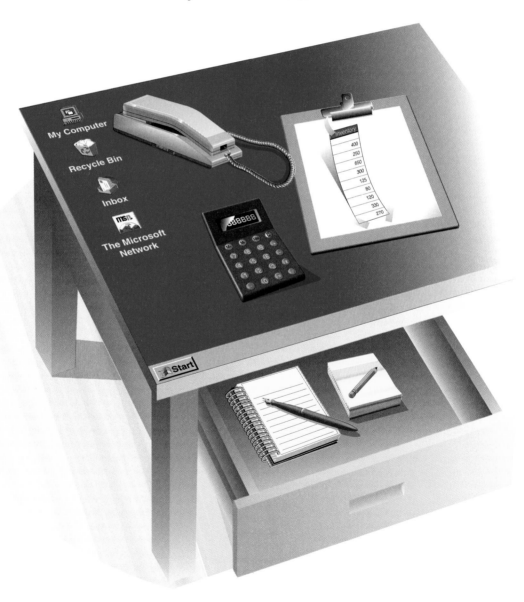

CHAPTER 15: WINDOWS ACCESSORIES

USING THE CALCULATOR

**Windows provides
a calculator you
can use to perform
calculations.**

USING THE CALCULATOR

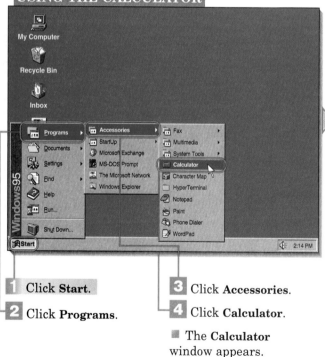

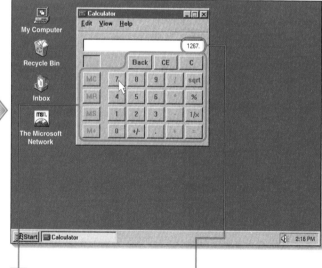

1 Click **Start**.

2 Click **Programs**.

3 Click **Accessories**.

4 Click **Calculator**.

■ The **Calculator**
window appears.

5 To enter information
into the Calculator, click
each button as you would
press the buttons on a
hand-held calculator.

*Note: You can also use
the numeric keypad on
your keyboard to enter
information.*

■ This area displays
the numbers you
enter and the results
of calculations.

TIP

To use the number keys on the numeric keypad, Num Lock must be on. To turn this setting on, press **Num Lock** on your keyboard.

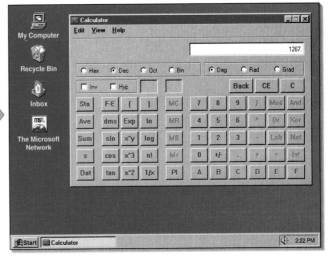

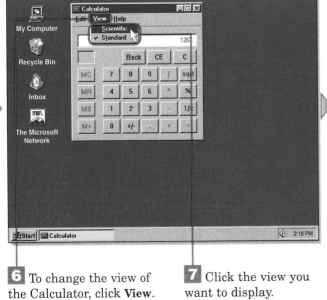

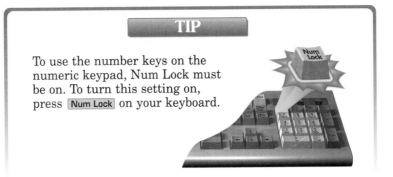

6 To change the view of the Calculator, click **View**.

7 Click the view you want to display.

■ In this example, the **Scientific** view of the Calculator appears.

■ You can use the **Scientific** view to perform more complex mathematical calculations, such as averages and exponents.

USING NOTEPAD

You can use Notepad to create simple documents such as notes and messages.

Although Notepad does not offer many of the features found in popular word processors, Notepad uses fewer of your computer's resources.

USING NOTEPAD

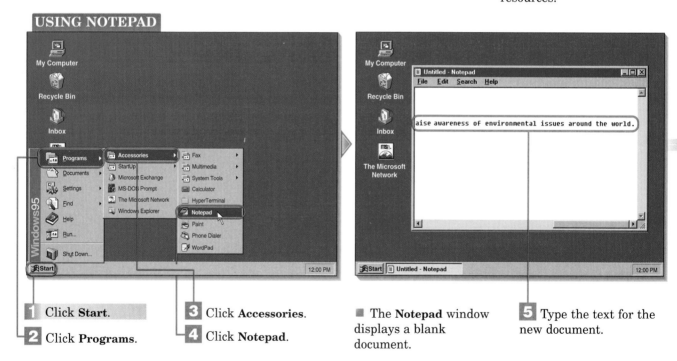

1 Click **Start**.

2 Click **Programs**.

3 Click **Accessories**.

4 Click **Notepad**.

■ The **Notepad** window displays a blank document.

5 Type the text for the new document.

You can quickly insert the
current time and date into
a document.

Press **F5** on your keyboard to insert
the time and date at the location of the
insertion point.

*Note: If Notepad inserts the wrong time
or date, you may need to adjust your
computer's clock. To adjust your
computer's clock, refer to page 102.*

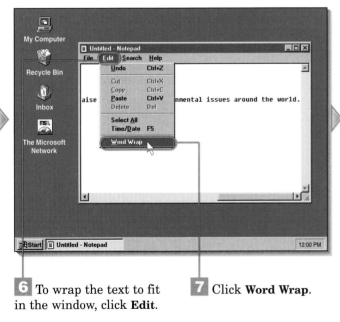

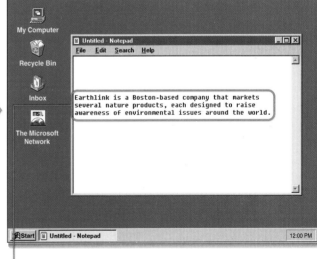

6 To wrap the text to fit
in the window, click **Edit**.

7 Click **Word Wrap**.

Notepad wraps
the text to fit in the
window.

*Note: To save the
document so you can
later review and make
changes to the
document, refer to
page 40.*

USING THE CLIPBOARD

The Clipboard is an area of your computer's memory that temporarily stores information. You can use the Clipboard Viewer to display the contents of the Clipboard.

When you cut or copy information in a document or use the Print Scrn key to make a copy of the screen, Windows places the information in the Clipboard.

USING THE CLIPBOARD

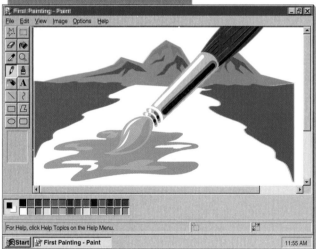

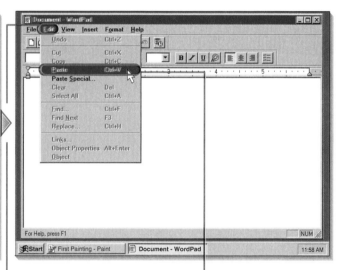

In this example, we use the Clipboard to temporarily store a copy of the screen.

1 Press `Print Scrn` on your keyboard to copy the screen.

■ Windows places a copy of the screen in the Clipboard.

2 Open the document you want to display the screen.

Note: To open a document, refer to page 70.

3 To place the contents of the Clipboard in the document, click **Edit**.

4 Click **Paste**.

■ The screen appears in the document.

TIP

The Clipboard stores one item at a time. As soon as Windows places a new item in the Clipboard, the new item replaces the current item. When you shut down Windows, the item in the Clipboard is deleted.

VIEW CONTENTS OF THE CLIPBOARD

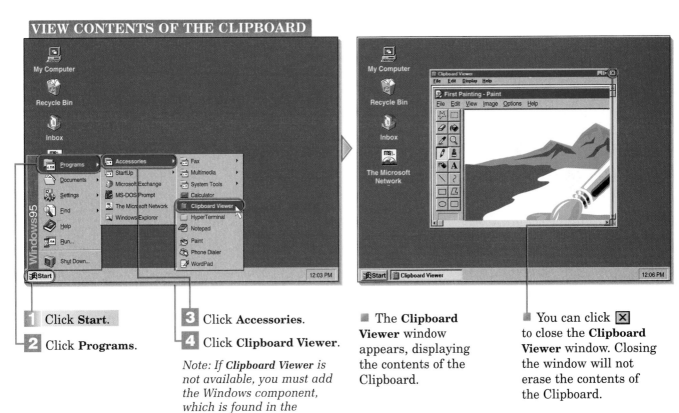

1 Click **Start**.

2 Click **Programs**.

3 Click **Accessories**.

4 Click **Clipboard Viewer**.

Note: If Clipboard Viewer is not available, you must add the Windows component, which is found in the Accessories category. To do so, refer to page 186.

■ The **Clipboard Viewer** window appears, displaying the contents of the Clipboard.

■ You can click ☒ to close the **Clipboard Viewer** window. Closing the window will not erase the contents of the Clipboard.

USING PHONE DIALER

You can have Phone
Dialer dial telephone
numbers for you and
store phone numbers
you frequently call.

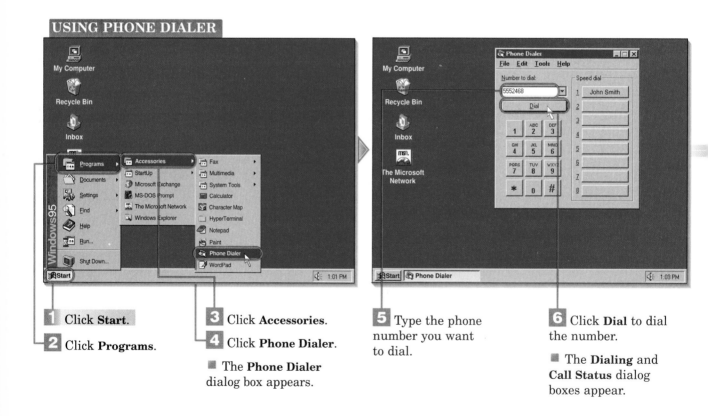

USING PHONE DIALER

1 Click **Start**.

2 Click **Programs**.

3 Click **Accessories**.

4 Click **Phone Dialer**.

■ The **Phone Dialer**
dialog box appears.

5 Type the phone
number you want
to dial.

6 Click **Dial** to dial
the number.

■ The **Dialing** and
Call Status dialog
boxes appear.

To have Phone Dialer dial
telephone numbers for you,
you must plug your telephone
into the modem's socket at
the back of your computer.
The modem plugs into the
telephone line socket on
your wall.

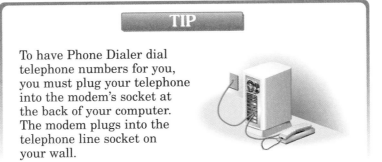

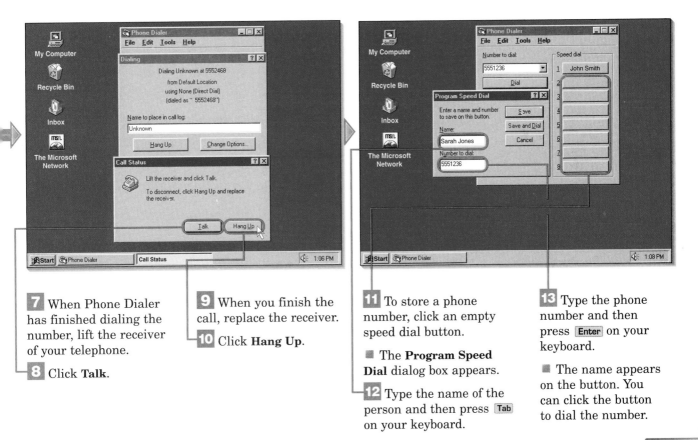

7 When Phone Dialer
has finished dialing the
number, lift the receiver
of your telephone.

8 Click **Talk**.

9 When you finish the
call, replace the receiver.

10 Click **Hang Up**.

11 To store a phone
number, click an empty
speed dial button.

■ The **Program Speed
Dial** dialog box appears.

12 Type the name of the
person and then press Tab
on your keyboard.

13 Type the phone
number and then
press Enter on your
keyboard.

■ The name appears
on the button. You
can click the button
to dial the number.

USING WORDPAD

WordPad is a word processor you can use to create documents such as letters and memos. WordPad offers many of the features found in more powerful word processors.

START WORDPAD

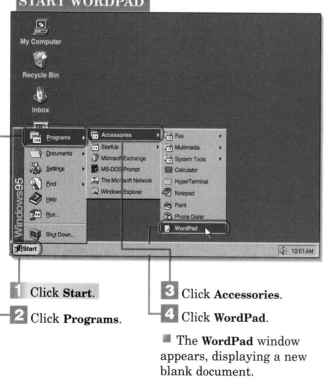

1 Click **Start**.

2 Click **Programs**.

3 Click **Accessories**.

4 Click **WordPad**.

■ The **WordPad** window appears, displaying a new blank document.

■ The flashing insertion point indicates where the text you type will appear.

5 Type the text for your document.

■ Press Enter on your keyboard only when you want to start a new paragraph.

Note: In this example, the size of text was changed to make the text easier to read. To change the size of text, refer to page 258.

You should save your document to store it for future use. This lets you later retrieve the document for reviewing and editing.

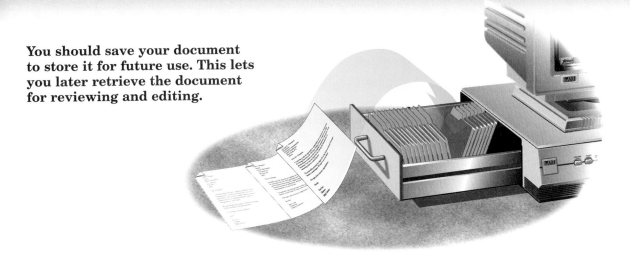

SAVE A DOCUMENT

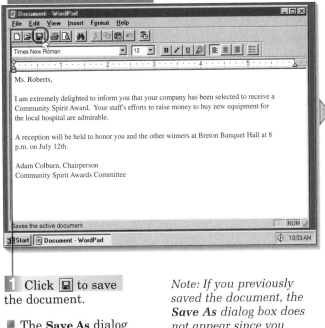

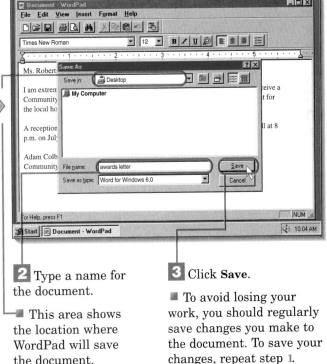

1 Click 🖫 to save the document.

■ The **Save As** dialog box appears.

Note: If you previously saved the document, the ***Save As*** *dialog box does not appear since you have already named the document.*

2 Type a name for the document.

■ This area shows the location where WordPad will save the document.

3 Click **Save**.

■ To avoid losing your work, you should regularly save changes you make to the document. To save your changes, repeat step **1**.

USING WORDPAD

You can easily add new text to your document and remove text you no longer need. You can also reorganize your document by moving text from one location to another.

EDIT TEXT

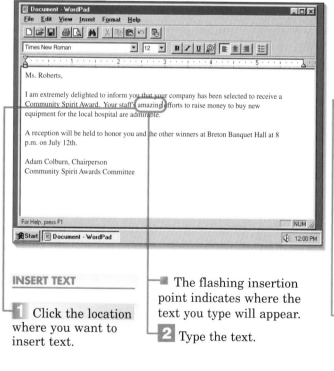

INSERT TEXT

1 Click the location where you want to insert text.

■ The flashing insertion point indicates where the text you type will appear.

2 Type the text.

DELETE TEXT

1 Drag the mouse I over the text you want to delete.

2 Press Delete on your keyboard to remove the text.

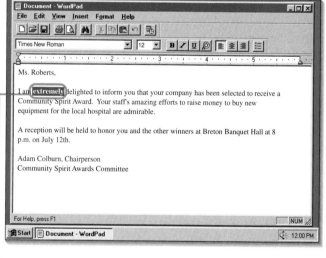

■ To delete one character at a time, click to the left of the first character you want to delete. Press Delete on your keyboard for each character you want to remove.

Copying text can help you edit your document. If you plan to make major changes to a paragraph, you may want to copy the paragraph before you begin. This gives you two copies of the paragraph—the original paragraph and a paragraph with the changes.

■ To copy text, perform steps **1** to **3** below, except press and hold down `Ctrl` on your keyboard as you perform step **3**.

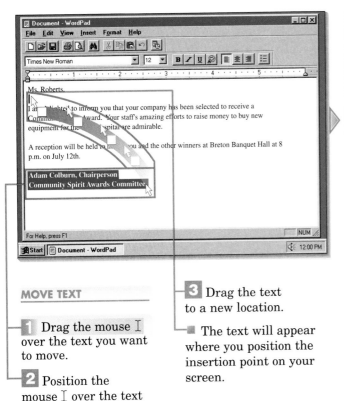

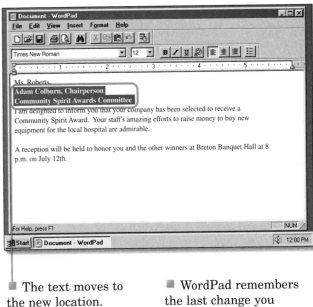

MOVE TEXT

1 Drag the mouse I over the text you want to move.

2 Position the mouse I over the text (I changes to ⇗).

3 Drag the text to a new location.

■ The text will appear where you position the insertion point on your screen.

■ The text moves to the new location.

■ WordPad remembers the last change you made, so you can cancel a change you regret. In this example, click ⟲ to immediately undo the move.

USING WORDPAD

You can enhance the appearance of the text in your documents by using various fonts, sizes and styles. You can also align the text in different ways.

FORMAT CHARACTERS

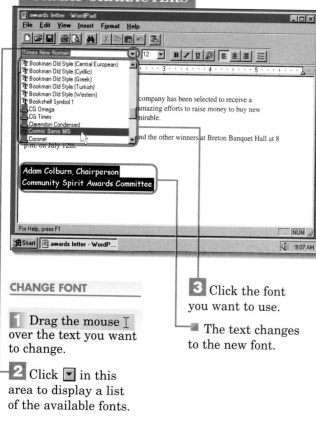

CHANGE FONT

1 Drag the mouse I over the text you want to change.

2 Click ▼ in this area to display a list of the available fonts.

3 Click the font you want to use.

■ The text changes to the new font.

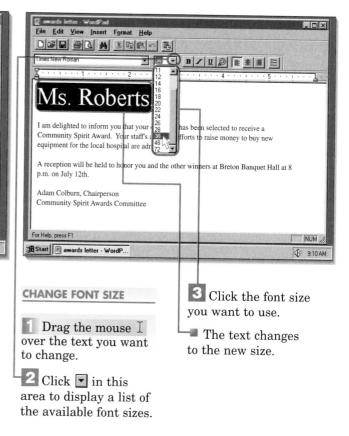

CHANGE FONT SIZE

1 Drag the mouse I over the text you want to change.

2 Click ▼ in this area to display a list of the available font sizes.

3 Click the font size you want to use.

■ The text changes to the new size.

Before formatting text in your document, you must first select the text you want to work with. Selected text appears highlighted on your screen.

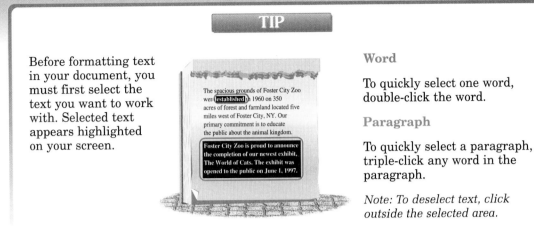

The spacious grounds of Foster City Zoo were established in 1960 on 350 acres of forest and farmland located five miles west of Foster City, NY. Our primary commitment is to educate the public about the animal kingdom.

Foster City Zoo is proud to announce the completion of our newest exhibit, The World of Cats. The exhibit was opened to the public on June 1, 1997.

Word

To quickly select one word, double-click the word.

Paragraph

To quickly select a paragraph, triple-click any word in the paragraph.

Note: To deselect text, click outside the selected area.

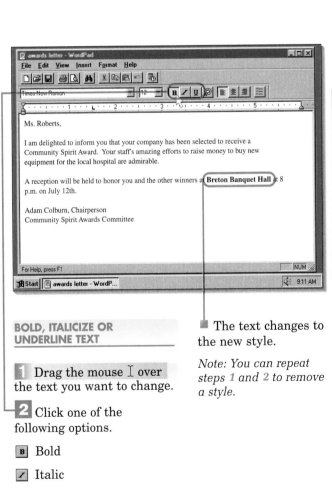

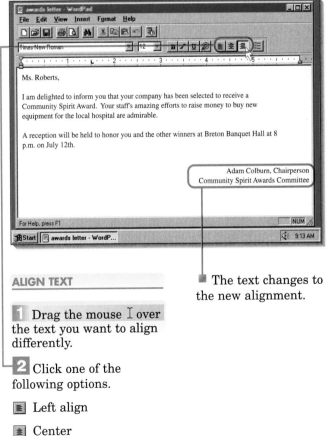

BOLD, ITALICIZE OR UNDERLINE TEXT

■1 Drag the mouse I over the text you want to change.

■2 Click one of the following options.

B Bold

I Italic

U Underline

■ The text changes to the new style.

Note: You can repeat steps 1 and 2 to remove a style.

ALIGN TEXT

■1 Drag the mouse I over the text you want to align differently.

■2 Click one of the following options.

▤ Left align

▥ Center

▦ Right align

■ The text changes to the new alignment.

INSERT SPECIAL CHARACTERS

You can add special characters to your documents which are not available on your keyboard. You can copy the special characters from Character Map and paste them into your documents.

Most word processors have a built-in feature that allows you to insert special characters. Character Map is ideal to use with programs that do not offer this feature.

INSERT SPECIAL CHARACTERS

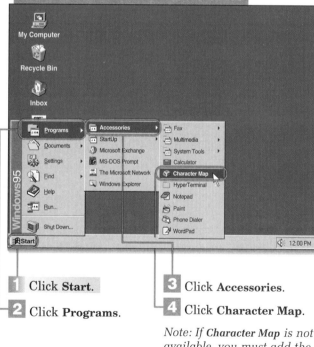

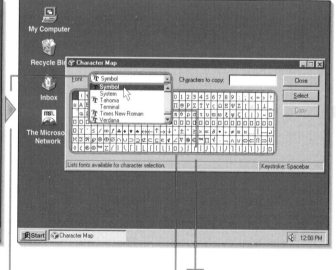

1 Click **Start**.

2 Click **Programs**.

3 Click **Accessories**.

4 Click **Character Map**.

Note: If Character Map is not available, you must add the Windows component, which is found in the Accessories category. To do so, refer to page 186.

■ The **Character Map** window appears.

5 Click this area to select the font you want to display.

6 Click the font that contains the characters you want to display.

■ This area displays the characters for the font you selected.

If you find the characters in the Character Map window hard to see, you can display an enlarged version of a character.

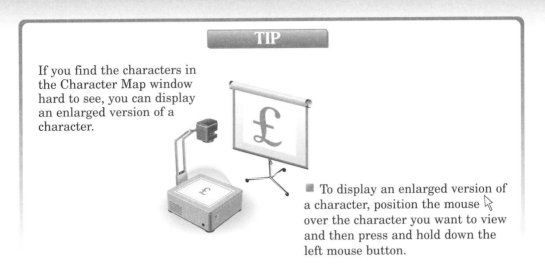

■ To display an enlarged version of a character, position the mouse over the character you want to view and then press and hold down the left mouse button.

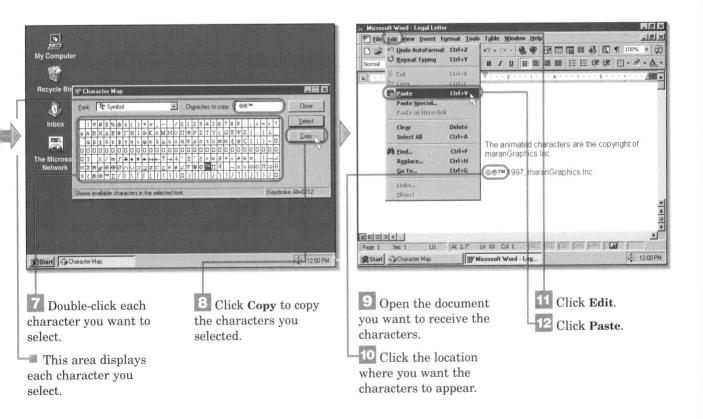

7 Double-click each character you want to select.

■ This area displays each character you select.

8 Click **Copy** to copy the characters you selected.

9 Open the document you want to receive the characters.

10 Click the location where you want the characters to appear.

11 Click **Edit**.

12 Click **Paste**.

PLAY GAMES

Windows includes several games
you can play on your computer.
Games are a fun way to improve
your mouse skills, hand-eye
coordination and reflexes.

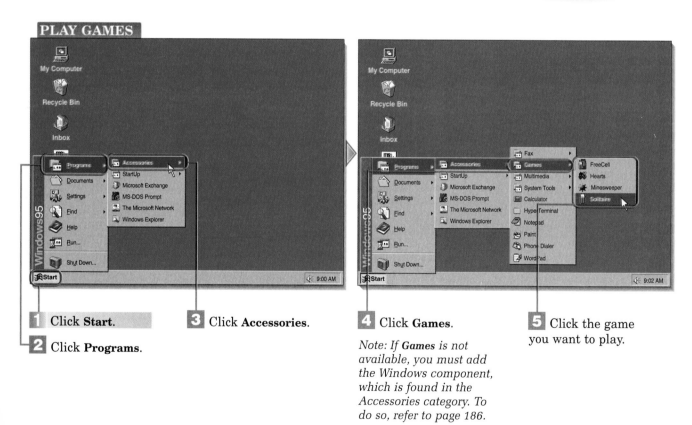

1 Click **Start**.

2 Click **Programs**.

3 Click **Accessories**.

4 Click **Games**.

*Note: If Games is not
available, you must add
the Windows component,
which is found in the
Accessories category. To
do so, refer to page 186.*

5 Click the game
you want to play.

Windows includes two other card games—FreeCell and Hearts.

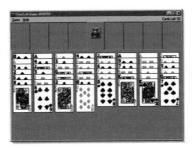

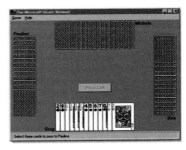

FREECELL

FreeCell is a single-player card game.

HEARTS

Hearts is a card game that you can play by yourself or against someone on the network.

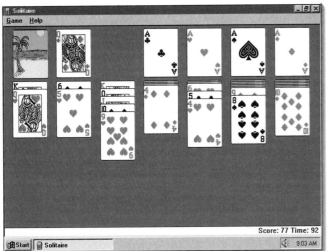

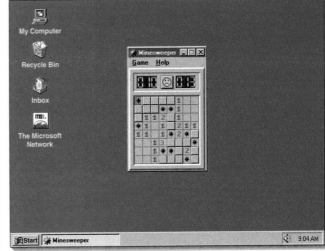

SOLITAIRE

Solitaire is a classic card game that you play on your own. You try to put all the cards in order from ace to king in four stacks, one stack for each suit.

MINESWEEPER

In Minesweeper, you try to locate all of the mines without actually uncovering them.

**In this chapter you will learn
how to use Briefcase to work with files
while you are away from the office.**

CHAPTER 16: BRIEFCASE

CREATE A BRIEFCASE

Briefcase lets you work with files while you are away from the office. When you return, Briefcase will update all the files you changed.

CREATE A BRIEFCASE

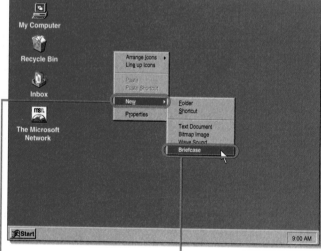

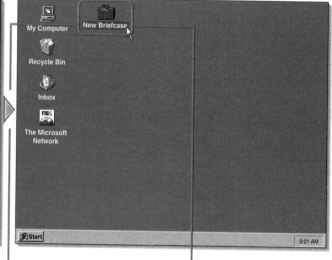

■ **1** Click a blank area on your desktop using the **right** button. A menu appears.

■ **2** Click **New**.

■ **3** Click **Briefcase**.

*Note: If **Briefcase** is not available, you must add the Windows component, which is found in the Accessories category. To do so, refer to page 186.*

■ A briefcase appears.

Note: You can rename the briefcase as you would any file. To rename a file, refer to page 68.

■ **4** To view the contents of the briefcase, double-click the briefcase.

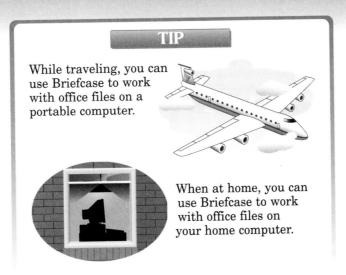

TIP

While traveling, you can use Briefcase to work with office files on a portable computer.

When at home, you can use Briefcase to work with office files on your home computer.

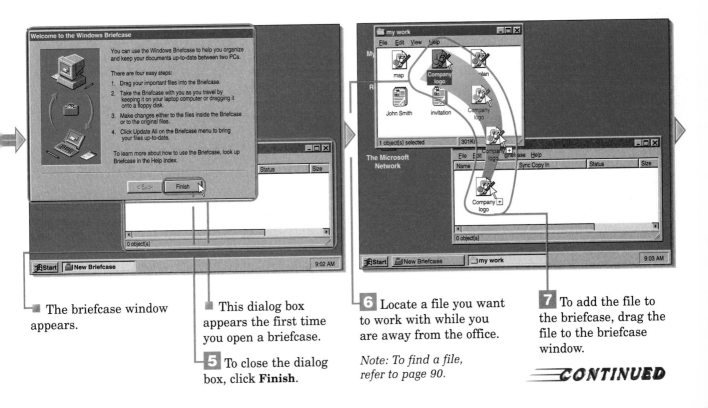

■ The briefcase window appears.

■ This dialog box appears the first time you open a briefcase.

5 To close the dialog box, click **Finish**.

6 Locate a file you want to work with while you are away from the office.

Note: To find a file, refer to page 90.

7 To add the file to the briefcase, drag the file to the briefcase window.

CONTINUED

CREATE A BRIEFCASE

You can move a briefcase you created to a floppy disk. A floppy disk lets you transfer the briefcase files to your home or portable computer.

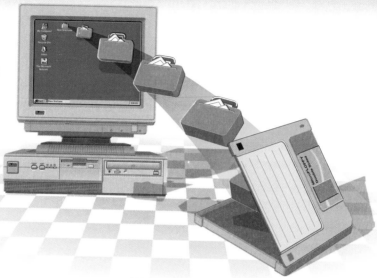

CREATE A BRIEFCASE (CONTINUED)

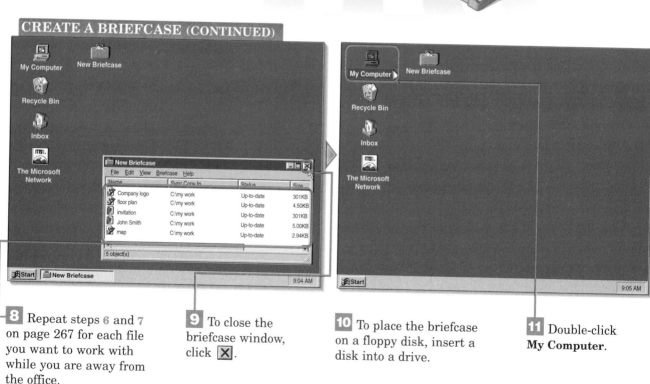

8 Repeat steps **6** and **7** on page 267 for each file you want to work with while you are away from the office.

9 To close the briefcase window, click ☒.

10 To place the briefcase on a floppy disk, insert a disk into a drive.

11 Double-click **My Computer**.

TIP

You can also use Direct Cable Connection to transfer office files to a briefcase on a portable computer. This is faster than using a floppy disk to transfer files and is ideal for transferring a large number of files.

Note: For information on Direct Cable Connection, refer to the Direct Cable Connection chapter starting on page 310.

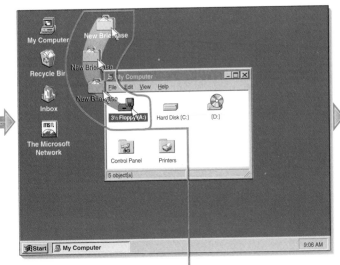

◼ The **My Computer** window appears.

12 To place the briefcase on the floppy disk, drag the briefcase to the drive containing the disk.

◼ The floppy disk now contains the briefcase.

◼ The briefcase disappears from your screen.

13 Remove the floppy disk from the drive. You can now use the floppy disk to transfer the files to your home or portable computer.

Note: To work with briefcase files, refer to page 270.

269

WORK WITH BRIEFCASE FILES

When traveling or at home, you can work with briefcase files as you would any other files on your computer.

WORK WITH BRIEFCASE FILES

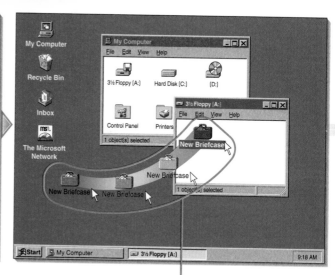

1 On your home or portable computer, insert the floppy disk containing the briefcase.

2 Double-click **My Computer**.

■ The **My Computer** window appears.

3 Double-click the drive containing the floppy disk.

■ The contents of the floppy disk appear.

4 To move the briefcase from the floppy disk to your desktop, drag the briefcase to a blank area on the desktop.

IMPORTANT

Do not rename the files in the briefcase or the original files on your office computer. If you do, Briefcase will not update the files.

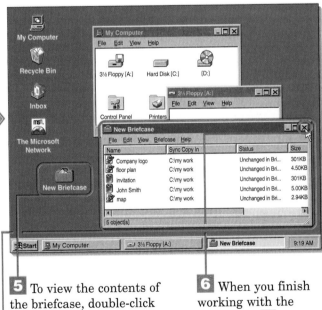

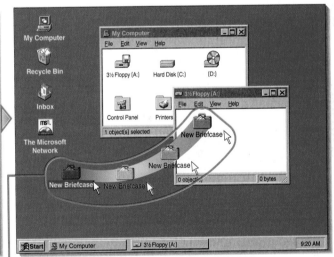

5 To view the contents of the briefcase, double-click the briefcase.

■ The contents of the briefcase appear. You can now work with files in the briefcase as you would any file.

6 When you finish working with the files, click ☒ to close the briefcase window.

7 To return the briefcase to the floppy disk, drag the briefcase to the floppy disk window.

8 Remove the floppy disk from the drive. You can now use the floppy disk to return the files to your office computer.

Note: To update the files you changed, refer to page 272.

UPDATE BRIEFCASE FILES

When you return to your office, you can quickly update the files you changed.

UPDATE BRIEFCASE FILES

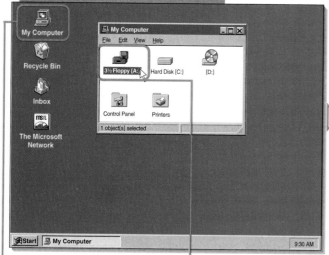

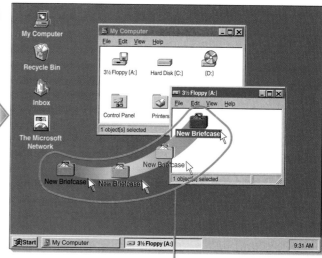

1 On your office computer, insert the floppy disk containing the briefcase.

2 Double-click **My Computer**.

■ The **My Computer** window appears.

3 Double-click the drive containing the floppy disk.

■ The contents of the floppy disk appear.

4 To move the briefcase from the floppy disk to your desktop, drag the briefcase to a blank area on the desktop.

Windows compares the files in the briefcase to the files on your office computer to decide which files need to be updated.

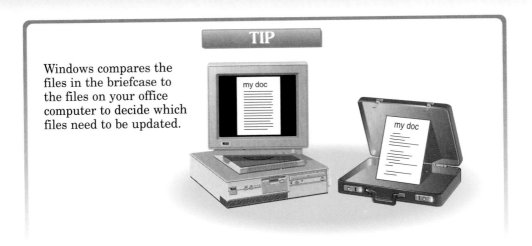

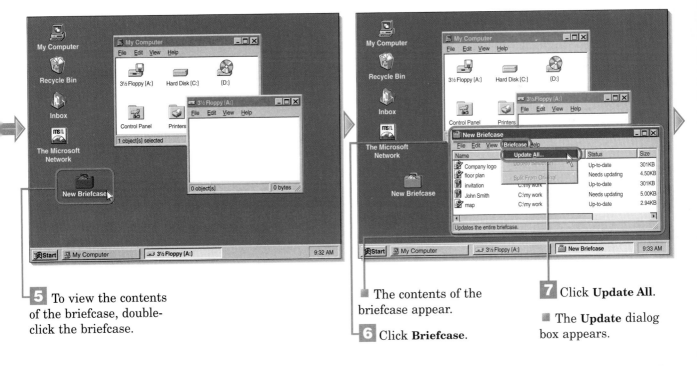

5 To view the contents of the briefcase, double-click the briefcase.

■ The contents of the briefcase appear.

6 Click **Briefcase**.

7 Click **Update All**.

■ The **Update** dialog box appears.

CONTINUED

UPDATE BRIEFCASE FILES

Windows tells you exactly which files need to be updated.

UPDATE BRIEFCASE FILES (CONTINUED)

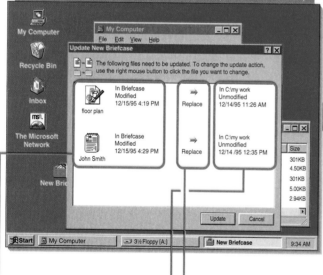

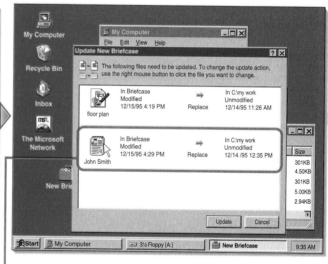

This area displays the name of each file that needs to be updated.

This area displays the way Windows will update each file.

This area displays the status of each file on the office computer.

8 To change the way Windows will update a file, click the file using the **right** button. A menu appears.

TIP

You can create a new briefcase every time you want to work away from the office.

Delete an old briefcase as you would delete any file.

Note: Deleting a briefcase does not remove the original files from your computer.

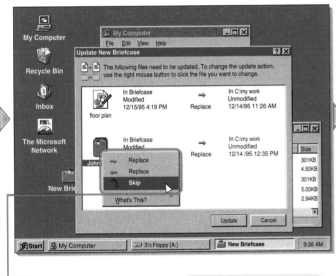

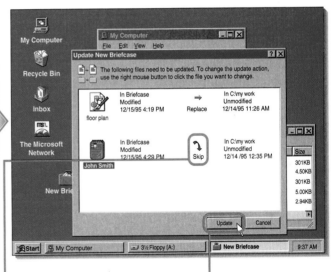

9 Click the way you want Windows to update the file.

→ **Replace**
Replace office file with briefcase file.

← **Replace**
Replace briefcase file with office file.

↰ **Skip**
Do not update file.

■ This area displays the way Windows will now update the file.

10 To change the way Windows updates other files, repeat steps 8 and 9 for each file.

11 To update the files, click **Update**.

275

**In this chapter you will learn
how to use a network to share
information and equipment.**

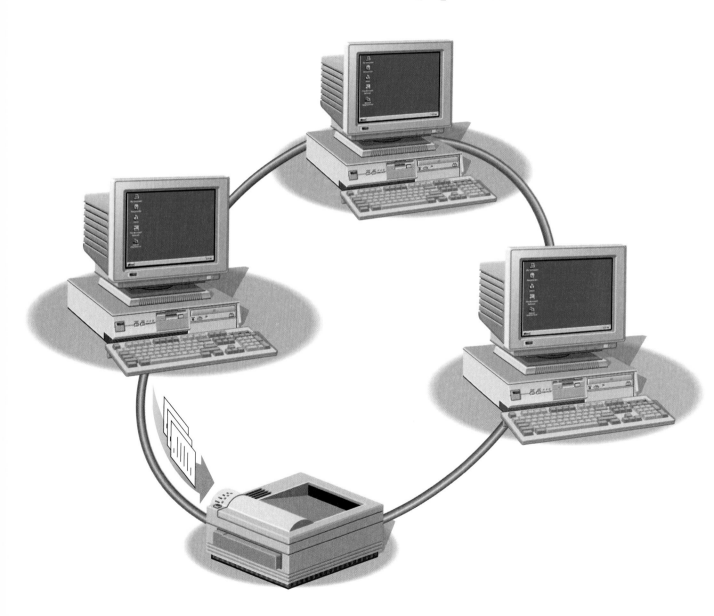

CHAPTER 17: NETWORKS

INTRODUCTION TO NETWORKS

A network is a group of connected computers that allow people to share information and equipment.

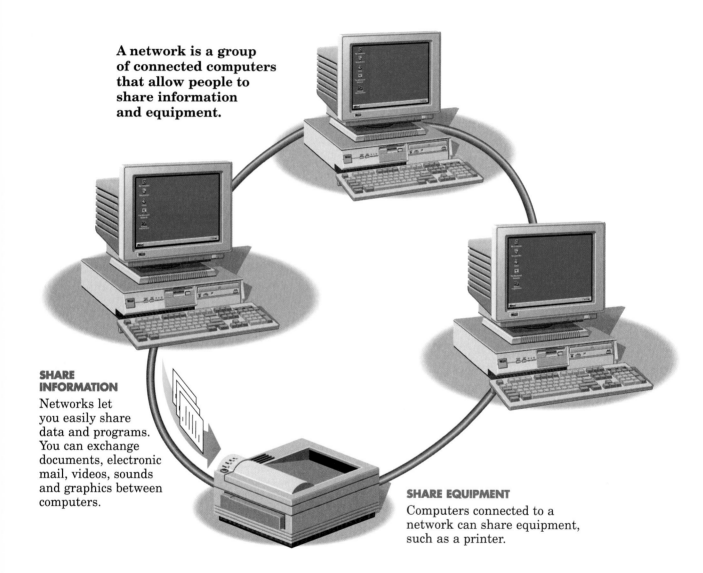

SHARE INFORMATION

Networks let you easily share data and programs. You can exchange documents, electronic mail, videos, sounds and graphics between computers.

SHARE EQUIPMENT

Computers connected to a network can share equipment, such as a printer.

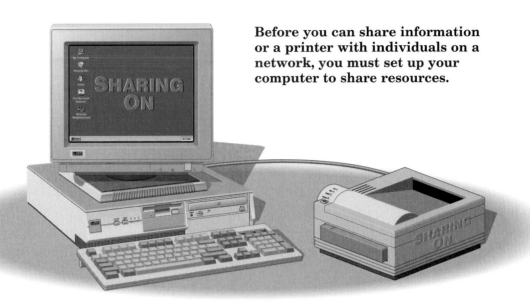

Before you can share information or a printer with individuals on a network, you must set up your computer to share resources.

TURN ON SHARING

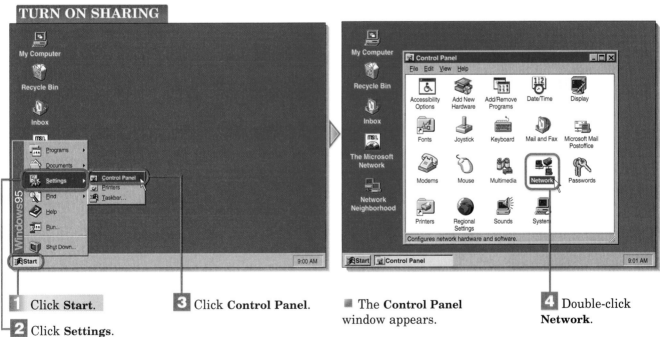

1 Click **Start**.

2 Click **Settings**.

3 Click **Control Panel**.

■ The **Control Panel** window appears.

4 Double-click **Network**.

CONTINUED

TURN ON SHARING

You can choose to give individuals
on a network access to your files
and/or printer.

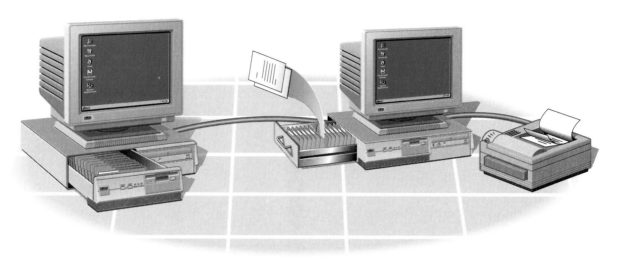

TURN ON SHARING (CONTINUED)

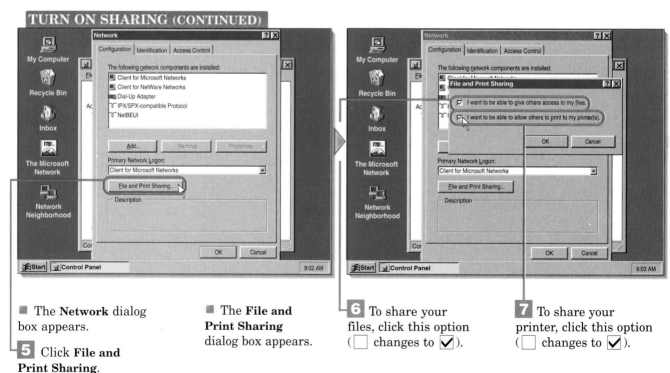

■ The **Network** dialog
box appears.

5 Click **File and
Print Sharing**.

■ The **File and
Print Sharing**
dialog box appears.

6 To share your
files, click this option
(☐ changes to ☑).

7 To share your
printer, click this option
(☐ changes to ☑).

TIP

**Once you set up your computer
to share information and/or a printer, you must specify
exactly what you want to share.**

■ To specify the information
you want to share, refer
to page 284.

■ To specify the printer
you want to share, refer
to page 288.

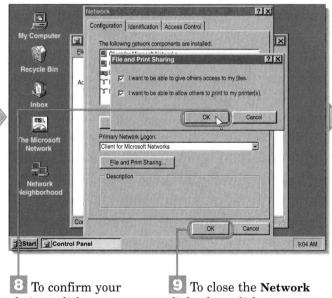

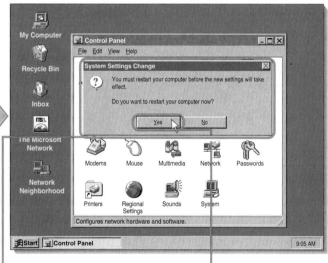

8 To confirm your
choices, click **OK**.

9 To close the **Network**
dialog box, click **OK**.

■ The **System Settings
Change** dialog box appears,
telling you that Windows
needs to restart your
computer before the new
settings will take effect.

10 To restart your
computer, click **Yes**.

NAME YOUR COMPUTER

You can change the
name of your computer
on a network.

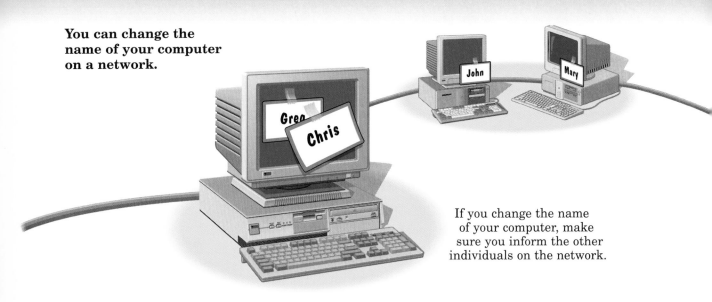

If you change the name
of your computer, make
sure you inform the other
individuals on the network.

NAME YOUR COMPUTER

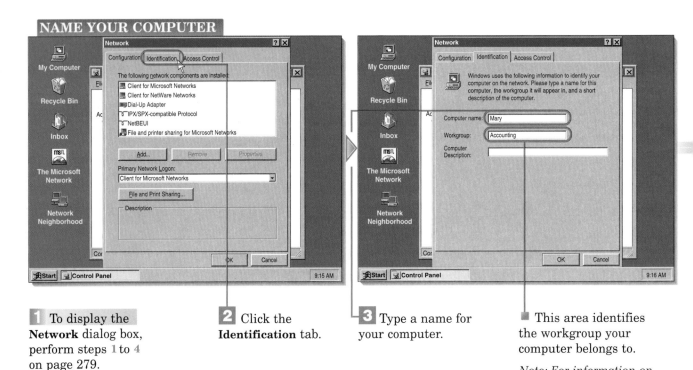

1 To display the
Network dialog box,
perform steps 1 to 4
on page 279.

2 Click the
Identification tab.

3 Type a name for
your computer.

■ This area identifies
the workgroup your
computer belongs to.

*Note: For information on
workgroups, refer to the
Tip on page 283.*

TIP

A **workgroup** is a group of computers on a network. Small companies usually have one workgroup. Larger companies have many workgroups, such as accounting, inventory and marketing, to better organize information.

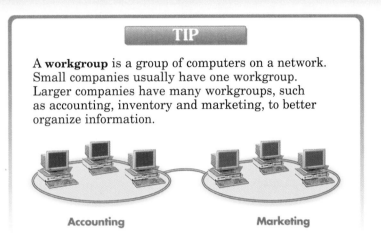

Accounting　　　　　　**Marketing**

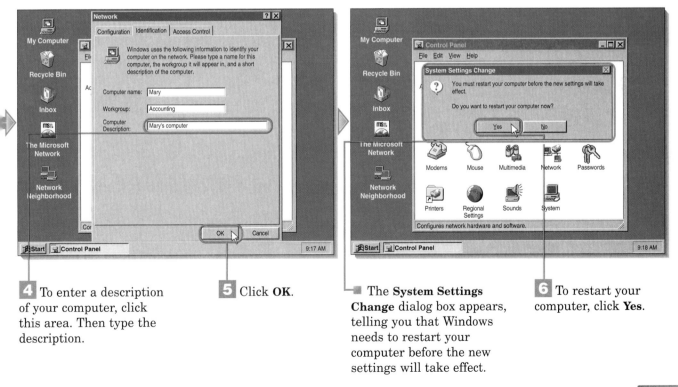

4 To enter a description of your computer, click this area. Then type the description.

5 Click **OK**.

■ The **System Settings Change** dialog box appears, telling you that Windows needs to restart your computer before the new settings will take effect.

6 To restart your computer, click **Yes**.

283

SHARE INFORMATION

You can specify exactly
what information you want
to share with individuals
on a network.

SHARE INFORMATION

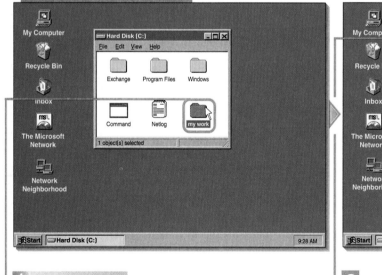

1 Click the folder
you want to share.

2 Click **File**.

3 Click **Sharing**.

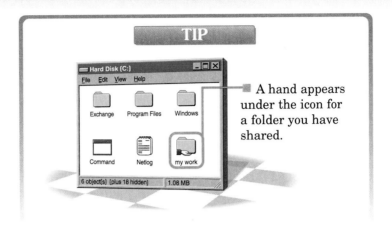

■ A hand appears
under the icon for
a folder you have
shared.

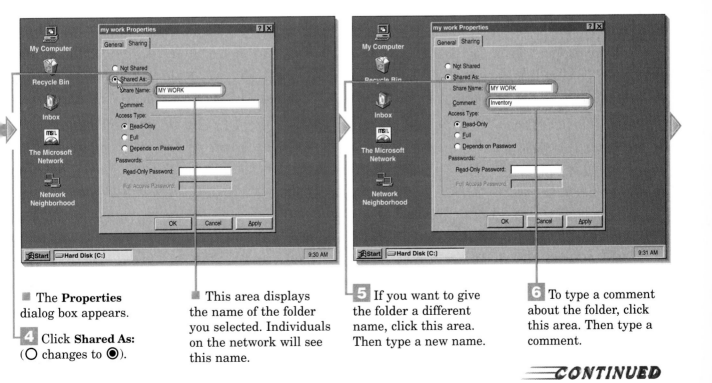

■ The **Properties**
dialog box appears.

4 Click **Shared As:**
(○ changes to ◉).

■ This area displays
the name of the folder
you selected. Individuals
on the network will see
this name.

5 If you want to give
the folder a different
name, click this area.
Then type a new name.

6 To type a comment
about the folder, click
this area. Then type a
comment.

CONTINUED

285

SHARE INFORMATION

You can give individuals on a network one of three types of access to your information.

Read-Only

All individuals on the network can read, but not change or delete, information.

SHARE INFORMATION (CONTINUED)

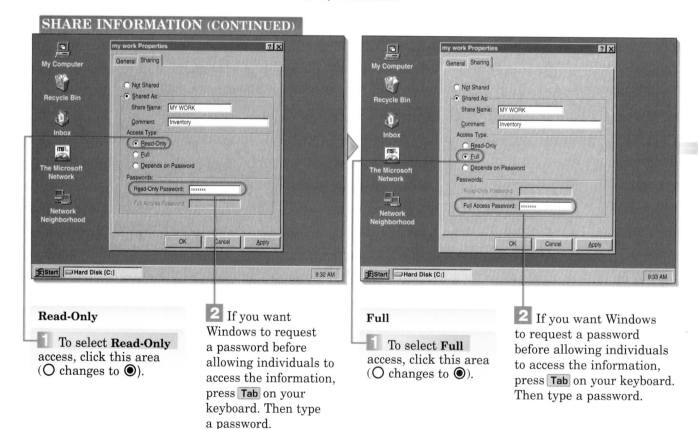

Read-Only

1 To select **Read-Only** access, click this area (○ changes to ◉).

2 If you want Windows to request a password before allowing individuals to access the information, press Tab on your keyboard. Then type a password.

Full

1 To select **Full** access, click this area (○ changes to ◉).

2 If you want Windows to request a password before allowing individuals to access the information, press Tab on your keyboard. Then type a password.

Full

All individuals on
the network can read, change
and delete information.

Depends on Password

Some individuals on the network get
Read-Only access, while others get Full
access. The type of access depends
on which password they enter.

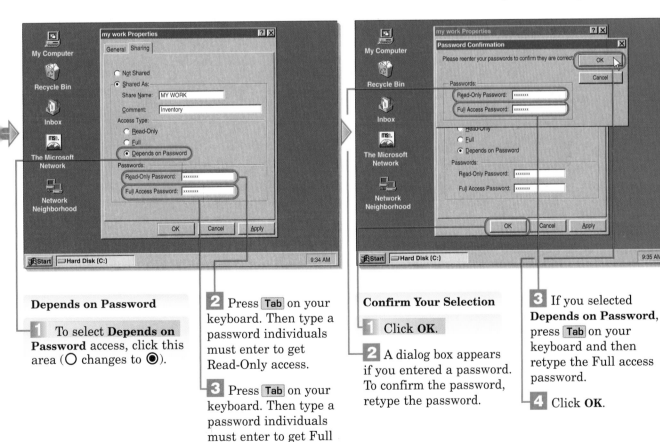

Depends on Password

1 To select **Depends on Password** access, click this area (○ changes to ◉).

2 Press Tab on your keyboard. Then type a password individuals must enter to get Read-Only access.

3 Press Tab on your keyboard. Then type a password individuals must enter to get Full access.

Confirm Your Selection

1 Click **OK**.

2 A dialog box appears if you entered a password. To confirm the password, retype the password.

3 If you selected **Depends on Password**, press Tab on your keyboard and then retype the Full access password.

4 Click **OK**.

SHARE A PRINTER

You can share your printer with other individuals on a network.

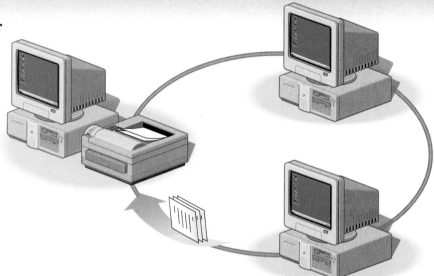

SHARE A PRINTER

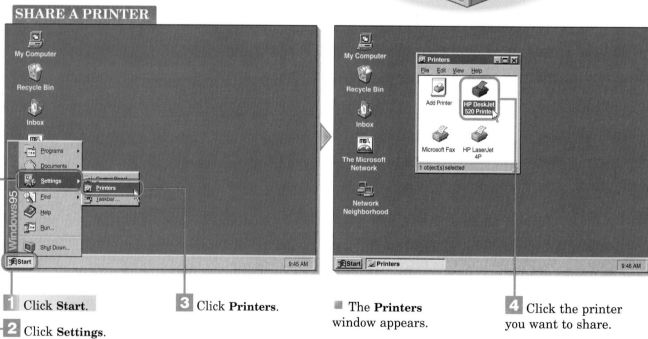

1 Click **Start**.

2 Click **Settings**.

3 Click **Printers**.

■ The **Printers** window appears.

4 Click the printer you want to share.

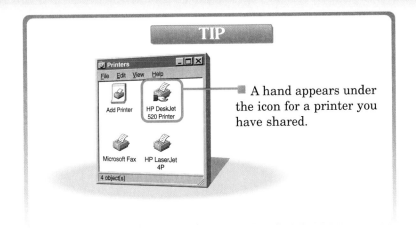

A hand appears under the icon for a printer you have shared.

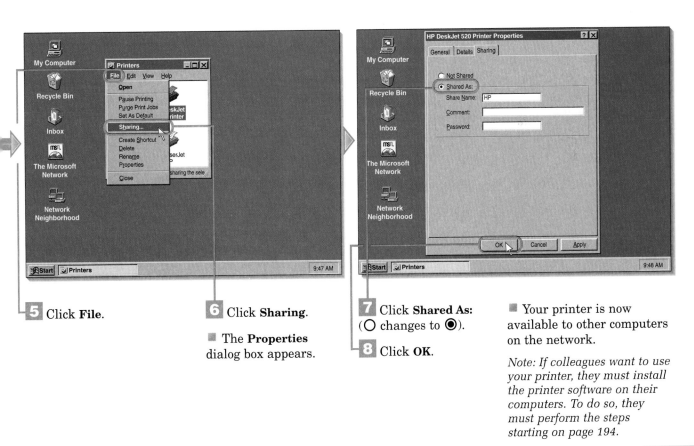

5 Click **File**.

6 Click **Sharing**.

■ The **Properties** dialog box appears.

7 Click **Shared As:** (○ changes to ◉).

8 Click **OK**.

■ Your printer is now available to other computers on the network.

Note: If colleagues want to use your printer, they must install the printer software on their computers. To do so, they must perform the steps starting on page 194.

SET THE DEFAULT PRINTER

If you have access to more than one printer, you can choose one to automatically print your documents.

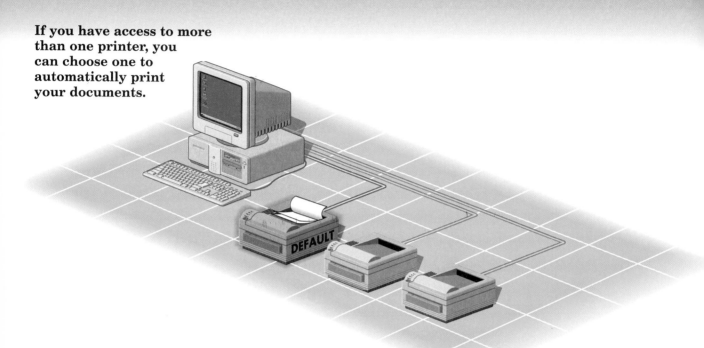

SET THE DEFAULT PRINTER

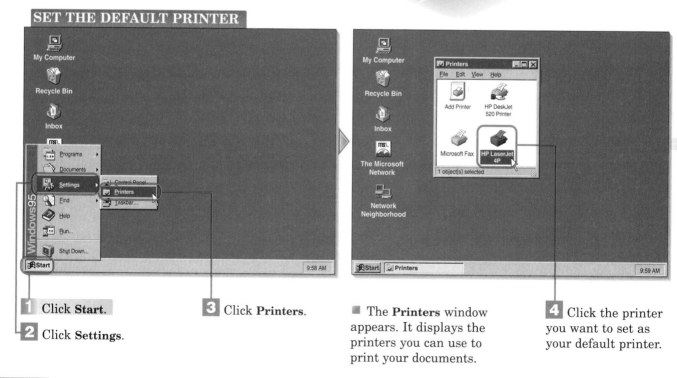

1 Click **Start**.

2 Click **Settings**.

3 Click **Printers**.

■ The **Printers** window appears. It displays the printers you can use to print your documents.

4 Click the printer you want to set as your default printer.

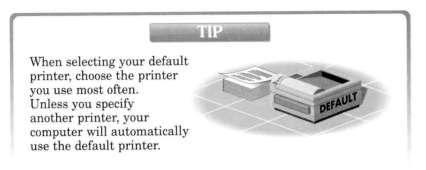

TIP

When selecting your default printer, choose the printer you use most often. Unless you specify another printer, your computer will automatically use the default printer.

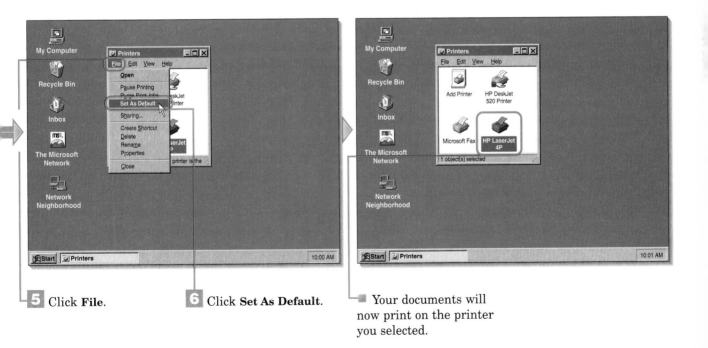

5 Click **File**.

6 Click **Set As Default**.

■ Your documents will now print on the printer you selected.

BROWSE THROUGH A NETWORK

You can easily browse through the information available on your network.

BROWSE THROUGH A NETWORK

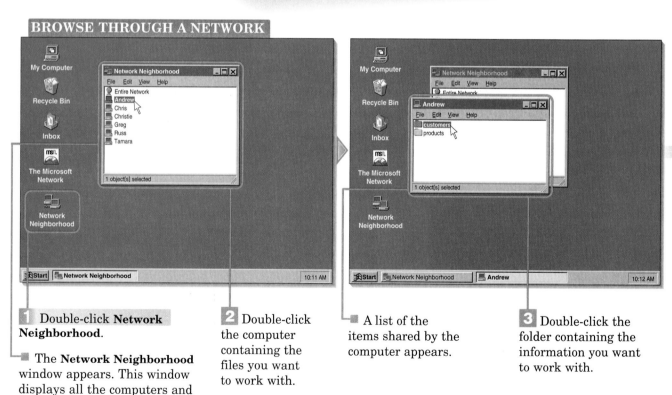

1 Double-click **Network Neighborhood**.

■ The **Network Neighborhood** window appears. This window displays all the computers and printers in your workgroup.

2 Double-click the computer containing the files you want to work with.

■ A list of the items shared by the computer appears.

3 Double-click the folder containing the information you want to work with.

■ **My Computer** lets you browse through the contents of your own computer.

■ **Network Neighborhood** lets you browse through the contents of other computers on the network.

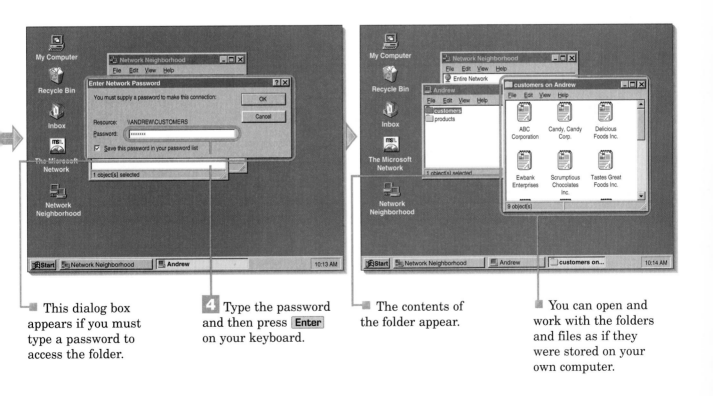

■ This dialog box appears if you must type a password to access the folder.

4 Type the password and then press **Enter** on your keyboard.

■ The contents of the folder appear.

■ You can open and work with the folders and files as if they were stored on your own computer.

FIND A COMPUTER

You can quickly locate a computer on a network. This is especially useful if your network consists of hundreds of computers.

FIND A COMPUTER

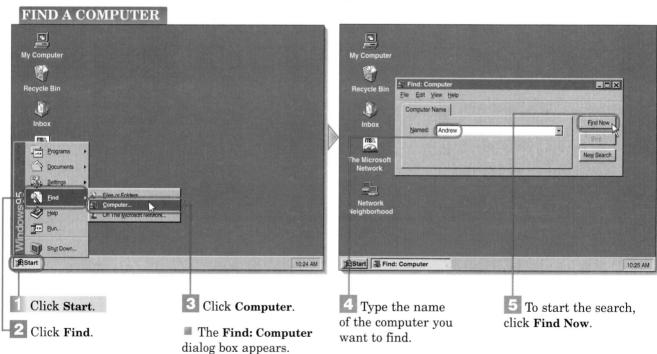

1 Click **Start**.

2 Click **Find**.

3 Click **Computer**.

■ The **Find: Computer** dialog box appears.

4 Type the name of the computer you want to find.

5 To start the search, click **Find Now**.

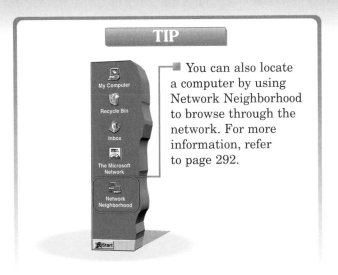

■ You can also locate a computer by using Network Neighborhood to browse through the network. For more information, refer to page 292.

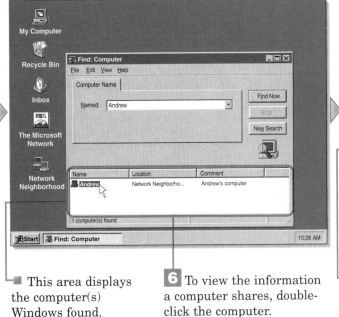

■ This area displays the computer(s) Windows found.

6 To view the information a computer shares, double-click the computer.

■ A list of the items shared by the computer appears.

■ You can open and work with the folders and files as if they were stored on your own computer.

Note: You may be asked to type a password to access some shared items.

**In this chapter you will learn
how to access information on a computer at work
when you are at home or traveling.**

CHAPTER 18: DIAL-UP NETWORKING

INTRODUCTION TO DIAL-UP NETWORKING

INTRODUCTION

**When at home or traveling,
you can use Dial-Up Networking to access
information on a computer at work.**

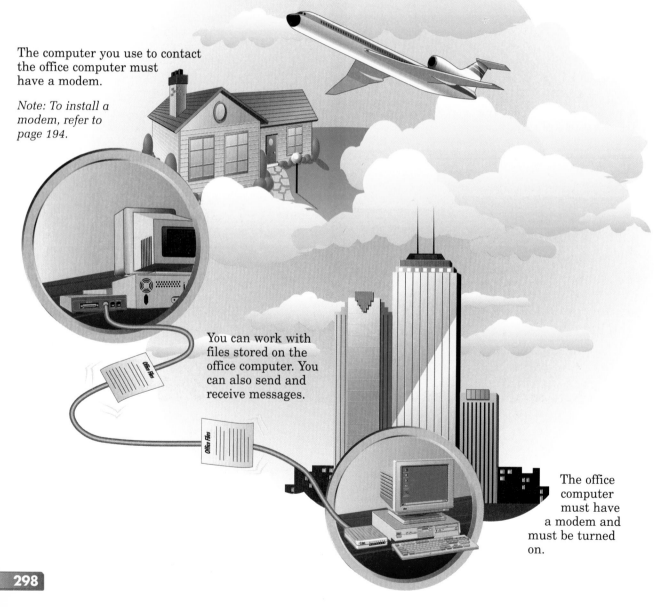

The computer you use to contact the office computer must have a modem.

Note: To install a modem, refer to page 194.

You can work with files stored on the office computer. You can also send and receive messages.

The office computer must have a modem and must be turned on.

298

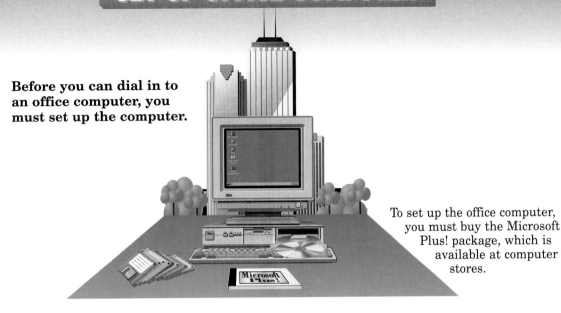

Before you can dial in to an office computer, you must set up the computer.

To set up the office computer, you must buy the Microsoft Plus! package, which is available at computer stores.

SET UP OFFICE COMPUTER

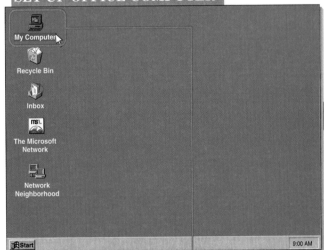

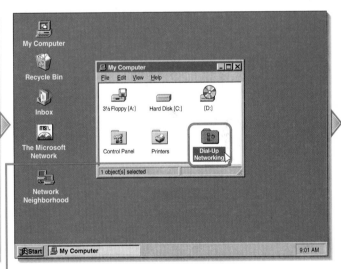

Perform the following steps on the office computer.

1 Double-click **My Computer**.

■ The **My Computer** window appears.

2 Double-click **Dial-Up Networking**.

*Note: If **Dial-Up Networking** is not available, you must add the Windows component, which is found in the Communications category. To do so, refer to page 186.*

*When you add Dial-Up Networking, you may be asked to provide a computer and workgroup name. For information on workgroups, refer to the **Tip** on page 283.*

CONTINUED

SET UP OFFICE COMPUTER

You can assign a password
so only those people who
know the password can
access information stored
on the office computer.

SET UP OFFICE COMPUTER (CONTINUED)

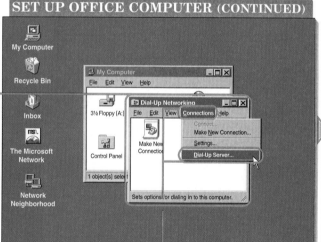

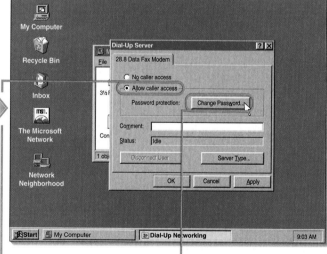

■ The **Dial-Up
Networking** window
appears.

*Note: If the Welcome to
Dial-Up Networking or Make
New Connection dialog box
appears, press* Esc *on your
keyboard to close the
dialog box.*

3 Click **Connections**.

4 Click **Dial-Up Server**.

*Note: If Dial-Up Server
is not available, you
must install the Dial-Up
Networking Server
component from the
Microsoft Plus! package.*

■ The **Dial-Up Server**
dialog box appears.

5 Click **Allow caller
access** (○ changes to ◉).

6 To assign a password,
click **Change Password**.

IMPORTANT

**When you dial in to an office computer,
you can only access information
shared by the computer.**

■ To turn on sharing on the
office computer, refer to page 279.

■ To specify what information
you want the office computer
to share, refer to page 284.

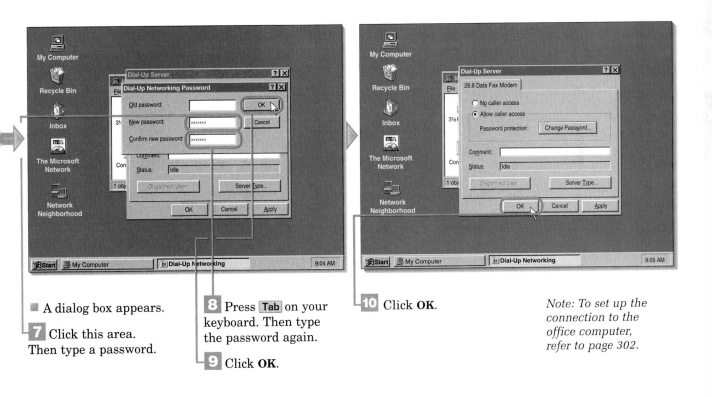

■ A dialog box appears.

7 Click this area.
Then type a password.

8 Press **Tab** on your
keyboard. Then type
the password again.

9 Click **OK**.

10 Click **OK**.

Note: To set up the
connection to the
office computer,
refer to page 302.

SET UP CONNECTION TO OFFICE COMPUTER

Before connecting to the office computer, you must tell Windows about the computer you want to contact.

SET UP CONNECTION TO OFFICE COMPUTER

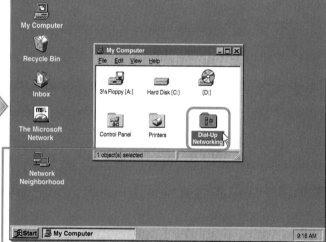

Perform the following steps on your home or portable computer.

1 Double-click **My Computer**.

▪ The **My Computer** window appears.

2 Double-click **Dial-Up Networking**.

*Note: If **Dial-Up Networking** is not available, you must add the Windows component, which is found in the Communications category. To do so, refer to page 186.*

*When you add Dial-Up Networking, you may be asked to provide a computer and workgroup name. For information on workgroups, refer to the **Tip** on page 283.*

To use Dial-Up Networking, both the office computer and the computer you use when at home or traveling must have a modem. Both computers must also be turned on.

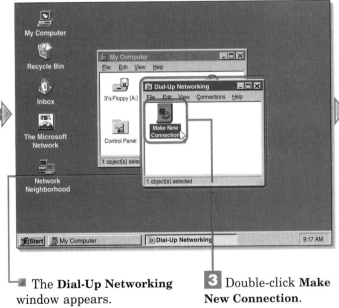

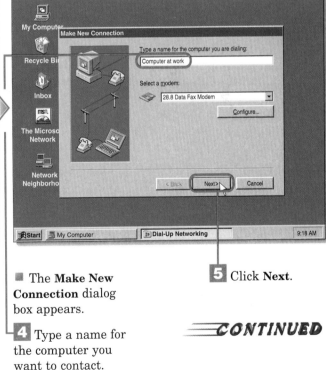

■ The **Dial-Up Networking** window appears.

*Note: If the **Welcome to Dial-Up Networking** dialog box appears, press* Esc *on your keyboard to close the dialog box. If the **Make New Connection** dialog box appears, skip to step 4.*

3 Double-click **Make New Connection**.

■ The **Make New Connection** dialog box appears.

4 Type a name for the computer you want to contact.

5 Click **Next**.

CONTINUED

303

SET UP CONNECTION TO OFFICE COMPUTER

Windows will store the information you enter about the office computer. This will help you quickly connect to the computer later on.

OFFICE COMPUTER INFORMATION

NAME:
Computer at work

PHONE No:
(415) 555-1234

SET UP CONNECTION TO OFFICE COMPUTER (CONTINUED)

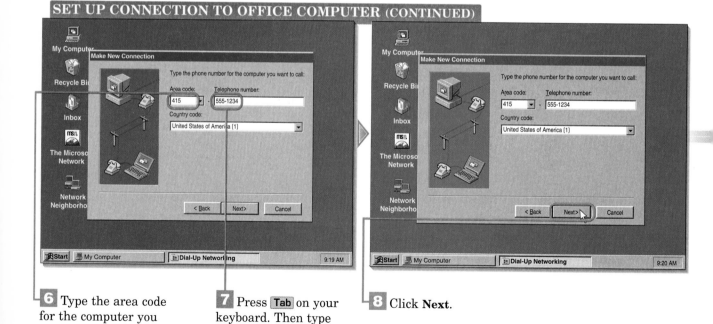

6 Type the area code for the computer you want to contact.

7 Press **Tab** on your keyboard. Then type the telephone number.

8 Click **Next**.

TIP

You only need to set up
a connection to an office
computer once. After the
connection is set up, you
can easily dial in to the
computer at any time. To
do so, refer to page 306.

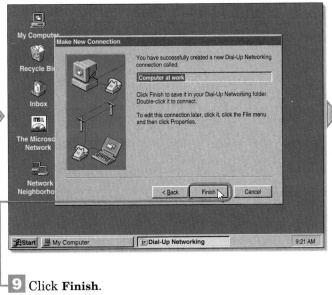

9 Click **Finish**.

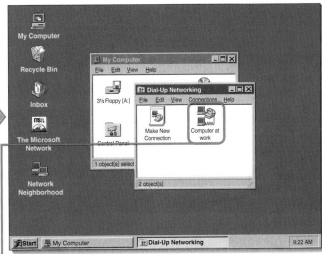

■ An icon appears for the
connection you set up.

*Note: To use this
icon to connect to
the office computer,
refer to page 306.*

DIAL IN TO OFFICE COMPUTER

After you set up a
connection to the
office computer,
you can dial in to
the computer to
access information.

DIAL IN TO OFFICE COMPUTER

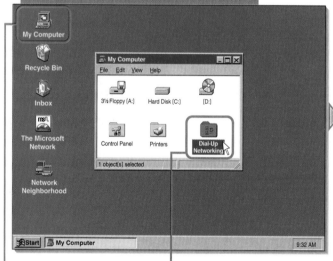

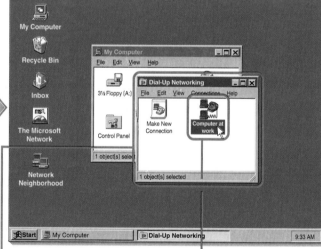

**Perform the following
steps on your home or
portable computer.**

1 Double-click
My Computer.

■ The **My Computer**
window appears.

2 Double-click **Dial-Up
Networking**.

■ The **Dial-Up Networking**
window appears, displaying
an icon for each connection
you have set up.

*Note: To set up a connection,
refer to page 302.*

3 To connect to a
computer, double-click
the icon for the
computer.

■ The **Connect To**
dialog box appears.

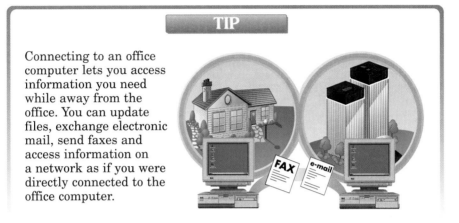

TIP

Connecting to an office computer lets you access information you need while away from the office. You can update files, exchange electronic mail, send faxes and access information on a network as if you were directly connected to the office computer.

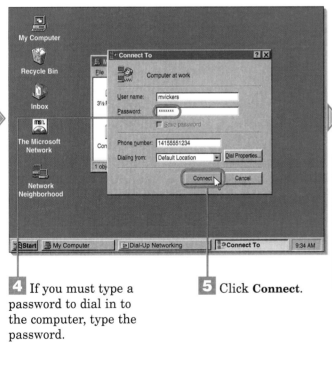

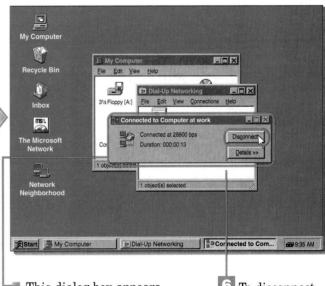

4 If you must type a password to dial in to the computer, type the password.

5 Click **Connect**.

◼ This dialog box appears when you are successfully connected to the office computer.

◼ You can use the Find feature to display the files shared by the office computer. For more information, refer to page 294.

6 To disconnect, click **Disconnect**.

**In this chapter you will learn
how to directly connect two computers
to share information.**

CHAPTER 19: DIRECT CABLE CONNECTION

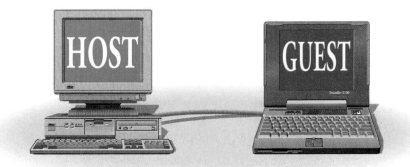

SET UP DIRECT CABLE CONNECTION

You can use a special cable to directly connect two computers to share information.

Guest

The guest is a computer that can access information on the host and the network attached to the host.

Cable

Make sure you plug the cable into both computers before performing the steps below. You can buy the required cable at most computer stores.

SET UP DIRECT CABLE CONNECTION

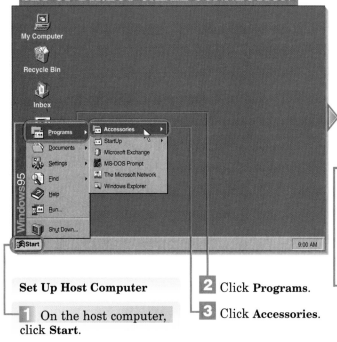

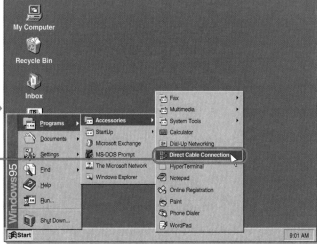

Set Up Host Computer

1 On the host computer, click **Start**.

2 Click **Programs**.

3 Click **Accessories**.

4 Click **Direct Cable Connection**.

Note: If **Direct Cable Connection** *is not available, you must add the Windows component, which is found in the Communications category. To do so, refer to page 186.*

When you add Direct Cable Connection, you may be asked to provide a computer and workgroup name. For information on workgroups, refer to the **Tip** *on page 283.*

Host

The host is a computer that provides information. Make sure the host is set up to share the information the guest wants to access.

■ To turn on sharing on the host computer, refer to page 279.

■ To specify what information you want the host computer to share, refer to page 284.

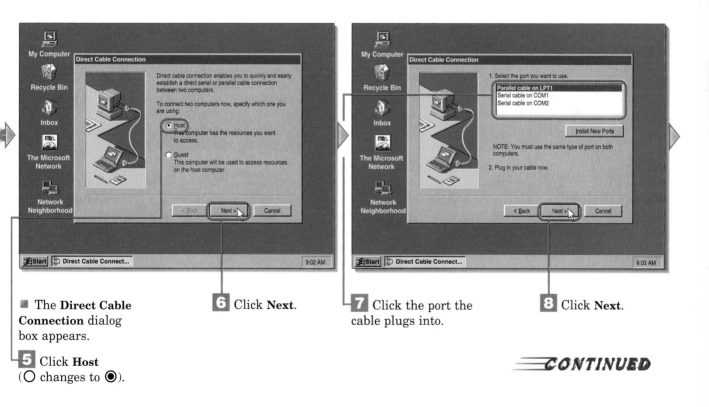

■ The **Direct Cable Connection** dialog box appears.

5 Click **Host** (○ changes to ⦿).

6 Click **Next**.

7 Click the port the cable plugs into.

8 Click **Next**.

CONTINUED

SET UP DIRECT CABLE CONNECTION

You must set up both the host and guest computers before the computers can exchange information.

SET UP DIRECT CABLE CONNECTION (CONTINUED)

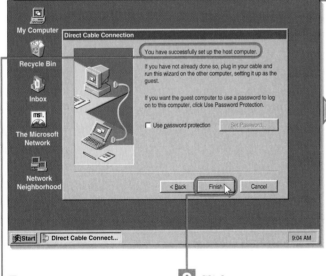

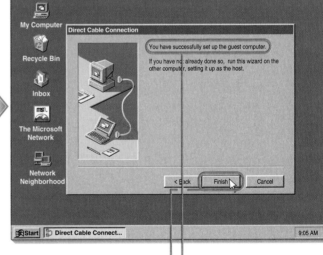

■ This message appears when you finish setting up the host computer.

9 Click **Finish**.

■ A dialog box appears, telling you the status of the connection.

Set Up Guest Computer

1 On the guest computer, perform steps **1** to **8** starting on page 310, selecting **Guest** in step **5**.

■ This message appears when you finish setting up the guest computer.

2 To connect the guest and host computers, click **Finish**.

TIP

You only need to set up a
direct cable connection
between two computers once.
After you set up a connection,
you can easily reconnect the
computers at any time.
For more information,
refer to page 314.

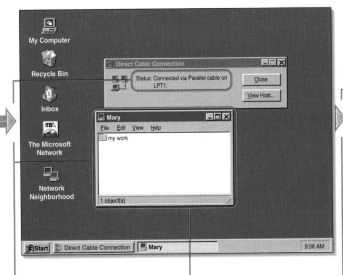

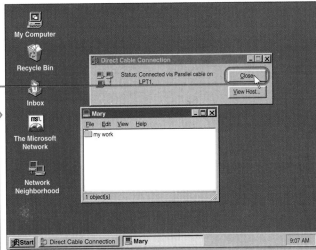

■ This message appears
when the computers are
successfully connected.

■ A window also appears,
displaying the items
shared by the host
computer.

■ You can open and work
with the folders and files
in the window as if the
information were stored
on the guest computer.

*Note: You can access
information on a network
connected to the host. To
find a computer on the
network, refer to page 294.*

Close the Connection

1 Click **Close**.

RE-ESTABLISH DIRECT CABLE CONNECTION

Once you set up a
direct cable connection
between two computers,
you can quickly exchange
information at any time.

RE-ESTABLISH DIRECT CABLE CONNECTION

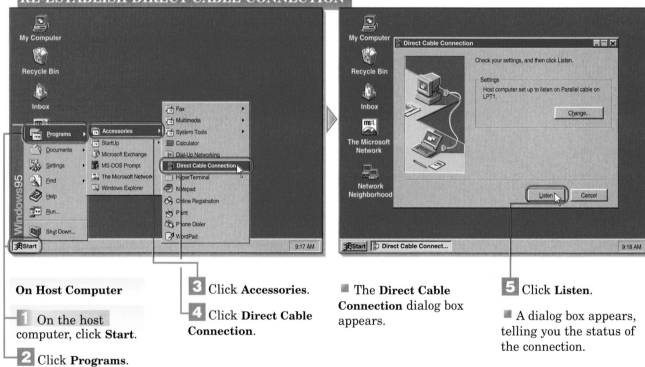

On Host Computer

1 On the host
computer, click **Start**.

2 Click **Programs**.

3 Click **Accessories**.

4 Click **Direct Cable
Connection**.

■ The **Direct Cable
Connection** dialog box
appears.

5 Click **Listen**.

■ A dialog box appears,
telling you the status of
the connection.

You can use Direct Cable Connection to transfer files from your office computer to a portable computer. This lets you use office files when at home or traveling.

If you want the files to update automatically when you return to the office, use the Briefcase feature.

Note: For information on the Briefcase feature, refer to the Briefcase chapter starting on page 266.

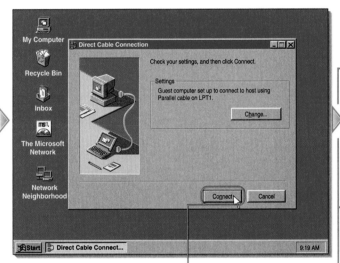

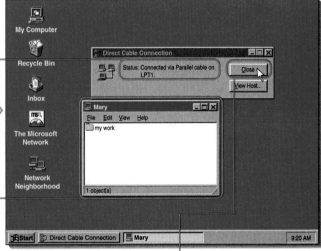

On Guest Computer

1 On the guest computer, perform steps 1 to 4 on page 314.

■ The **Direct Cable Connection** dialog box appears.

2 Click **Connect**.

■ This message appears when the computers are successfully connected.

■ A window also appears, displaying the items shared by the host computer. You can open and work with the folders and files in the window as if the information were stored on the guest computer.

Close the Connection

1 Click **Close**.

In this chapter you will learn about newer versions of Windows 95 and about many programs that can help you work more efficiently.

CHAPTER 20: ENHANCING WINDOWS 95

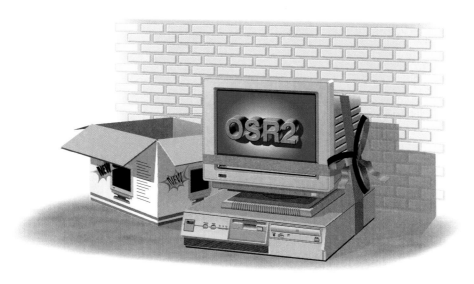

DISPLAY WINDOWS VERSION NUMBER

There are currently three versions of Windows 95. You can display the System Properties dialog box to find out which version you have.

System:
Microsoft Windows 95
4.00.950 B

DISPLAY WINDOWS VERSION NUMBER

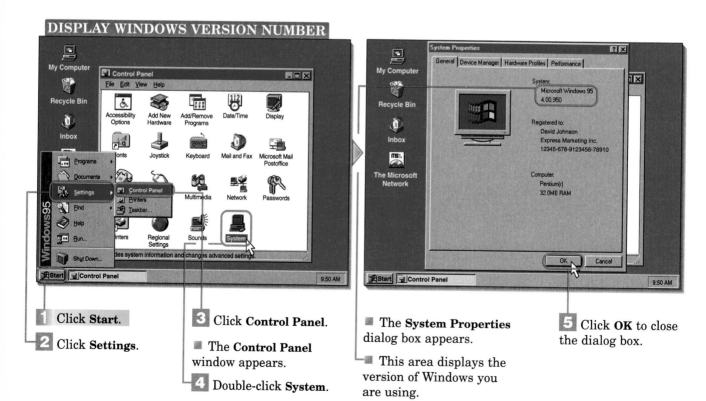

1 Click **Start**.

2 Click **Settings**.

3 Click **Control Panel**.

■ The **Control Panel** window appears.

4 Double-click **System**.

■ The **System Properties** dialog box appears.

■ This area displays the version of Windows you are using.

5 Click **OK** to close the dialog box.

WINDOWS 95 VERSIONS

WINDOWS 95

The original version of Windows 95 is identified by the number 4.00.950. This version is sold in computer stores as the Microsoft Windows 95 upgrade.

WINDOWS 95 VERSION A

The second version of Windows 95 is identified by the number 4.00.950 followed by the letter "a". Version A is created by installing Service Pack 1 to update and solve some of the problems found in the original version of Windows 95.

You can get Service Pack 1 by contacting Microsoft or by downloading it from the Windows 95 Service Packs page at:

www.microsoft.com/windows95/info/service-packs.htm

Some computers are sold with this version already installed.

WINDOWS 95 OSR2

The most recent version of Windows 95 is identified by the number 4.00.950 followed by the letter "B". This version is called OSR2 (OEM Service Release 2). OSR2 has been released to hardware manufacturers and is only available when you purchase a new computer.

INTRODUCTION TO WINDOWS 95 OSR2

Windows 95 OSR2 contains many enhancements to previous versions of Windows. OSR2 was designed to work with the newest types of hardware devices and is only available with the purchase of a new computer.

Although you cannot purchase OSR2 to update your existing version of Windows, you can obtain individual OSR2 components for free from Microsoft's Web site at:

www.microsoft.com/windows/pr/win95osr.htm

FAT32

The most important feature of OSR2 is FAT32. FAT32 is not available unless you purchase a new computer with OSR2. FAT32 is a new file system that improves the organization of data on your hard disk to reduce wasted space. FAT32 allows you to use hard drives larger than 2 GB (gigabytes).

WANG IMAGING

OSR2 includes the Wang Imaging program. Imaging allows you to turn paper documents into documents that can be used on your computer. You can use a scanner or a fax machine to read documents into your computer.

INTERNET EXPLORER

Internet Explorer 3.0 is included with OSR2. You can use Internet Explorer to browse through and view information on the World Wide Web.

OSR2 also includes an Internet Connection Wizard to help you quickly find and set up a connection to an Internet service provider so you can access the Internet.

INTERNET MAIL AND NEWS

Internet Mail and Internet News are both part of Internet Explorer and are also included with OSR2. You can use Internet Mail to send and receive e-mail messages with other people on the Internet. You can use Internet News to browse through and participate in discussion groups, called newsgroups.

NETMEETING

OSR2 also includes a program called NetMeeting. NetMeeting allows you to collaborate with other Internet users. After contacting other people using NetMeeting, you can have voice conversations over the Internet, transfer data and view and use a program stored on another person's computer.

INTERNET EXPLORER 4.0

You can use Internet Explorer 4.0 to access information on the Internet. Internet Explorer 4.0 enhances the way Windows 95 looks and acts.

Internet Explorer 4.0 is available free of charge at:

www.microsoft.com

BROWSE THROUGH INFORMATION

Internet Explorer 4.0 integrates the World Wide Web, your corporate network and your Windows 95 desktop so you can browse through information more efficiently. Internet Explorer 4.0 also provides enhanced security features so you can safely purchase items on the Internet.

EXCHANGE ELECTRONIC MAIL

Internet Explorer 4.0 includes Outlook Express, which enables you to exchange e-mail messages with people around the world. Outlook Express allows you to enhance your messages with graphics, animation and multimedia. The program also includes powerful search tools to help you find unknown e-mail addresses.

PARTICIPATE IN NEWSGROUPS

You can use Internet Explorer's Outlook Express to join discussion groups, called newsgroups, to meet people around the world with similar interests. There are thousands of newsgroups on many different topics.

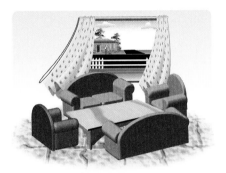

CREATE WEB PAGES

Internet Explorer 4.0 includes FrontPage Express, which allows you to create and edit your own Web pages. You can place pages you create on the Web so millions of people around the world can view your information.

PARTICIPATE IN CONFERENCES

Internet Explorer 4.0 includes NetMeeting, which lets you communicate with another person on the Internet. You can chat with a colleague, exchange files and work together on the same document.

Microsoft Chat is also included, so you can communicate with other people on the Internet using a comic strip format.

CHANGE CHANNELS

You can subscribe to channels that update on a regular basis. Each channel is a Web site that sends information from sources like Disney, ESPN and Time Magazine straight to your desktop.

You can receive constant updates while you work on other tasks. You select the type of information you are interested in and how often you want to receive the information.

MICROSOFT OFFICE 97

Microsoft Office 97 includes programs that can help you accomplish many tasks.

Microsoft Office 97 Standard Edition includes Word, Excel, PowerPoint and Outlook. The Professional Edition includes all of these programs, plus Access.

Office Assistant

All of the Office 97 programs provide the Office Assistant to help you perform tasks. The Office Assistant can offer tips, step-by-step instructions and answer questions you ask.

Microsoft IntelliMouse Support

Office 97 programs are designed to take advantage of the new IntelliMouse, which has a wheel between the left and right buttons. Moving this wheel lets you quickly scroll through information on the screen.

Internet Support

Each Office 97 program has features that help you take advantage of the World Wide Web. You can make documents you create available on your company intranet or the Web.

Word 97 is a word processing program that lets you create letters, reports, memos and newsletters quickly and efficiently.

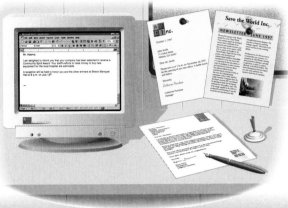

Word 97 offers many features that help you work with text in a document. The program can automatically format text and check for spelling and grammar errors as you type. You can use Word 97 to neatly display information in tables and produce personalized letters for each person on a mailing list.

EXCEL 97

Excel 97 is a spreadsheet program that helps you organize, analyze and present data.

Excel 97 lets you efficiently enter, edit and change the appearance of data in your worksheets. The program also provides powerful tools to calculate and analyze your data. You can create colorful charts using your worksheet data. The Chart Wizard helps you choose the correct type of chart for your needs and style the chart the way you want.

CONTINUED

MICROSOFT OFFICE 97 (Continued)

POWERPOINT 97

PowerPoint 97 is a program that helps you plan, organize and design professional presentations.

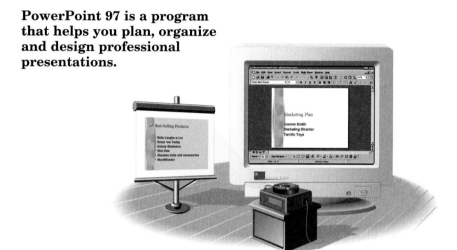

PowerPoint 97 provides many templates to help you quickly start creating effective on-screen and slide presentations. Presentations can include charts and graphics as well as sound and animation. You can create handouts for your audience and notes to help you deliver your presentation.

ACCESS 97

Access 97 is a database program that allows you to store and manage large collections of information.

Access 97 provides you with the tools you need to create an efficient and effective database, including tables, forms, queries and reports. The Database Wizard included in Access 97 helps you automatically set up more than 20 types of databases. You can use the pre-designed formats to give your forms and reports the look you want.

OUTLOOK 97

Outlook 97 is an information management program that helps you organize contacts, messages, tasks and appointments.

Manage Contacts

Outlook 97 provides an address book where you can store information about your contacts, such as phone and fax numbers as well as e-mail and Web page addresses.

Exchange E-mail

Outlook 97 lets you exchange e-mail messages with other people. You can preview your e-mail messages to quickly determine which messages you want to read first.

Keep Organized

You can create notes, task lists and record your activities in a journal. Outlook 97 allows you to drag and drop information. For example, you can easily drag an e-mail message onto your task list to remind you to reply to the message.

Manage People on a Network

You can use Outlook 97 to check the calendars of several people on a corporate network or intranet and schedule a meeting at a convenient time.

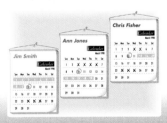

UTILITIES YOU CAN USE WITH WINDOWS 95

There are many utility programs available that you can use with Windows 95.

ADOBE ACROBAT AND ACROBAT READER

Adobe Acrobat allows you to create Portable Document Format (.pdf) files. These files allow you to display books and magazines on the screen exactly as they appear in printed form. Acrobat Reader is a program that allows you to view .pdf files. Adobe Acrobat and Acrobat Reader are available at:

www.adobe.com

ANTI-VIRUS

You can use an anti-virus program to reduce the risk of a virus infecting your computer. A virus is a program that can cause problems ranging from displaying annoying messages on your screen to erasing the information on your hard drive. McAfee offers evaluation versions of several anti-virus programs at:

www.mcafee.com

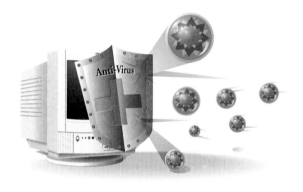

CLEANSWEEP

CleanSweep can help you free up space on your hard drive by finding unneeded files that you can remove. CleanSweep can also help you remove programs from your computer. There is a trial version of CleanSweep available at:

www.quarterdeck.com

FIRST AID

You can use First Aid to identify and solve problems with your computer. First Aid watches for memory and hard drive problems and can warn you when your hard drive is about to fail. There is a trial version of First Aid available at:

www.cybermedia.com

NORTON UTILITIES 2.0

Norton Utilities provides tools to help you perform hard drive maintenance tasks, such as defragmenting the drive and removing unneeded files. Norton Utilities also includes tools to help you recover lost files and protect against computer failure. You can purchase Norton Utilities at:

www.symantec.com

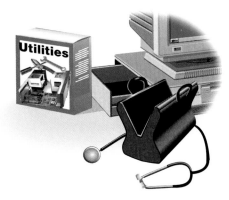

OIL CHANGE

Oil Change identifies the programs installed on your computer and lets you know when a manufacturer provides a free update at their Web site. You can have Oil Change automatically install the updates on your computer. There is a trial version of Oil Change available at:

www.cybermedia.com

CONTINUED

UTILITIES YOU CAN USE WITH WINDOWS 95 (Continued)

PAINT SHOP PRO

Paint Shop Pro is an inexpensive and easy-to-use graphics program you can use to view, edit and convert images from over 30 image formats. You can use Paint Shop Pro's drawing and painting tools to create your own pictures. A trial version of Paint Shop Pro is available at:

www.jasc.com

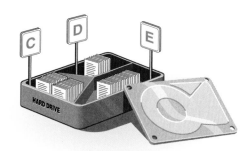

PARTITIONMAGIC

PartitionMagic can help you create, format, change and move your hard drive partitions. A partition is a part of the hard drive that is assigned a drive letter and acts as a separate hard drive. When you use PartitionMagic, you do not have to back up your data or reinstall Windows 95. You can purchase PartitionMagic at:

www.powerquest.com

POINTCAST NETWORK

The PointCast Network automatically transfers the latest news and information to your computer. You can tell PointCast whether you prefer local, national or international news.

You can also receive information about specific industries, companies, sports, horoscopes, lottery results and more. The PointCast Network is available free of charge at:

www.pointcast.com

POWERDESK

PowerDesk enhances the way Windows 95 looks and acts. Explorer Plus replaces Windows Explorer and offers new capabilities to help you work with files.

The PowerDesk Toolbar displays tools on your desktop that help you start your favorite programs and monitor your computer resources. There is a trial version of PowerDesk available at:

www.mijenix.com

QUICK VIEW PLUS

Windows 95 includes Quick View which allows you to preview a file without opening it. Quick View Plus enhances Quick View's capabilities by enabling you to preview more file types, such as Word 97 and Excel 97. There is a trial version of Quick View Plus available at:

www.inso.com

WINZIP

WinZip compresses files to make it easier and faster to transfer information from one computer to another. WinZip also helps you uncompress files.

Many of the files you transfer to your computer from online services and the Internet must be uncompressed. WinZip is available at:

www.winzip.com

331

INDEX

INDEX

OVER 4 MILLION

OTHER 3-D Visual SERIES

SIMPLIFIED SERIES

Windows 95 Simplified
ISBN 1-56884-662-2
$19.99 USA/£18.99 UK

More Windows 95 Simplified
ISBN 1-56884-689-4
$19.99 USA/£18.99 UK

Windows 3.1 Simplified
ISBN 1-56884-654-1
$19.99 USA/£18.99 UK

Excel 97 Simplified
ISBN 0-7645-6022-0
$24.99 USA/£23.99 UK

Excel For Windows 95 Simplified
ISBN 1-56884-682-7
$19.99 USA/£18.99 UK

Word 97 Simplified
ISBN 0-7645-6011-5
$24.99 USA/£23.99 UK

Word For Windows 95 Simplified
ISBN 1-56884-681-9
$19.99 USA/£18.99 UK

Office 97 Simplified
ISBN 0-7645-6009-3
$29.99 USA/£28.99 UK

Creating Web Pages Simplified
ISBN 0-7645-6007-7
$24.99 USA/£23.99 UK

World Wide Web Color Yellow Pages Simplified
ISBN 0-7645-6005-0
$29.99 USA/£28.99 UK

Internet and World Wide Web Simplified 2nd Edition
ISBN 0-7645-6029-8
$24.99 USA/£23.99 UK

Computers Simplified, Third Edition
ISBN 0-7645-6008-5
$24.99 USA/£23.99 UK

Netscape 2 Simplified
ISBN 0-7645-6000-X
$19.99 USA/£18.99 UK

The 3-D Visual Dictionary of Computing
ISBN 1-56884-678-9
$19.99 USA/£18.99 UK

WordPerfect 6.1 For Windows Simplified
ISBN 1-56884-665-7
$19.99 USA/£18.99 UK

FOR CORPORATE ORDERS, PLEASE CALL: 800-469-6616

S A T I S F I E D   U S E R S !

EACH YOURSELF VISUALLY SERIES

**Teach Yourself Computers
and the Internet VISUALLY**

ISBN 0-7645-6002-6
$29.99 USA/£28.99 UK

**Teach Yourself
Office 97 VISUALLY**

ISBN 0-7645-6018-2
$29.99 USA/£28.99 UK

COMING SOON!

Teach Yourself Netscape Communicator VISUALLY

ISBN 0-7645-6028-X $29.99 USA/£28.99 UK

Teach Yourself Networking VISUALLY

ISBN 0-7645-6023-9 $29.99 USA/£28.99 UK

**Teach Yourself the Internet and
World Wide Web VISUALLY**

ISBN 0-7645-6020-4
$29.99 USA/£28.99 UK

**Teach Yourself
Access 97 VISUALLY**

ISBN 0-7645-6026-3
$29.99 USA/£28.99 UK

Visit our Web site at:
http://www.maran.com

FOR CORPORATE ORDERS, PLEASE CALL: 800-469-6616

The fun & easy way to learn about computers and more!

**Windows 3.1 For Dummies,™
2nd Edition**
by Andy Rathbone

ISBN: 1-56884-182-5
$16.95 USA/$22.95 Canada

**MORE Windows
For Dummies™**
by Andy Rathbone

ISBN: 1-56884-048-9
$19.95 USA/$26.95 Canada

**Personal Finance
For Dummies™**
by Eric Tyson

ISBN: 1-56884-150-7
$16.95 USA/$22.95 Canada

**PCs For Dummies,™
2nd Edition**
*by Dan Gookin &
Andy Rathbone*

ISBN: 1-56884-078-0
$16.95 USA/$22.95 Canada

FOR MORE INFO OR TO ORDER, PLEASE CALL ▶ **800-762-2974**   For volume discounts & special orders please
call Tony Real, Special Sales, at 415-312-0644

**DOS For Dummies,®
2nd Edition**

by Dan Gookin

ISBN: 1-878058-75-4
$16.95 USA/$22.95 Canada

**The Internet
For Dummies™**

*by John Levine &
Carol Baroudi*

ISBN: 1-56884-024-1
$19.95 USA/$26.95 Canada

FINALIST
*Ninth Annual
Computer Press
Awards ≥ 1993*

**Macs For Dummies,™
2nd Edition**

by David Pogue

ISBN: 1-56884-051-9
$19.95 USA/$26.95 Canada

FOR MORE INFO OR TO ORDER, PLEASE CALL ▶ 800-762-2974

For volume discounts & special orders please
call Tony Real, Special Sales, at 415-312-0644

IDG BOOKS ®

TRADE & INDIVIDUAL ORDERS

Phone: **(800) 762-2974**
or **(317) 895-5200**
(8 a.m.–6 p.m., CST, weekdays)
FAX : **(317) 895-5298**

EDUCATIONAL ORDERS & DISCOUNTS

Phone: **(800) 434-2086**
(8:30 a.m.–5:00 p.m., CST, weekdays)
FAX : **(817) 251-8174**

CORPORATE ORDERS FOR 3-D VISUAL™ SERIES

Phone: **(800) 469-6616**
(8 a.m.–5 p.m., EST, weekdays)
FAX : **(905) 890-9434**

Qty	ISBN	Title	Price	Total

Shipping & Handling Charges

	Description	First book	Each add'l. book	Total
Domestic	Normal	$4.50	$1.50	$
	Two Day Air	$8.50	$2.50	$
	Overnight	$18.00	$3.00	$
International	Surface	$8.00	$8.00	$
	Airmail	$16.00	$16.00	$
	DHL Air	$17.00	$17.00	$

Subtotal _____

CA residents add applicable sales tax _____

IN, MA and MD residents add 5% sales tax _____

IL residents add 6.25% sales tax _____

RI residents add 7% sales tax _____

TX residents add 8.25% sales tax _____

Shipping _____

Total _____

Ship to:

Name _____

Address _____

Company _____

City/State/Zip _____

Daytime Phone _____

Payment: ☐ Check to IDG Books (US Funds Only)
☐ Visa ☐ Mastercard ☐ American Express

Card # _____ Exp. _____ Signature _____

maranGraphics™